M000251728

THE ENLIGHTENED EDGE FOR LEADERS:
IGNITE THE POWER OF YOU

"Barbara Bouchet's book reflects her long experience at showing people how to get out of their own way. Her uniquely supportive yet challenging approach facilitates connection with self and others. She leads the reader through a series of practical exercises and specific examples that outline a process for transformation. She also makes it clear that this path is best traveled with someone who is skilled in guiding others. I recommend Barbara and this book as guides along the path."
—Hannah S. Wilder, PhD, MCC, President, Advantara® Global Executive Learning and Coach Certification Institute

"I read this book hoping to find some tools and tips that would be helpful in my coaching practice. I did not expect the profound insight it gave me about my own life. I highly recommend you read it twice - once for yourself and once for the leaders in your life."
—Jillian Ihsanullah, PhD, Principal Consultant, Linkage, Inc.

"*The Enlightened Edge for Leaders* provides life-changing tools and techniques that touch all aspects of our lives, at work and at home. Barbara leverages her professional experiences to provide insights into both the internal and interpersonal dynamics that are constantly at play. I highly recommend this book to anyone who wants to take the next step toward self-realization."
—Edith Feild, Sr. Director, Integrations, Philips Women's Healthcare

"No one I know is as qualified as Barbara to share wisdom on the connections between personal growth and leadership capability. I've personally experienced the depth of her insight and know there are so many people who would also find her help a turning point in their careers and lives."
—Daniel K. Oestreich, consultant and co-author, *Driving Fear Out of the Workplace* and *The Courageous Messenger*

THE ENLIGHTENED EDGE
FOR LEADERS

THE
ENLIGHTENED EDGE
FOR LEADERS

IGNITE THE POWER OF YOU

BARBARA BOUCHET

SEATTLE, WASHINGTON

Published by
Blue Orb Publishing
P.O. Box 77458, Seattle, WA 98177

Requests for permission should be directed to
permissions@BlueOrbPublishing.com
Blue Orb Publishing, P.O. Box 77458, Seattle, WA 98177

    ISBN: 978-0-9824569-0-3
    LCCN: 2010910465

Printed in the United States of America

To the luminous being within you.
To everyone I have ever loved, even imperfectly.
To all the great teachers and provocateurs in my life.
To my sweetest loves, my husband Ron, and son Derek.
To the boundless creative force that fuels my existence.

CONTENTS

ACKNOWLEDGMENTS

THIS book might not have emerged had it not been for the early catalytic prompts from enthusiastic teachers, mentors, clients, family members and friends. I give my deepest thanks to all those who offered their support, patience, encouragement, and feedback. Words aren't enough to express my deeply felt gratitude for the innumerable nudges and pushes along the way, and especially for the sustenance offered during the dry spells when faith ran dim. They truly have made this book possible.

Thanks to Garth Alley, Susan Daffron, John Eggen, Howard Greenfield, Jon Haass, Rob Holdford, Dan Oestreich, Stephanie Reynolds, Alan Steinborn, Scott Verrette, and Connie Weiseth for their support through long conversations, coaching, troubleshooting, specific suggestions, introductions, technical tools and friendship.

For helping me to come forward in my own leadership and to express the fullness of my heart, I offer the deepest gratitude to Barbara De Angelis. She is a blessing in my life.

My special thanks to Joseph Anderson, Judy Eekhoff, Edee Feild, Alex Fisher, Bert Holland, Marti Lyttle, Jillian Ihsanullah, Brent Mullins, Sunjeev Pandey, Sonja Rothfuss, Victoria Scarlett, Hannah Wilder, and David York for their thoughtful reading of the final draft of the book and their insightful feedback.

Thank you to Lisa Carlson for preliminary editing, Seth Schulman for his insightful development comments, Susan Lang for copy editing, and Bonnie Myhrum for proofreading. Kathi Dunn, Hobie Hobart and Sevda Holland also offered valuable feedback on the cover.

I give thanks to the many authors who have given me permission to use their brilliant quotes in order to support and enhance my material.

If I have overlooked naming someone who has contributed to this book, please accept my apology and know that no act of kindness goes unnoticed. For my clients whom I won't name and whose privacy I protect, please know that you have enriched my life, my work, and my heart.

I wish to thank my family and especially my son Derek, for his candid feedback and good taste with endless testing of titles and evolving ideas for the book cover.

Most special thanks goes to my husband and best friend, Ron. Through the many hours, days, weeks, and months of intensive writing and re-writing, Ron offered fundamental, absolutely necessary support, preparing and delivering countless guilt-free meals to me in front of the computer, graciously accepting the many weekends when play was sacrificed to writing, and lastly, courageously acting as the first reader and editor of every draft of the book. I'm enormously grateful for his honesty, persistence and patience, especially when I received the feedback in a less than stellar way. (Yes, I also struggle at times with the reactive patterns you'll read about.) He has graciously shared me with my other great love, creative activity. Thank you so much Ron, for tending the hearth while my time, focus, and energy have been absorbed in this huge project.

For the growth I've gained through this intensive creative process, I want to honor the invisible, but steady hand that has guided me. It has consistently offered the fiery spark of inspiration and illumination that fuels all my creative activity. For this, I also give thanks.

INTRODUCTION

THE world needs you! It needs more people like you, people who are ready to ignite their power as leaders. Perhaps you feel that your capacity as a leader hasn't yet been fully realized. You may have a partial vision of something more you could accomplish, for others and for yourself. No doubt you have struggled to get where you are and know that getting to the next level will require added effort. You may suspect that not all obstacles are external—some may be internal.

This book can help you identify and change whatever holds you back from being a more effective leader. This is a guide for making a powerful shift from a foundation that is guarded and limited to one that is rooted in expanded and realistic possibilities, a place I call the enlightened edge.

The enlightened edge is a working space that becomes available when you challenge what is limited and distorted and you stand behind what is expanded and true. For example, when a leader challenges a crippling lack of confidence with a powerful assertion of personal and professional value, his or her enlightened edge expands. Or when a highly capable yet caustic leader develops greater sensitivity to others when communicating performance expectations, that person works with his or her enlightened edge.

Most people live their lives without ever tapping into their potential, which bubbles quietly below the surface, systematically suppressed and diverted. You have probably had glimpses of your own potential. Now you have an opportunity to activate and effectively use it.

The enlightened edge is different for each person. It can illuminate where you are in your development and point to the next stage in your growth as a leader. Working with your enlightened edge will strengthen the clear vision and presence that support powerful and positive action. As you unlock the power and spirit that already reside within you, you'll see yourself and others in a new light. Igniting your potential will enable you to lead others in a way that also ignites their potential. You'll find faster and better ways to manage yourself, manage others, and get results.

Leaders who don't look inward may not fulfill their potential, despite their best efforts. By doing the work outlined in this book, you'll discover what may be limiting you and what could liberate you. You will identify your blind spots, fill in the gaps, and learn to recover gracefully from mistakes. Your work will provide a foundation for working with both the light and the dark aspects of who you are, so you can lead with deep, inner confidence.

As a leader, you can't afford to deceive yourself or operate in a relationship vacuum. This book will show you how to influence others with integrity and vision, so they will be inspired to follow you. You'll learn how to strengthen the clear thinking and clear feeling necessary for highly effective communication. This process will assist you in building collaborative relationships; you'll be prepared for challenging conversations and discover how to get difficult relationships back on track.

Until now, many of the models and processes outlined in this book, such as the **Limited You** and the **Essential You**, Shadow Gratification™, Reactive Patterns, Relational Patterns, and the Contact Zone™ have been available only through the coaching or training I offer to executives and professionals. This book now makes available to you the same information that has helped CEOs, vice presidents, directors, managers, business owners, independent professionals, and entrepreneurs become even more capable, wise, and balanced leaders.

I have worked as a psychotherapist, adult educator, executive coach, and organization consultant for over twenty-five years. I own my own business, was executive director of a non-profit corporation, started a consulting firm, and have been an associate with other consulting firms.

As a coach and consultant, I've worked with leaders in large companies, among them Microsoft, Costco, Amazon, and Philips Healthcare, as well as many smaller companies and non-profit organizations. I provide executive coaching, leadership and team development, group coaching, strategic planning, and conflict resolution, and frequently am relied upon as a trusted advisor. I have also worked privately and confidentially with many leaders in health care, global e-commerce, engineering, information solutions, banking, business law, global investing, environmental protection, education, food supply, and the ministry.

This broad experience with clients has made it possible for me to provide the many examples used throughout the book. The confidentiality of my clients (both individuals and companies) has been protected in these case studies. No company names are used. The names of all individuals have been changed. Gender, appearance, and occasionally the industry have been altered in order to ensure privacy. In some cases, superficial themes have been fictionalized, but all central themes are rooted in actual client experience.

My clients have consistently been my greatest source of information and inspiration. They have allowed me into the privacy of their lives, their relationships, and their organizations with the often unspoken but most intimate of questions: *"Can you help me with this?"* This question deserves an authentic, specific response and has always challenged me to bring forward the best resources available.

I have drawn on years of observing, experimenting, and learning in order to distill the best practices and processes presented in this book. They are backed by the efforts of innumerable helping professionals in the areas of psychology, coaching, and organization development and draw on ancient spiritual traditions as well. I have tested them repeatedly in my own work with hundreds of clients.

Psychological and spiritual influences have been intertwined for most of my life and have helped illuminate the path for my work. I was raised Catholic, by a mother who took both a mystical and psychodynamic view of experience. I discovered Martin Buber (*I-Thou*) when I was fourteen, Buddhism when I was fifteen, and shortly after that, Sigmund Freud and Carl Jung.

However, it was the human potential movement and the discovery of transpersonal psychology that sparked my commitment to psycho-spiritual integration. In my late twenties, I concluded my graduate work, became a psychotherapist, and moved into a leadership role in creating a regional psychosynthesis training center, working especially with health care professionals.

This period marked a powerful convergence of psychology with spiritual influences such as Buddhism, mystical Christianity, eastern philosophy, and yogic practices. These approaches and ideas became part of the background for an ongoing practice of meditation, body awareness, intuitive listening, and creative expression.

As I moved deeper into my practice as a psychotherapist in my thirties, I was influenced by social exchange theory, systems theory, and existentialism. Body-feelings-mind integration continued to be important and tools like guided imagery and Eugene Gendlin's focusing technique were quite valuable.

As a seasoned psychotherapist I became more interested in object relations theory, self-psychology, character disorders, shame, and the intransigent aspects of personal change. These points of reference dovetailed with relational psychology, especially in my work with couples, business partners, and groups.

In my forties I entered a period of creative awakening, and *The Artist's Way* by Julia Cameron was a welcome catalyst. I drew inspiration from creative thinkers and artists of all types, especially from literary fiction writers, and wrote an as-yet-unpublished novel.

About ten years ago, as my focus shifted to complex business challenges and the emerging field of coaching, I received formal training as a coach. I focused a great deal on emotional intelligence, communication, work-life effectiveness, and especially leadership development. These perspectives and the need to create practical solutions for leaders led to the creation of this book.

My approach draws on established psycho-spiritual principles and proven techniques for increasing:

- Visibility, impact, and influence
- Emotional, relational, and political intelligence

- Balance, renewal, and work-life effectiveness
- Strategic thinking and visioning
- Communication and conflict resolution skills

This book asks you to reflect, to consider new perspectives, to try new behaviors, and to believe in your potential. Each chapter has one or more exercises, several questions for reflection, and multiple suggestions for taking action. Allow yourself adequate time to explore these areas of investigation and discovery. Doing so will ensure that you get maximum benefit from this material.

This book was written with one goal: to show you how to become a more powerful and mindful leader who is deeply anchored in your inner truth and the core of your being. It will create the basis for a shift in identity that will expand how you see yourself and the world.

Part One focuses on two very different aspects of who you are:

- The **Limited You**, which is guarded, limited, and reactive
- The **Essential You**, which is expanded, powerful, and relational (rooted in a respectful relationship with others)

Part One will help you understand how these very different levels of identity operate. You'll learn to identify four reactive patterns, used by the **Limited You,** and four corresponding relational patterns, used by the **Essential You.**

In Part Two you'll develop the tools that will help you shift from the **Limited You** to the **Essential You** and anchor your effectiveness as a leader. You'll expand your ability to:

- Learn from your life, mistakes, and pain
- Work with the reality of what is going on in the here and now, rather than denying or defying it
- Contain, accept, and care for the Limited You as you challenge its limiting stories
- Hold creative tension and work with it creatively to ignite your power
- Work skillfully in the Contact Zone™ (the space where people connect and have significant impact)
- Increase your leadership presence and vision

Part Two will also show you how to use skill, integrity, and grace to collaborate with and influence others, even those who are difficult or frustrating.

If you are an executive or a manager or have been identified as a person with high potential, this book will help support and keep you on the fast track. If you are a business owner, entrepreneur, or leader of a non-profit, you'll find the tools to stabilize your work-life effectiveness and find realistic limits that can also contribute to the success of your organization. If you are a helping professional or human resources professional, you'll learn a very clear model for supporting the growth of others. If you are a social, political, or religious change agent, you'll find a way to inspire others by communicating your vision more effectively. If you dream of being a better leader or if you just want to grow personally so you can guide your family, this book will provide a map and a process for doing so.

Working with your enlightened edge will give you a distinct advantage at work, at home, and in any area of your life where you want to perform at your best. As your awareness expands and as you grow more enlightened, your improved vision will guide your actions, leading to wiser choices and actions, and, eventually, more joyful and life-affirming outcomes.

The world needs enlightened leaders who are willing and able to look honestly at who they are and what holds them back from having greater positive impact. This book will ask you to do the work to shift from a limited, guarded, constricted person to a person more fully alive and powerful—someone capable of rising to the occasion and becoming an inspiring and enlightened leader.

Barbara Bouchet, MEd
Seattle, Washington
BB@ContactPointAssoc.com

PART ONE:
THE INNER WORK
OF LEADERSHIP

Part One of **The Enlightened Edge for Leaders** will introduce you to the **Limited You**, which is guarded, limited, and reactive, and the **Essential You**, which is expanded, powerful, and relational (rooted in a respectful relationship with others). You'll learn about how the **Limited You** and the **Essential You** are constructed and what feeds them. It will become clear how working with both of these aspects of who you are supports enlightened leadership.

You will also be introduced to four reactive patterns and four corresponding relational patterns. You'll see how the **Limited You** uses the reactive patterns. The relational patterns, used by the **Essential You**, will provide you with specific alternatives that can act as antidotes for the reactive patterns.

1

THE LEADERSHIP CHALLENGE

Most powerful is he who has himself in his own power.
SENECA, Roman philosopher

THE world needs enlightened leadership from men and women who act from a high level of integrity, have a clear, compelling vision, create powerful, positive alliances, and work strategically for the greater good. We need as many people as possible to tap into their potential in order to address the complex and multi-layered challenges we face as a nation and as global citizens.

When you are energized, whole, centered, and grounded, your contribution has impact that resonates in powerful and positive ways. By responding to others and the world around you from the center of your being, you become part of something greater.

Many people want to be part of a larger effort to build something that supports life and the values they hold dear. This kind of building and rebuilding requires leadership, not just from the top down but also at all levels of an organization or community.

Even though we have faced dire social, economic, political, and environmental difficulties before, it's becoming increasingly clear that the challenges before us now cannot be solved in isolation from one another.

They also cannot be solved using the same thinking that created the problems in the first place.

Leadership starts with a transformative shift in awareness, and it starts with you. The enlightened you, the awake, mindful you, needs to become more powerful and active in the world. We need solutions that are informed by a wiser, kinder, more emotionally intelligent and creative mind. To bring this about requires focused inner work.

INNER WORK

The inner work outlined in this book will ask you to engage with reality in a grounded way and to incorporate new levels of responsibility, so you can handle complex leadership challenges with a clearer mind and heart. First, you'll be asked to focus internally in order to lead yourself and then to focus externally to lead others. This approach is a balanced blend of becoming softer in some ways and firmer in others. It asks you to look closely at who you are, how you operate in relationships, and how you deal with a wide variety of challenges.

Frequently, leaders who bypass internal work don't reach their full leadership potential, despite the best of intentions. Leaders who are self-aware, self-accepting, and self-disciplined have much greater success leading and inspiring others in constructive ways.

Not everyone will see the necessity of doing the work that leads to more enlightened leadership. Without sufficient motivation, there usually isn't enough fuel, energy, desire, or commitment to look inward.

People are often motivated when they have a life experience that touches them deeply and intensely. Emotional pain accomplishes this with amazing effectiveness. People often make the deepest changes as a result of learning from highly charged, painful emotional experiences such as:

- Feeling threatened, anxious, or humiliated by an event or situation
- Struggling with feelings of anger or aggression
- Experiencing a crisis in how you see yourself or others
- Feeling confused, stagnant, or purposeless regarding your life direction
- Losing something or someone very important to you

Each of these situations could be an entry point to learning and growing as a person and as a leader. During times of personal or professional upheaval or crisis, you have an opportunity to learn at a heightened level. Focusing on doing the inner work at these times can be very useful in bringing about positive changes.

The goal of this book is to assist you in bringing about a transformational shift. This is the transition from a reactive **Limited Self** to a more powerful, expanded **Essential Self** that is rooted in your inner essence. This shift from the **Limited You** to the **Essential You** is possible for anyone who does the inner work.

THE LIMITED YOU & THE ESSENTIAL YOU

Within the average person, enormous variability in moods, behaviors, beliefs, moral decisions, and spiritual well-being can be found. For example:

- One moment you like who you are, but at another moment you're disappointed in your behavior or performance.
- You are confident and inspiring in many situations but flat or insecure in others.
- Colors look bright and life is exciting on some days, while on other days life is dull or full of angst.
- You can think clearly, even brilliantly, at times but at other times you are hampered by reactions and distractions.

This variation is normal and to be expected. It is often the result of two different internal states or points of view: the **Limited You** and the **Essential You**. These two aspects of who you are represent two ends of a continuum; they exist at the same time, even though they may show up in sequence.

- *Can you think of moods that you cycle through?*
- *Are you aware of any contradictory and repetitive attitudes you have toward others?*

As a human being you exist at many levels at once and have many dimensions. The goal of this book is to help you consciously and effectively focus on two dimensions of your identity: a limited sense of self and one that is more free and more effective. As you get more familiar with these different, diverse aspects of who you are, it becomes easier to shift from one level to another.

A look at the anatomy of the **Limited You** and the **Essential You** will give you a way to understand these two versions of yourself and help clarify the nature of what needs to shift in order for you to become a more enlightened leader.

THE LIMITED YOU

At the center of the **Limited You** is a *core insecurity*, which is the deepest fear you have about who you really are and your place in the world. In order to protect itself from this deep fear, the **Limited You** creates *defensive strategies* like control, blame, angry defiance, passive compliance, and avoidance. These behaviors and attitudes surround and isolate the core insecurity. They act as a "lockdown" on the core insecurity so it doesn't come forward and disrupt what is going on in your life. Defensive strategies can protect you from feelings and internal states that are very uncomfortable or anxiety provoking.

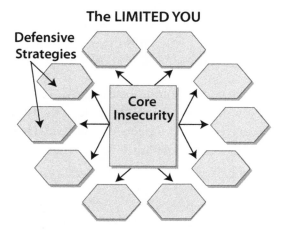

The **Limited You** represents what holds you back. It limits your ability to be positive and constructive. Even though some people can have a powerful impact while operating mostly out of the **Limited Self**, the results often tend to be negative and have a destructive effect on others. In a similar way, some people can use their **Limited Self** to generate a great deal of energy and power, but it is tenuous and not sustainable over time.

The **Limited You** operates under a seductive and self-limiting set of illusions. Once you dispel these illusions, you can more easily see what is true, clearly assess what is needed and take action accordingly. If you think you don't have a **Limited You**, consider the possibility that this could be a defensive frame of mind, and that it could be limiting you. Even though skepticism can be useful when considering a new point of view, remaining open to a new possibility is even more important.

> *The LIMITED YOU restricts and undermines your power and positive impact.*

Realizing there is something to grapple with internally can be unsettling. At the same time, by simply acknowledging the **Limited You**, you can experience some liberation and a new sense of possibility. The whole point of understanding the **Limited You** is to more effectively manage it and become increasingly free of it.

Because defensive strategies and core insecurities are very well established, they cannot be wished away or made to vanish through simple positive thinking. It's necessary to fully understand your core insecurity, update it with an adult mind, and bring it into alignment with what is true. When you become more conscious of the **Limited You**, you'll discover that it won't operate as subversively, outside of your awareness, and that it will have less power to hold you hostage.

> *I was forced to go to a positive thinking seminar. I couldn't stand it. So I went outside to the parking lot and let half of the air out of everybody's tires. As they came out I said, "So...are your tires half full or half empty?"*
>
> ADAM CHRISTING,
> comedian

Working with the **Limited You** in the ways we are discussing will relieve you of much anxiety. You may notice a sense of lightness, a more complete perspective, and an enhanced sense of humor. This inner work will release within you the kind of personal power that comes from feeling peaceful at your core, in the depths of your being. Working with the **Limited You** opens the door to the **Essential You**, which frees you from needless limitation by exploring and anchoring what is really true about yourself.

THE ESSENTIAL YOU

The **Essential You** is structured in a way that is similar to the **Limited You**, but with a different quality and a different outcome. At its center is a *core truth* that accepts reality (what is going on in the here and now), honors the potential for growth, and is relational. A core truth always has integrity and can come into focus when you are feeling and thinking clearly and openly.

Integrative anchors are behaviors, processes, and skills that reinforce the core truth and assist you in staying strong, clear, and connected. They anchor your potential in specific, actionable ways and help hold the **Essential You** in place, so it can bring its expanded perspective to your everyday life. The following diagram illustrates the **Essential You** with integrative anchors that surround and support the core truth.

The ESSENTIAL YOU

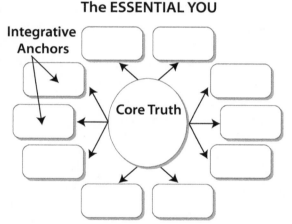

Since the **Essential You** is based on truth rather than illusion, it is truly powerful. The **Essential You** is rooted in the core of your being and represents the best of who and what you are. It grounds, inspires, and elevates you, all at the same time.

The **Essential You** operates from a foundation of relational awareness that acknowledges the interconnectedness and value of all living beings. As a result of this perspective, the **Essential You** engages respectfully with everyone.

The **Essential You** draws out the best in other people and uses power in ways that don't require coercion. Although coercion gets certain results, it is a primitive mechanism that you can replace with more sophisticated and effective skills. When you operate from the **Essential You**, your personal power and presence are benign and your impact more positive and powerful.

> *The ESSENTIAL YOU expands and supports your power and positive impact.*

THE SHIFT

This model and these fundamental concepts will get clearer as you read on. The important thing right now is to consider the possibility that both the **Limited You** and the **Essential You** are operating simultaneously with very different agendas that can either limit or expand your effectiveness.

For most people, self-image or identity usually doesn't change easily since it is anchored in so many important experiences. But it *can* change. In fact, how you see yourself will probably *have* to change if you are to become more effective as a leader.

To really ignite your full power, it's necessary to accurately see how the **Limited You** can distort reality, misuse power (even without intending to), and alienate others to constrict your leadership power and presence.

> *Change yourself, change the world. Trying to change the world without changing our mind is like trying to clean the dirty face we see in the mirror by scrubbing the glass. However vigorously we clean it, our reflection will not improve. Only by washing our own face and combing our own unkempt hair can we alter the image. Similarly, if we want to help create conditions that foster peace and well-being in the world, we first need to reflect these qualities ourselves.*
>
> CHAGDUD TULKU RINPOCHE, Tibetan Buddhist teacher[2]

As you continue to read, understand, and work through the exercises, you'll develop the skills to clearly and objectively observe the **Limited You** and the mechanisms that reinforce it. The part of yourself that holds you back will then be less able to operate unnoticed behind the scene, and you'll be free to make choices you didn't even know you had, especially as you refine these skills.

This shift from the illusions of the **Limited You** to your true nature as the **Essential You** is like throwing off a heavy, scratchy overcoat that has been weighing you down, irritating you, and draining your energy. When it's gone, you feel lighter, freer. Your personal power and who you are naturally can expand and radiate like sunshine.

Instead of masking your inner being with defensive strategies that protect your core insecurity, the **Essential You** reveals who you truly are at your core. This expands your leadership presence, giving you a greater capacity to inspire and lead others in any area of your life where you need to have significant influence.

The subtle but powerful shift to the **Essential You** is facilitated when you:

- Realize many of your core insecurities are not true
- Stop relying on your defensive strategies
- Align with your essence
- Stand behind the truth about what is real and true for you

Your potential as an enlightened leader depends on repeated choices to engage deeply with who you are at multiple levels.

PACE YOURSELF

The transformation from the **Limited You** to the **Essential You** is a fundamental type of change. It is a shift in identity that will change how you see yourself and how others see you. It won't happen overnight and you can expect some setbacks along the way. It is helpful to be reasonable, patient, and understanding with yourself. Identity isn't created all at once, nor is it instantly changed.

Almost everyone has moments in which the inner work gets foggy, doesn't seem worth it, or is sidelined. These are the times when limiting patterns creep in to undermine your potential. Draw on your commitment to work with your enlightened edge, and trust your inner truth at these moments. Doing so will help you remain confident and constructive, even while wrestling with the **Limited You**.

Humans are complex and multi-layered, and change takes place on many levels at once. Effort in one area will translate into several related areas, leading to some pleasant surprises, but not always the ones you expect.

Change is also non-linear. When it doesn't happen on your time line, be firm and kind with yourself. Maybe you need to become more invested and take more risks. Or maybe you need to pull back and consolidate new behaviors and attitudes. Find the pace that is comfortable but still challenging.

Working with your enlightened edge is a long-term commitment that extends far beyond the scope of this book. If you find yourself discouraged or giving yourself a hard time, consider getting assistance from a coach, therapist, friend, or trusted colleague. Getting help is not a sign of weakness. It is a smart strategy that can save you time and help you get out of your own way.

You now have some preliminary information on the **Limited You** and the **Essential You**, as well as what is involved in making the shift. In order to make this more tangible, let's turn to an exercise and a practical approach to your leadership challenges.

YOUR LEADERSHIP GOALS

Establishing some initial goals will help to make the shift from the **Limited You** to the **Essential You** more actionable. It will also give you a way to measure your progress as you continue. When you establish leadership goals specific to your life-work situation, the pathway to achieving them becomes clearer. As the obstacles in your path come into focus, you can use them as fuel for further work.

This next exercise will support you in focusing on one of your personal leadership goals. Often leadership goals are professional or technical, but at this point let's focus on leadership skills that are personal or interpersonal.

Defining these initial goals will help you apply what you're learning as you read on, so please don't skip this step. Write something down as you work through the exercise, even if it's a bit vague. Your goals will get clearer as you go.

Exercise: Identify A Personal Leadership Goal

Think about who you are and your potential as a leader. Imagine what you would look and act like if your leadership were more focused, positive, and unencumbered. Imagine feeling very alive and energized. As you think about this, consider:

- ▸ Feedback you have received from co-workers, family, and friends
- ▸ The effect you'd like to have on others
- ▸ What you want to accomplish before you die
- ▸ The way you've always wanted to be
- ▸ The way you are when you're at your best

What is the one change that would make the greatest impact in your effectiveness as a leader? Write down the goal in two different ways:

I want to be more:

_____

_____

I want to be less:

_____

_____

Now imagine you have fulfilled the goal as fully as possible. Accept it, feel it, revel in it. Write down the best thing about how you feel.

_____

_____

How did you feel about doing this exercise? If the exercise helped strengthen a sense of clarity and vision, hold on to it; we will build on that. In upcoming chapters we will look at what has held you back from fulfilling this goal so far. For now, focus on the goal in front of you. Begin to act as though it is already fulfilled.

ACT AS THOUGH

This technique of operating as though the goal is already fully realized is a highly effective means to clear away internal obstacles.[3] Thinking about, believing in, and visualizing your goals may introduce a possibility, but that isn't enough to make them a reality. Specific action is necessary.

For example, the urge to run a marathon might start with the idea and the belief that you can really do it. Buying running shoes might be a preliminary activity, but until you start regular running and *acting as though* you are going to run the marathon, it won't happen.

> **When you ACT AS THOUGH something has already taken place, you set the stage for that to actually occur.**

When you act on your potential, you activate it. This doesn't guarantee you'll achieve your goal, but it is a necessary precursor. So, you may train for the marathon but still might not have the endurance or physical characteristics to make it a reality. But you will have begun the process of investing in your potential and will have some new experiences and information to guide your next steps.

Your potential is waiting to be activated. If you *act as though* you are already successful with your goal for just one day, you will be amazed at the difference. This is a very practical way not only to remember your goal and strengthen a *can-do* attitude, but also to help you develop the skills needed for making your goal a reality.

> *Tentative efforts lead to tentative outcomes. Therefore, give yourself fully to your endeavors. Decide to construct your character through excellent actions and determine to pay the price of a worthy goal. The trials you encounter will introduce you to your strengths. Remain steadfast... and one day you will build something that endures; something worthy of your potential.*
>
> EPICTETUS, Greek philosopher

Let's say, for example, you establish a goal of being less terse and more approachable in your communication. As you work toward this goal, you *act as though* you are a clear, thorough, friendly communicator, and that others appreciate it. An outcome of this could be the realization that projects are moving more smoothly toward completion. This realization could in turn make it much easier to continue to *act as though*, which brings you closer to your goal.

You probably already have experience with *acting as though* because it is an indispensable part of preparing for a new level of responsibility or promotion. For example, to get ready for an executive role, you need to act as though you already have the presence and skills to carry out the new role. By acting as though, you carry yourself differently and others see you differently as well.

LEAD YOURSELF FIRST

Acting as though is a first step in mobilizing a deeper source of reliable, sustainable, personal power. To tap further into this power, you must look inward and develop a comfortable relationship with what you find. This inward search for greater self-knowledge is a necessary part of developing character. Even if your character is quite solid, a good look inside will help you see where you can improve and where you may need more support.

> Inspire trust by first leading yourself and then leading others.

As a leader you ask others to change in important ways. To inspire others to follow, you need to demonstrate that you are not only worthy of being followed, but that you have done your own work and have, to some extent, walked in the shoes of those you are leading.

> ◆ What experiences have you gone through in the past that have helped your personal growth as a leader?
> ◆ How are they relevant to you today?

A strong commitment to your personal growth[4] in any situation establishes you as not only credible but trustworthy to others. When you can show others that you are willing and able to lead yourself, they are much more inclined to trust you.

LEADERSHIP: A PRECIOUS TRUST

When others agree to follow you, they are choosing to rely on you in some way. The terms of agreement are rarely outlined, but implicitly those individuals trust you to do something beneficial for them or for something they care about.

In some situations, leadership is formal and exercised through the authority of a role. In other situations, it is informal and often exercised through casual conversations. Even though leadership can be associated with positions of power or authority, it does not depend on role or position. It can take place any time you need to make a difference.

Leadership can occur with a dynamic presentation or with a pow-erfully placed comment. It can take place in a boardroom, in a grocery line, at a public meeting, or at home. But when it does occur, it generates an implicit agreement between you and the person following your lead. This is an agreement to trust. And it is precious because the person trusting you gives you the power to affect him or her in some way.

> *Leadership and personal power are not dependent on role or position.*

When someone occupies a position of power or formal authority, the trust placed in that individual is rooted in a social or organizational agreement. This agreement gives power to the person with authority. And in exchange, that person provides a service.[5] For example, a police officer provides protection and security; a teacher provides knowledge and skill building; a nurse provides comfort and medical treatment; and a minister provides inspiration and guidance. In each case, there is implicit trust that the person with the power will fulfill the expectations of the role and won't betray that trust.

It doesn't always work out that way. Sometimes trust is betrayed, and power is easily misused. Often this is due to lack of centered per-sonal power. Working with your enlightened edge ensures that your leadership relies more on an internal, benevolent source of power and less on the sketchy and sometimes misused power that goes with a role or position.

Ideally, people with formal authority and positions of power have well-developed personal power and a solid connection with the core of who they are. In practice, this is too often *not* the case. Let's look at James, as an example.

James

James was in his mid-forties with red hair, sparkling blue eyes, and a lithe, lean body. Some people saw him as highly attrac-tive, but others found him too intense. Two years ago he was promoted to CEO of a product-based business within a large, global corporation.

He first became a manager in his early thirties, and at that time showed promise as a leader. He had a ton of energy, good instincts for business, and the know-how to use his power to create results. He was promoted repeatedly and gained a great deal of authority as he ascended through the ranks.

However, his high level of authority as CEO masked his leadership limitations. James was not a well-developed leader. The gaps in his personal power became apparent when he became overly upset and angry. Sometimes he misused his authority by unfairly punishing those around him with threats. All of this damaged his credibility.

Perhaps you know someone like James? I'll continue to refer to James and his journey as a leader throughout Part One of this book. You'll learn more about what happened to him and the steps he took to transform his leadership. The changes he made didn't happen easily or quickly; they were hard won, substantial, and a clear demonstration of the enlightened edge of leadership.

We've taken an initial look at the importance of inner work, the value of leading yourself first, the **Limited You** and the **Essential You**, and the role of trust in leadership. If you did the "Identify a Personal Leadership Goal" exercise, keep it in focus as you continue. You'll develop more tools for achieving both this goal and others, as you continue to read, learn, and do the suggested exercises.

We'll spend the rest of this chapter looking at the defining characteristics of your essence and the enlightened edge.

ESSENCE: YOUR CORE

The key to success is the **Essential You**. At the heart of the **Essential You** is your essence, which resides in the core of who you are. Some people describe essence as deep within the body. Some say it's in your heart. Some say it's in your head or above your head. You can visualize it in many ways, but your essence is who you fundamentally are. You may experience it in moments when your mind is still and alert, or when your heart feels full and radiant. Your essence is embedded unconditionally in the fabric of your being, rain or shine, happy or sad, powerful or powerless, man or woman, leader or not.

Essence is ineffable; that is, it is incapable of being fully described or expressed. But it is associated with qualities and abilities that can be described, such as natural grace, perspective, centeredness, the ability to observe, and the feeling of aliveness.

Natural Grace

If your essence had a signature, it would be natural grace—the bright, benevolent, magnetic presence that you radiate when you're anchored in the **Essential You**. This presence is visible and palpable to others, affecting them in both obvious and subtle ways.

Natural grace is intrinsically attractive to most people. When they see someone else who is linked to their essence in this way, they will tend to trust that person and want to be around him or her. A leader who embodies natural grace is often charismatic and inspires others to follow.

> *Natural grace is the source of benevolent presence.*

You'll find that natural grace is positively contagious. It flows through you to the people you touch, and through them to the people they touch. In this way, natural grace links us together in a positive, expanded, and powerful way, making it possible to move toward challenging goals even when tension mounts and obstacles seem insurmountable.

Observer

Your essence gives you the ability to observe and to be aware of many different aspects of yourself, others, and the world you live in.

> *Apart from the pulling and hauling stands what I am, Stands amused, complacent, compassionating, idle, unitary…Both in and out of the game, and watching and wondering at it.*
>
> WALT WHITMAN, poet

The internal observer gathers awareness in a neutral, non-reactive way. It doesn't judge but instead remains impartial about what it observes. The observer simply witnesses.

This innate capacity to observe usually operates invisibly, behind the scenes. And it is linked with many other important functions, like choice, will, intention, and the ability to take action.

The inner observer also plays a hidden but vital role in your ability to be present, mindful, and purposeful. The observer fuels you with the awareness necessary to interact effectively with your environment and to provide leadership.

> ◆ Have you ever reflected on who within you can observe you?
>
> ◆ Can you think of a time when having greater awareness led to an increased sense of freedom?

Aliveness

As you connect with your essence and respond to it, you will probably feel more creative and energetic. Your essence is a limitless resource of vitality and power. You may already have discovered that it is easier to take initiative when you're feeling energized from deep inside.

When you're ignited in this way, you may also discover a deeper desire to create or build something better. Creative energy springs from the same deep reservoir that gives you life energy.

The following exercise can be very invigorating and is an important one for leaders. It can be used to find renewal and balance, especially in the middle of a hectic, high-demand life.

Exercise: Really Alive

Breathe deeply and sink into your body, letting your shoulders drop as you breathe. Remember the times when you felt *really alive*. The following list suggests some possibilities for reflection. Consider those times when you felt:

- ▶ Physically challenged (racing, biking, climbing, skiing)
- ▶ Emotional intensity (confrontation, performance, intimate encounter)
- ▶ Creatively stimulated (building something, creating something that is meaningful)
- ▶ Mentally absorbed in some focus or process (new idea, detailed plan)
- ▶ Doing anything you really love to do

Make note of two or three times when you felt especially alive.

_____

_____

_____

Reflect on how these experiences affected you. Were you energized? Did you become more focused? More relaxed? Stronger?

Describe briefly how you felt before, during, and after one of the more powerful experiences.

_____

_____

_____

As you continue to learn about the **Essential You**, return to the previous exercise. Doing so will reinforce awareness of potential for aliveness at physical, emotional, and conceptual levels.

- ◆ *How did the exercise work for you?*
- ◆ *What aspects were especially invigorating or empowering?*

Perspective

Perspective allows you to stand back and expand the range of what you can see. It helps you to see issues more clearly and from different points of view. When you're centered and linked with your essence, a more generous perspective is possible.

If you are struggling with a difficult situation, need to expand your vision, or develop new strategies, you need a bigger context. Perspective shows you the context for the current situation and can also help you create a new context. As a leader, you can then show others your vision of what is possible.

> *The greater danger for most of us lies not in setting our aim too high and falling short; but in setting our aim too low, and achieving our mark.*
>
> MICHELANGELO, Renaissance painter, sculptor, architect, engineer, and poet

By developing a solid connection with your center, you can consistently gain access to fresh energy and perspective. This will also help you manage yourself and others better. It will support getting the specific results you're trying to achieve, such as higher performance, clearer alignment with strategic goals, and less misplaced effort. In the long run, taking a few minutes to pull back and get perspective will be a faster path toward those results.

For example, if you're working on a creative project and the original direction is getting lost, it may be wise to step back and get perspective so you can either re-establish the original direction or intentionally shift your focus. This will save many lost hours of work that might not be on track with what is needed.

Centeredness

It's easy to get overly involved in the activity of life and forget about the center of your being. The center of your being, which is rooted in your essence, isn't an objective thing and so can't be described as a thing in time and space. It is a subjective state.

The center of your being can be described through qualities such as serenity, awareness, clarity, perspective, relatedness, compassion, presence, aliveness, integrity, purpose, and intention. These qualities are vital in making the shift from the **Limited You** to the **Essential You**. Techniques for centering will usually draw on one or more of these qualities.

Paying attention to your center will help you shape and guide your life. When things get rough, it is the serene, clear center within that can provide renewal and perspective. You can find greater purpose, direction, and clarity simply by listening to your own internal source. Finding a reliable pathway to your own internal center will support the transition from the **Limited You** to the **Essential You** in both obvious and subtle ways.

As you do the work suggested in this book, you'll discover and develop many paths back to your center. In the following example, Johanna illustrates how even painful emotions can help forge a connection with a deeper experience of centeredness.

Johanna

Johanna, an emergency room charge nurse at a large hospital on the West Coast, was the last person you would expect to see closing her eyes and turning inward. She was hard-driving but compassionate, and she loved the thrill of life-and-death situations when she could intervene and make a tangible difference.

But when she was thirty-five, life threw some disruptive events at her, all at once. Her husband was diagnosed with pancreatic cancer (with a deadly prognosis). Her sister, who was living with her, was going through a nasty divorce and trying to sort out the emotional and financial wreckage. Johanna's stress at work was mounting, with the familiar pattern of reduced resources and no reduction in patient services.

Johanna knew she was stressed, but when she saw a handful of her beautiful red hair swirling at the bottom of the shower and realized that her hair was falling out, she cried hard and long, in pain and despair. Feeling exhausted, miserable, humbled, and very open, she became aware of a sweet quietness inside and gravitated toward it.

It was like a warm presence that cradled her in a soothing, loving, and restful way. She rocked her body as she let herself melt into this feeling of being held by warmth and tenderness. Johanna described it as "...like all my raw, frayed ends were being smoothed out, one by one."

She started to feel better—more alive than she had in months. She continued to be drawn to the restoring, quiet place inside and found a way to come back to it regularly. In doing so, Johanna became more aware of her real priorities as she made important decisions. The practice of returning to her source sustained her through the chaos of her personal and professional life.

Although dramatic, Johanna's example isn't unusual. Often a crisis acts as a catalyst for opening up to the essence or center of who you are. But you don't need to wait for a crisis. Turning inward is a skill you can practice anytime. You'll be asked to turn inward in a variety of ways as you continue to read.

The **Essential You** is organized around your core truth, and draws fundamentally from your essence. The capacity to observe in a neutral way, experience aliveness, gain perspective, and to act from the center of your being are defining characteristics of your essence. Each of these capacities is necessary and will come into play when you work with your enlightened edge.

> ♦ *Focus for just a moment on the place in your body where you feel the most centered.*
> ♦ *Breathe into this place. As you inhale, expand and open up to the core of your being, your source of support. As you exhale, let yourself relax and receive.*

THE ENLIGHTENED EDGE

The enlightened edge is a working space where you challenge what is limited and distorted and stand behind what is expanded and true. Working with your enlightened edge will bring you to your growth edge as a leader. There, your awareness expands toward what is more true, whole, and relational. It provides the presence, perspective, vision, and wisdom to offset needless harm, limitation, and reactivity.

The following diagram illustrates how current awareness can yield to an expanded awareness. That new awareness then becomes part of the enlightened edge.

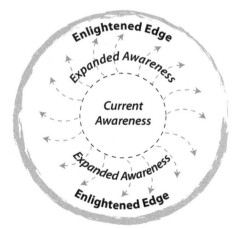

Your enlightened edge comes into focus when you expand your current awareness and work with the information that comes with new awareness. In the previous example, Johanna had a new experience that she returned to over and over again. Every time she did so, she was working with her enlightened edge.

You can also expand your enlightened edge when you have an inspired vision and decide to make it a reality. This usually brings you into contact with others, when it is sometimes difficult to stay connected, relational, and non-reactive. Whenever you deal with an aspect of reality you would like to see improved, you test and stretch your enlightened edge.

Tamara is an example of a leader who encountered her enlightened edge through a social issue.

Tamara

Tamara was an elected member of the city council in a suburb of a large city. Through her work with the public schools, she came across some new information regarding the obesity problem in children nationwide and in her state in particular. With two of her own grandkids in elementary school, she had heightened attention to issues related to children.

As she became aware of the scope of the problem, Tamara saw the gaping need for better nutrition in the schools. She stretched beyond her own self-interest and immediate comfort zone and developed a vision for revamping the lunch program for public schools.

Along the way, Tamara needed to work skillfully with others, especially when faced with so many competing needs that also required funding. But she persisted and finally, after many months of effort, she found a way to work with the schools to provide healthy, tasty, affordable lunches, and special funding for children who couldn't afford school lunches.

At several junctures Tamara chose to continue to stay open to new information and feedback, work constructively with frustrating situations and people, and stay true to her vision. The school lunch project kept her in touch with her enlightened edge. But her commitment to working with that edge was the key to her success.

At this point, it will be useful to think about your own enlightened edge and to make note of any challenges and goals that have come into focus. This will help you apply what you're learning to what is most important to you.

> ◆ *What have you read about so far that is most intriguing to you as a leader?*
> ◆ *How do you think the **Limited You** is affecting your leadership?*
> ◆ *How could further development of the **Essential You** affect your leadership?*
> ◆ *What areas of your life could use more expanded awareness?*

The leadership challenge asks you to shift your base of power from the **Limited You** to the **Essential You**. To accomplish this, you'll need to understand at a fairly deep level how the **Limited You** functions. You'll need to expand your awareness both conceptually and emotionally as you work with your enlightened edge. By learning as much as you can about yourself and the **Limited You**, you'll become better equipped to first lead yourself and then others.

The next two chapters will give you a chance to look closely at the **Limited You**. As you gain awareness, you'll begin to see new possibilities for yourself. Chapter 4 will then focus on the **Essential You** and how to shift from what is illusory and limiting to what is true and expansive.

2

THE LIMITED YOU & CORE INSECURITIES

Nothing in life is to be feared, it is only to be understood.
Now is the time to understand more,
so that we can fear less.

MARIE CURIE, physics and chemistry Nobel Prize winner

B ECOMING free of the **Limited You** is a tremendous relief. You'll find that a huge weight has been lifted when you release yourself from the fears, beliefs, and assumptions that can limit and hold you back from fulfilling what you really want to accomplish. Usually these fears are rooted in a deep insecurity that may not seem rational but somehow persists.

Recall from Chapter 1 that the **Limited You** is organized around a core insecurity. Surrounding this vulnerable core is a powerful cluster of defensive strategies that become activated when something threatens to trigger the core insecurity. These protective defensive strategies prevent you from experiencing the uncomfortable feelings associated with the core insecurity. But they also profoundly limit you, because they close off access to deeper sources of strength.

THE ENEMY?

The **Limited You** creates blind spots when it operates outside your awareness or field of vision. However, as you expand your field of vision and get feedback on blind spots, you won't be blindsided or held back by what can feel like your own worst enemy—the **Limited You**, with its carefully arranged layers of protection.

Even though the **Limited You** can seem like an enemy, it's important to work with and understand it. With greater understanding, you'll find that it's easier to feel compassion for aspects of yourself that are difficult to accept. Keep in mind that the tendency to attack yourself is an indication that the **Limited You** is in charge. The **Essential You** doesn't attack; its actions are completely constructive.

> *We have met the enemy and he is us.*
>
> POGO, comic strip character created by Walt Kelly

It takes courage to look at how you limit yourself. This is where you face what is illusory in order to reveal what is true and enduring. As you acknowledge your fear and wrestle with it, you'll find your enlightened edge. The process of looking at the **Limited You** isn't for the fainthearted. But it *is* necessary for effective leadership.

> *The ESSENTIAL YOU never attacks the LIMITED YOU.*

The **Limited You** may at times seem unacceptable or impossible to deal with. It can be like a shadow self that you try to push away or ignore. No one really wants to feel his or her core insecurity or be under its influence. People often go to extremes to keep it hidden. But invariably, when something triggers the **Limited You**, you can find yourself feeling, thinking, and acting in ways you don't like or may regret.

> ♦ Do you remember a time when you really had to struggle to overcome a fear that you knew was not rational?
> ♦ Did it take courage or effort to work through the fear?

Let's take a deeper look at James, who lost a lot of ground due to his **Limited Self.** You'll also see that he claimed ground as he courageously looked at his core insecurity and his defensive strategies. He took on a new level of responsibility for himself.

James, continued from page 15

When James came into his new role as CEO of one organization among many in a global technology corporation, he knew
that there was a lot of cleanup work to be done. The previous
CEO had left a very messy situation at multiple levels. James
needed to deliver significant results in his new role in order to
remain a viable player with other CEOs in the parent organization. And he also had an expensive lifestyle to support. The
thought of not succeeding never crossed his mind.

It was "war" for James. In the first six months, he replaced
five of his ten VPs. The organization reeled from the impact.
Casualties were a predictable part of his game plan. He anticipated the reactions, was prepared for them, and charged ahead.

In his drive to succeed at gaining recognition, money, and
control, he became reckless and didn't pay much attention to
how he treated others. When he caught a glimpse of damage
done to others, he either turned a blind eye or blamed others
for being weak.

He absolutely could not stand vulnerability in anyone. He
couldn't see his own vulnerability and felt contempt when he
saw it in others. It never occurred to him that his own insecurities were driving him. Nor was he aware that his organization
was very close to disaster.

James didn't even consider that something was amiss until
after his organization ran headlong into a product delivery crisis.
This occurred after a peer from another business line sabotaged
him in ways he didn't see coming, and after he lost two of his
most talented and creative senior engineers to the competition.

When a friend suggested that he get some serious coaching,
he found the idea absurd. A few weeks later, the CEO of his
parent company threatened to fire him for poor business performance. He also received feedback from the human resources
department of the parent company about his punishing leadership style and how inappropriate it was for the future direction
of the global organization.

Finally, James was willing to really look at himself. Before
that, he had been only vaguely aware of a persistent, gnawing

uneasiness in his gut and chest that he didn't want to think about. This unshakable discomfort was linked with the acute need to keep pushing, no matter what. He was operating in the middle of a blind spot fueled by his core insecurity.

But James had a very difficult time admitting that he was insecure about *anything*. It just *wasn't* how he saw himself. He saw himself as strong, super-strong in fact, and able to dominate or control as needed.

However, one of James's greatest strengths had always been his commitment to learning from mistakes and to creating innovative solutions. Once he decided to apply these principles to himself, his self-awareness took a major leap.

James discovered that at his core he felt terribly inadequate and powerless to get what he really needed from others. It was a very childlike, frightening feeling.

Surrounding this core insecurity was a thick layer of behaviors and strategies that made sure he didn't have to feel this fear. These strategies included being insensitive, ruthless, hypercritical of weakness, unreasonable, and punishing when others disappointed him or didn't pay him the proper respect.

Despite his long track record culminating in his position as a CEO and his driving personality style, James was plagued by his core insecurity, which was:

> *"I am inadequate and powerless to get what I really want from others."*

James also used strategies like blaming, avoiding feedback, criticizing others, and feeding his insatiable materialism to protect himself from feeling powerless and inadequate. Yet, paradoxically and predictably, none of the strategies provided any real relief. Most of his strategies alienated him from others, further reinforcing the deep fear and bad feeling he had inside.

The following diagram illustrates his core insecurity and some of the defensive strategies he used to keep his core insecurity from surfacing.

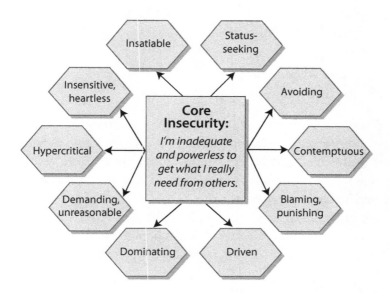

After James began to look at his insecurity and his defensive strategies, he started to feel free of their grip. He began taking responsibility for rebuilding his identity along new lines, using many of the processes in this book. He eventually became an inspiration to others for how change can occur.

You may know some people like James. Do you recognize any of his tendencies in yourself? If you do, remember that this is not the whole story or the whole truth. There is more to James than his **Limited Self**, and there is more to you. The **Essential Self** exists deeply and powerfully.

LESS TRUE OR MORE TRUE

In searching out what is true, the half-truths will more easily come into focus. You'll then have an opportunity to update what is less true with what is more true.*

---

* The *More True You Worksheet* can help you identify what is true for you at a deep level and use that information to take constructive action. The result is a powerful shift toward greater integrity and success with your goals. You can download the worksheet for free by going to **http://contactpointassoc.com/moretrue.html**

As you move through this chapter, working with the **Limited You**, it's very useful to distinguish:

♦ Fiction from fact
♦ Fantasy from reality
♦ Past from present

These are not hard or rigid distinctions, but they are vital to your work with the enlightened edge and to anchoring the **Essential You**. The **Limited You** can be very sloppy about facts, truth, reality, and the here and now. This lack of rigor feeds into the distortions of the **Limited You** in a pronounced way.

We will spend more time with these distinctions indirectly in this chapter and more directly in later chapters. Chapter 8 especially will include a much more thorough discussion of reality and fantasy.

UNCONSCIOUS FEARS

Based on my experience with a wide cross-section of talented leaders, I have found that core insecurities are usually rooted in the formative experiences of childhood. These experiences almost always refer to some fear about who you are or your place in the world. They are filtered through a child's mind and tucked away into an unconscious part of the psyche.

These unconscious fears then stay under the surface of awareness, operating irrationally but powerfully. They usually aren't updated through an adult mind. But as you shift from the **Limited You** to the **Essential You**, you'll update some deep, even irrational beliefs and fears.

Core insecurities aren't what defeat people. Everyone has insecurities. This is normal. Whether you are aware of it or not and whether you deal with it directly or not, the real problem arises when an underlying insecurity is covered up, remains unconscious, is allowed to operate subversively, and as a result, keeps you from fulfilling your potential. This situation leaves you trapped and unable to have any real measure of freedom from the core insecurity.

CHILD'S VIEW

Strange as it may sound, you are held hostage to a child's view of the world until you take responsibility for updating it. Most people, leaders included, live in an adult body but are frequently controlled by the black-white thinking of a child, especially in times of emotional stress or tension with others.

When a stressor creates sufficient threat, it activates primitive parts of the brain that trigger core insecurities and the **Limited You**. Emotional reactions linked with the instinct for survival then replace clear or creative thinking.

> ◆ *Can you recall a time when you were extremely stressed?*
> ◆ *Do you remember feeling insecure, anxious, agitated, aggressive, or emotionally less mature than usual?*

Even though core insecurities tend to be rooted in the past, it isn't necessary to go back and relive your childhood. Based on my experience, one time through is usually quite sufficient for most people! Any relevant patterns from childhood are alive and well in the here and now. All you need to do is look honestly for current patterns of thinking, feeling, and relating that are primitive or childlike. Then it's a matter of updating and correcting what isn't true.

RECOGNIZE FALSE STORIES

Your core insecurity is always a distortion of the reality of who you really are. Even though your core insecurity may tell you something about an experience you had in the past, it also distorts reality and the truth in a significant way.

Core insecurities don't represent the full truth. Your core insecurity will almost always amplify a very intense, even traumatic aspect of your experience. It will then form an erroneous conclusion about who you are or how others are. It will distort your perceptions and use them to create false stories to support what appears to be true. The result is a very convincing illusion.

Your core insecurity always distorts the truth

If your core insecurity was formed when you were young, as it was for most people, it will be rooted in the primitive thinking, limited options, and survival needs of a child. The result is a disabling insecurity, a story from your past that has been driving much of the difficulty in accomplishing your as-yet-unrealized goals in life.

Once you see your insecurity as telling a story rather than telling the truth, you can gain freedom from its disabling control. The story can tell you about your experience at one point in time, but it isn't equipped to tell the truth about here and now.[1]

> *Freedom is what you do with what's been done to you.*
>
> JEAN-PAUL SARTRE,
> existentialist philosopher
> and writer

Let's look at Shirley, a leader with a disabling story that is clearly linked to her formative years.

Shirley

Shirley was a director of nursing in a regional medical center. She was single and in her mid-forties. She had a pensive but gentle manner that masked her long-standing fear that she was really incompetent and couldn't make a difference. This dated back to when she was seven years old: her mother was in a car accident and almost died.

For many months, her mother was depressed and in severe pain. Shirley, being just a child, was unable to relieve her mother's pain or to make it all better. She felt emotionally adrift with the sudden loss of her mother's attention. This was compounded by the loss of her father's attention as well, since he spent even more time at work, avoiding his wife and the powerlessness he felt around her.

Shirley coped by trying hard to be very good at everything she did and making things as nice as possible for her mother. She was an excellent student, read to her mom every night, learned to cook simple desserts, cleaned the house, and even created shopping lists for her father. This was part of a developing pattern of tending to the needs of her parents. Her mom and dad rewarded her for being such a great kid but were unaware of how anxious and responsible Shirley felt whenever something went wrong.

As an adult, Shirley became a workaholic and often got up in the middle of the night to clean, respond to email, or make lists when she couldn't sleep. She didn't consciously feel inadequate. She was only aware of a chronic pattern of tension in her shoulders and uneasiness in her chest. Her primary way to relieve the discomfort was to work until she was exhausted.

Her pattern of caretaking and overworking kept her from feeling the full force of her deep fear of incompetence, but these behaviors also kept her bound to her fear. She was never free of her insecurity because it took so much energy to avoid feeling what was always lurking just below the surface.

The following diagram illustrates Shirley's **Limited Self.** Notice the core insecurity concerning competence (which is very common with highly competent people) and the surrounding behaviors and tendencies that serve as defensive strategies.

Do you see how Shirley's childhood experiences became part of a story that is embedded in her core insecurity? We'll return to Shirley in the next chapter, where you'll see how she found her core truth and started to build integrative anchors for her **Essential Self.**

PATTERNS FOR CORE INSECURITIES

Core insecurities follow some common patterns. They usually:

- ◆ **Dismiss or defy reality** in a way that can often have aggressive overtones. For example, a core insecurity that says "I am all alone" defies the reality that there are indeed people who are available to provide support.

- ◆ **Bypass a more complete truth** by making a sweeping generalization, distort some aspect of what is going on, or delete significant information. For example, a core insecurity that says "I always fail" makes a sweeping generalization that leaves out information about successes and distorts a more complete view of self.

- ◆ **Limit growth** in yourself and others, often by taking a narrow perspective or one that is self-defeating. For example, a core insecurity that says "I can't handle what I feel" sets up a narrow range for tolerable emotions, which limits the ability to process and manage difficult emotional states.

- ◆ **Attack yourself or others** through unchecked reactivity, polarization, and primitive responses to stress. For example, a core insecurity that says "I am stupid" takes a hostile position toward self. A core insecurity that says "I hate the world" takes an aggressive stance that is focused outward.

Each of the above themes will be expanded upon in later chapters. For now, keep them in mind when reflecting on your core insecurity. They can point the way to the core of the **Limited You**. This insecure, strategically defended part of yourself needs your adult, mature mind and heart to help it out of the mess it's in.

MORE THAN ONE CORE INSECURITY?

It's useful to focus on one central insecurity in order to become free of its grip. However, what is central in one situation might be not be the same in another situation or at another point in time. Humans are complex and not neatly organized. You could view yourself as having one core insecurity or several. But practically speaking, if you go deep enough in your inner exploration and self-assessment, you'll probably be able to find one core insecurity that prevails in most of the challenging situations that you face.

If it seems that there really are several core insecurities screaming for attention, focus on the one that makes you the most uncomfortable and that utilizes the most defensive strategies. When it comes to core insecurities, it's better to simplify and focus rather than get distracted by too many points of vulnerability.

For some people, the next exercise is the most challenging and probably the most important one as well. It asks you to bring forward and expose the shadowy areas you'd probably rather not look at. Remember that this is not the whole truth about you. When you put information about yourself on paper, in a distilled form, rather than allowing a vague feeling or thought to control from the shadows, you can really work with it. You can draw on your ability to observe in an impartial way and become curious about what you see. This will help to create a more expanded perspective.

In the next exercise, you'll be asked to pay attention to the signals from your body. Find a quiet place where you won't be interrupted. Give yourself at least thirty minutes or more. If you're not used to listening to your body, allow some extra time for the early part of the exercise.

Keep in mind, this exercise may be one of the most difficult, but in the end it may also the most valuable. It is certainly crucial. Dive deep inside and gather as much information as you can.

Exercise: Identify Your Core Insecurity

PART 1: Explore

There is a connection between the sensations in your body and your experiences and emotions. Many people, especially those in Western cultures, have been trained to ignore this connection. For example, many of us pay little attention to "gut feelings" as a source of information.

However, in this exercise, we will use the linkage between body sensations and your emotional experience to discover valuable information.

This exercise will provide a cornerstone for your enlightened edge. Start by finding a peaceful, undisturbed environment in which you can relax.

Section A

Begin to explore any areas of your body where you feel uneasy, unsettled, insecure, or closed off. Pay special attention to the places in your body where the feelings are most intense. The sensations you experience could include rumbling, tingling, tension, discomfort, pain, heat, or cold. These parts of your body carry useful information about the **Limited You**.

Note the areas of your body and your sensations as you go through this exercise. These "body clues" will help you to pinpoint what your individual issues are and where they show up in your body. This will make them easier to identify in the future. Spend some time with this. It's worth it!

Write down the sensations and locations you noticed.

_____

_____

_____

Section B

Breathe into your body and think about:

- Areas of your life where you have failed
- Ways in which you don't feel good about yourself
- Qualities in yourself that you wish weren't there
- Anything else about you that is challenging to accept

Write down the three things that are most difficult to accept.

1. _____

2. _____

3. _____

Section C

Keep breathing and listen to your body. What would be the most hurtful, critical, frightening, or infuriating thing someone could say about you? Write down three things they might say.

1. _____

2. _____

3. _____

Section D

Continue to breathe deeply. Imagine you are feeling extremely defensive or misunderstood. What is it that you might say about yourself at these moments? Write down three things you might say.

1. _____
2. _____
3. _____

Section E

If someone attacked your character and you could do nothing to defend yourself, how do you imagine you might feel about yourself? Write down three things you might feel.

1. _____
2. _____
3. _____

PART 2: Identify Your Core Insecurity

Review all you have just written down. Recall that your core insecurity is the deepest fear you have about who you really are and your place in the world. It will also be the most personal, enduring, and destructive story you tell yourself at critical moments.

Your core insecurity will tend to:

- ▸ Dismiss or defy reality in some way
- ▸ Bypass truth
- ▸ Limit growth in yourself and others
- ▸ Be reactive and non-relational with yourself and others

Examples of core insecurities might be:

- ▸ I am a fraud and will be found out
- ▸ I have no worth and can't be accepted
- ▸ There is something wrong with me at the core
- ▸ I am completely alone
- ▸ I will always fail at what means the most to me

Get as honest with yourself as possible and write down what you believe to be your core insecurity. Distill it into as few words as possible.

My core insecurity is:

_____
_____
_____
_____
_____

Now take a deep breath and remember that this is **not** the truth about you. It is just your fear, and while it does reflect some aspect of your experience, it is not an accurate statement about all of you.

Whew! That exercise probably was not easy, especially if you were being honest with yourself. Congratulations on staying with it! This information will help you shift from the **Limited You** to the **Essential You**, and as you continue to read, it will also show you where the **Limited You** most needs your assistance.

If you didn't get very far with the exercise, pick it up again at another time. Or notice if there was a part where you felt stuck. Perhaps a conversation about that section with someone you trust would be useful. Keep in mind that the **Limited You** usually doesn't want to be exposed, so it may not want to do the exercise at all. If you stay kind and firm with your intention to work with this, it will get clearer as you go on.

If you haven't done so already, this might be a good time to take a break and do something that is energizing and life-giving.

♦ *What is it about **your life** that you feel good about?*
♦ *What is it about **you** that you feel good about?*

It's a good idea to keep the above in mind any time you're working with the **Limited You**. Self-examination can be intense!

To gather further information, you could also enlist others in your investigation of your basic insecurity. For example, you could ask several people you trust and who care about you to describe your top three strengths and limitations. You may find that the feedback is more encouraging and less discouraging than expected because other people are often more positive about you than you are about yourself.

If you feel especially gutsy, you could also ask these trusted friends or colleagues if they see any blind spots or fatal flaws. Blind spots are especially important to look at since they often point directly to the basic insecurity. However you go about it, getting feedback from others can be a useful adjunct to self-reflection.

♦ *How do you feel about the previous exercises?*
♦ *Do you sense you are "onto something"?*

New awareness of sensations, emotions, experiences, and realizations can be very useful. As you continue to move toward the enlightened edge, you'll find that this kind of information will support deep transformation.

After doing this exercise, many people immediately ask, "What do I do about this?" Good question. We'll get to that. First, you need to understand a few more things about the **Limited You**, so you can more wisely and effectively manage your core insecurity and defensive strategies. You'll then be better equipped to identify your core truth and stabilize the integrity of the **Essential You**. This deeper understanding is necessary if you are to transform your core insecurity.

In the next chapter you'll learn about the pervasive and entrenched nature of defensive strategies. This knowledge will help you identify and make sense of your own reactions and behaviors. You'll see how they operate and how you reinforce them on a regular basis.

3

REACTIVITY & DEFENSIVE STRATEGIES

*The important thing is this: to be willing at any moment
to sacrifice what we are for what we could become.*

CHARLES DUBOIS, naturalist

THE biggest challenge in dealing with the **Limited You** isn't your core insecurity. It is the cluster of defensive strategies that protect you from experiencing your core insecurity. Your defensive strategies act as insulation, to keep the core insecurity at bay, but they also limit access to your full potential. They rob you of personal power and limit your ability to think, feel, and learn.

The solution provided by defensive strategies is at best short-term. In the short run, defensive strategies protect you from the acute (sharp, intensely painful) experience of your core insecurity. In the long run, however, those same defensive strategies reinforce your core insecurity. They create a chronic (gnawing, persistently painful) condition of being diminished by behaviors that lack integrity.

Defensive strategies are always reactive, with an element of destructiveness. They can also be attractive, compelling, and even seductive.

41

When acted on in the real world, they have the potential to wreak havoc with other people, systems, and organizations. Defensive strategies can destroy relationships and careers. And even though they keep you from feeling acute pain, they never get rid of the chronic uneasiness associated with the core insecurity.

Defensive strategies tend to:

♦ Compensate for the core insecurity
♦ Have a short-term or narrow focus that excludes the bigger picture
♦ Limit clear thinking and the ability to learn
♦ Be at the expense of other people
♦ Defy reality or address it in an aggressive way
♦ Be self-defeating in the long run

Some of the more widely used defensive strategies are coercion, blaming, shaming, angry defiance, passive compliance, avoidance of responsibility, rescuing, (more about that in Chapter 5) and excessive control. We'll look more closely at these behaviors and how to offset them in this chapter and the remainder of Part One.

You have the power to dramatically change your behaviors. The **Limited You** really does struggle to do the best it can, and it really needs your help! As you learn more about this shadowy world, you'll be able to shine a light on it, and then be equipped to carve a path for moving out of it. You'll see how the **Essential You** can emerge in the middle of all of this.

IMPAIRED INFORMATION PROCESSING

When gripped by fear, the **Limited You** activates defensive strategies for short-term survival. Even though these reactive, short-term strategies may be poor choices for the long run, the **Limited You** finds it difficult to see that clearly in the moment.

♦ *Can you recall a time when you felt threatened (perhaps regarding a relationship or financial investment) and tried to ease the fear through a short-term but unwise solution?*
♦ *How did this work out?*

Reactivity can be blinding, rendering even a smart person unable to think or feel clearly, and incapable of anticipating long-term consequences. When reflexive defensive strategies take over, the ability to process information is also seriously challenged. The result can be difficulty thinking strategically, deeply, or broadly. Judgment, decision making, and overall leadership capacity are hampered.

> *If we don't change the direction we're going, we're likely to end up where we're headed.*
>
> CHINESE PROVERB

Decisions made in a reactive frame of mind are usually distorted, harmful, confused, or ineffective. Wise, grounded decision making is based on gathering appropriate information and then processing that input in an unbiased, clear fashion. None of this is possible if you're feeling threatened or defensive.

Long-term success requires not just clear thought but the ability to learn. For learning to take place, there must be enough freedom from fear of negative consequences to allow learning and new awareness to emerge. This includes the freedom to make mistakes and learn from them without undue fear.

> *Reactivity inhibits strategic thinking, clear decision making, and the ability to learn from mistakes.*

- ◆ Can you think of a time when you made a serious mistake and felt terrible about it, but managed to get past the bad feelings and learn something?
- ◆ Do you recall what helped you to get past the bad feelings?
- ◆ Did it involve neutralizing your insecurity in some way?

High reactivity leads to high anxiety, which interferes with learning at many levels. Innovation and the ability to make well-considered improvements can be short-circuited simply because the climate of fear is too intense and the ability to think clearly has disappeared. A focused commitment to learning, in a variety of ways, will help with this and is the main theme of Chapter 7.

REACTIVITY & "NORMAL CRAZY"

Reactions tend to create conflict and disconnection. They make it difficult to process what is going on internally, interpersonally, and organizationally, and they contribute to the ugliness that is often associated with office politics.

Reactivity is amplified when people emotionally bounce off each other in destructive or unproductive ways. For example, a manager makes an offhanded, needlessly critical comment about one of her direct reports in a staff meeting and that person takes offense. He reacts with irritation and embarrassment and makes an accusing comment about the manager's competence. His peer hears this and reacts further by making assumptions about the manager's motives. A nasty rumor starts about how the manager got her job in the first place. The rumor gets back to the manager through a poorly informed but talkative peer who can't name names. The manager is furious and gets very irritable, making even more off-handed critical comments at whomever she suspects of questioning her competence.

This kind of crazy scenario is all too common. Being reactive interferes with work, communication, and relationship effectiveness. Fear and aggression don't mix with productive interpersonal contact. On the other hand, work is more productive when reactivity is at a minimum and people can communicate with each other in meaningful, healthy ways.

Pervasive reactivity can be thought of as craziness that has become *normal* because it's ubiquitous and embedded into everyday activity. Extra stressful, bad days are often marked by *normal crazy* activity.

The shaky foundation generated by too much reactivity leaves a person or organization vulnerable. The preoccupation with anxiety and a *normal crazy* environment can leave you unprepared to recognize or deal effectively with real external threats. Competitors can easily exploit this vulnerability. And there may be needless exposure to a looming crisis.

You are more powerful on many levels when you are less reactive. Less reactivity translates into less stress, less mishandled tension, and a greater ability to relate effectively to others.

Fortunately, it is possible to reduce the general level of reactivity in your own life and in the life of your organization. You can do this by becoming aware of your triggers and by working with alternatives to your defensive strategies.

TRIGGERS FOR REACTIVITY

When you're in a reactive state, it's helpful to understand what triggered that state. Identifying your triggers can help create a context for where, when, and with whom you are most likely to become reactive.

> ◆ *Have you ever felt strong, confident, and secure one moment and then a moment later felt nagging doubt creeping in, or your gut starting to churn with anxiety?*
>
> ◆ *Were you able to identify what triggered the uncomfortable feeling?*

Triggers are events, experiences, situations, people, and activities that activate a state of alarm or threat. They stimulate core insecurities, which in turn activate defensive strategies.

Triggers usually come from "out there" and are often beyond our control. They tend to activate some kind of reactivity. For example, rumors of a re-organization could trigger a feeling of trepidation, which might relate to a core insecurity concerning safety.

Almost anything can become a trigger under the right circumstances. Triggers often activate other triggers, creating clusters that typically generate a high level of reactivity both within an individual and between people.

Consider the situation in which a young, inexperienced manager is in a staff meeting with his peers and their director. The director asks some challenging questions that trigger the manager's insecurity about having enough knowledge. The insecurity in turn activates a defensive strategy that comes back hard and fast with data and details that unintentionally expose his peers to deeper scrutiny. This triggers, in his peers, a feeling of threat and anger about being exposed. They view him as having engaged in hostile overkill. Their competitiveness is activated and they gather their own ammunition in defense. Trigger begets trigger and it can snowball very quickly.

Triggers can be external, as in the example of the inexperienced manager in the staff meeting, but some triggers are internal. For example, blushing, a rapid heartbeat, aggressive impulses, unwanted thoughts, or unexplained feelings of shame are all internal triggers.

These triggers can be especially confusing and can activate many defensive strategies.

Kayla is an example of someone who developed a great deal of insight about her triggers.

Kayla

Kayla was VP of global marketing for a large beverage company. Her work involved a great deal of travel, with long meetings and even longer days. While traveling she frequently lacked adequate sleep, had a poor diet, and exercised very little. This was a serious challenge because she traveled more than fifty percent of the time.

Work-life balance was important to Kayla, but it took a back seat to her travel schedule. She had a thirteen-year-old son and a husband who didn't travel for work. Even though her son wasn't being neglected, she still felt guilty about her time away. She felt even worse when her son's grades started to drop dramatically and his attitude seemed to be changing for the worse.

When at home, she hovered over her son and frequently second-guessed her husband's parenting decisions. At work, and especially while traveling, she alternated between being amiable and outgoing and then suddenly irritable and mildly aggressive. Her behavior was confusing to others, especially her global partners, who thought it was because she was an American. But in spite of her mercurial moods, she was highly effective.

As Kayla began to work with her reactions, she wondered what was triggering her mood and behavior changes. She saw that at home her son's sullenness was a trigger, as was her husband's casual response to the boy's failing grades. These triggers activated her guilt and fear, and her headlong flight into hovering and micromanaging.

At work, the biggest triggers by far were sleep deprivation and all-too-frequent drops in blood sugar when she was traveling. During meetings she had lapses in concentration and word finding. It was very frightening to be so foggy and off her game. She compensated by becoming demanding, critical, and edgy.

As Kayla saw how powerful these triggers were, she realized she needed to address them in some new way. At work she started to insist on more reasonable flight times and more recovery time between meetings. She made sure she had high-quality food and nutritional supplements with her at all times. She also got a prescription for sleeping pills and used them when she knew she really had to sleep.

At home it was more complicated, but she joined with her husband to address what was going on with her son. They were able to intervene early in a budding drug problem.

Being aware of your triggers can help you find sure footing when looking at your reactions. This awareness gives you an alternate way to see what is happening. Any time you can see more clearly, you can intervene and disrupt what might otherwise be an automatic reaction.

Since almost anything can act as a trigger, you have no control over when and how an event may trigger a response in you. The control comes with *how* you respond to the trigger. The **Limited You** will be reinforced if you respond reactively. The **Essential You** will be reinforced if you find a way to successfully manage your reactivity and defensive strategies.

Remember, it's how you work with your insecurities and challenge your defensive strategies that will bring you freedom from the **Limited You** and define you as a leader.

Let's return now to James. You'll see how he worked with his enlightened edge and created new, more productive options.

James, continued from page 27

Recall that James, with his competitive, punishing, and occasionally ruthless approach to challenges, initially had no awareness of his core insecurity. He denied that he had any insecurity. It was only after getting substantial feedback about his performance and leadership style that he recognized there was a problem. At that point, reality disrupted his fantasy of total control, and he realized he could lose his job if something didn't change fast.

When he agreed to be coached, he still blamed others, but wondered about himself too. This was progress for James! As he started looking at himself, he didn't like what he saw.

When James came face to face with his core insecurity (*"I am inadequate and powerless to get what I really want from others."*), he immediately engaged his best defensive strategy, which was to attack. In this case, he attacked himself emotionally. He hated his insecurity. He tried to abolish it the same way he tried to get rid of any other obstacle.

Abolishment didn't work. The insecurity was still there. He finally realized he had to accept that he would sometimes feel inadequate and powerless when he wanted something from others. He learned to accept the reality that sometimes he would get what he wanted and sometimes he wouldn't. This was very bitter medicine for James.

James had been avoiding reality in many ways, and now he had to deal with the loss of his favorite fantasy (total control) before he could start to deal with reality in a constructive way.

It was difficult for James to acknowledge having any dependence on others. It was not a position he would allow himself to be put in if he could help it. He was much more at ease dominating and coercing others; this kept any feelings of dependency at bay.

As James faced his hatred of being dependent, he recalled that as a child he had no choice in being dependent on his authoritarian parents. They persistently shamed him with their hypercritical standards. He felt overwhelmingly powerless to get their approval, which left him with an unbearable sense of inadequacy. As a result, his dependency and the feelings of inadequacy and powerlessness that went with it, terrified him.

But as he looked with an adult perspective at the fear he had as a child, he realized he could learn to tolerate feeling powerless. He found that he still didn't like it, but he wouldn't be completely overwhelmed and could survive it.

With this new ability to accept less than total control, he found it easier to accept and respect the legitimate limitations of other people. It also became easier to not attack or devalue people who triggered his insecurity.

Can you appreciate how difficult it was for James to face his core insecurity? It was a formidable challenge for him to give up some of his defensive strategies, but he did, and he became more resilient in the process. It wasn't handed to him. He had to work with his enlightened edge.

There are myriad ways to avoid acknowledging your core insecurity. When someone triggers your insecurity, any number of defensive strategies can pop up. We'll spend the rest of this chapter focusing on more ways to view and recognize the activity of the **Limited You**. It tries to survive in the best way it can, maneuvering through any number of triggers and defensive strategies, including coercion and Shadow Gratification™.

SHADOW GRATIFICATION: TOXIC JUICE

Defensive strategies are activated in order to protect you from your core insecurity, but they are reinforced through Shadow Gratification™.*
Shadow Gratification™ takes place when you engage a defensive strategy and receive some kind of enjoyment from it. This enjoyment or satisfaction will, by definition, be at the expense of someone else or some part of you.

Shadow Gratification™ makes defensive strategies juicy and enjoyable. The juice is pleasurable and you may feel more powerful, but because someone gets hurt or is diminished, it's toxic juice. Shadow Gratification™ feeds reactivity and the **Limited You**.

Shadow Gratification™ is also extremely seductive because you can be fooled into thinking that the harm done to *others* doesn't really hurt *you*, or that the harm done to *you* doesn't hurt *anyone else*. But

---

* Shadow Gratification™ is part of *The Contact Zone™: Power & Influence* board game. For more information on the game, go to **http://contactpointassoc.com/boardgame.html**. The free *Expand Your Personal Power in the Contact Zone™* tips series includes suggestions for dealing with Shadow Gratification™. For more information, go to **http://contactpointassoc.com**.

it does. It fuels and strengthens the **Limited You**. This always hurts you and others in the long run.

Gratification itself isn't the problem. Healthy gratification can be wonderful. For example, setting the record straight on an important issue and being heard can be gratifying. Helping someone who thrives through your guidance can also be gratifying. Gratification is only a problem when you get it at the *expense* of someone else or something of value.

Some examples of Shadow Gratification™ are:

* Ranting, attacking, blaming
* Manipulating through guilt
* Excessive and inhumane demands
* Unreasonable criticism and control
* Gossiping, spreading rumors
* Revenge, retaliating by going behind someone's back
* Stealing, taking credit for what isn't yours
* Rescuing, giving unasked-for advice
* Feeling and acting superior, having to be right, gloating
* Righteous idealism and moralism

Since Shadow Gratification™ feeds the **Limited You**, it is wise to be conscious of when and how you use these enticing defensive strategies. Ultimately, you must give up Shadow Gratification™ if you want to gain mastery over yourself and fully develop the **Essential You**.

> *You must relinquish toxic Shadow Gratification™ in order to fully develop the ESSENTIAL YOU.*

Practically speaking, you could start with the most compelling and destructive forms of Shadow Gratification™ and then focus on the ones that are less toxic. If you're willing to forego the pleasure that goes with some of your gratifying defensive strategies, these seductive but destructive strategies will start to drop away.

Addictions, which are highly compelling, usually have a strong element of Shadow Gratification™ that reinforces the **Limited You**. They are pleasurable and gratifying but always have a destructive component. Sometimes the cost to others is obvious; other times it's subtler. But it's always there.

> ◆ *What are one or two of your favorite and enjoyable defensive strategies?*
> ◆ *What is it about them that is pleasurable or gratifying?*
> ◆ *Do they protect you from feeling threatened or insecure?*

The cost of addictions may not be obvious because the habits are *so* pleasurable and gratifying. Substance abuse points to a very obvious addiction, but keep in mind that almost anything can be an addiction when it is used to pleasurably reinforce the **Limited You**.

If you stand straight, do not fear a crooked shadow.

CHINESE PROVERB

A word of caution: don't expect others to give up their Shadow Gratification™. They probably won't. Expecting them to do so won't serve you in the long run. All you can expect is to recognize it in yourself. Don't expect too much of yourself, either. Your goal probably isn't to be a saint; it's to be aware of choices and impact.

Brad's dilemma illustrates the seductive appeal of Shadow Gratification™ and how it can be both gratifying and part of a self-limiting, self-destructive pattern.

Brad

Brad was an assistant producer of digital business videos. He had a creative temperament and was known for high-quality work, but also for a demanding and super-critical work style. He was not advancing in his career and was alienated from his wife, who had another lover. His kids were grown and had moved out of state, and he had no male friends.

Brad was plagued by the fear (core insecurity) that he would never be good enough to do anything right. When working with others, he pushed toward perfectionism so he wouldn't look bad and be exposed as incompetent.

Brad found some Shadow Gratification™ through making fun of those who appeared incompetent. He was argumentative and had to be right, proving that he was the best. This gave him a momentary lift and relieved him of the discomfort of his insecurity.

No one liked being around Brad because he was so aggressive and annoying. So, even though he was smart and talented and had tremendous creative potential, most of his important relationships suffered significant damage.

Brad felt very uneasy right before sleep, when he was most vulnerable to his core insecurity. To relieve his discomfort, he played violent video games before going to bed. His addiction to these games kept the vulnerable feelings away and allowed him to feel gratified and triumphant, but it did nothing to help the core insecurity.

The growing anxiety about all of this fed the growling insecurity in his gut. Brad didn't know how to handle this unease on his own, and even as it got worse, he didn't seek help.

Can you see how Brad's core insecurity gave him short-term relief but actually made matters worse? The more he indulged in the Shadow Gratification™ associated with perfectionism, making fun of others, having to be right, being the best, and feeling triumphant in video games, the deeper he dug the hole he was in.

All of these forms of gratification served as Brad's defensive strategies and reinforced his **Limited Self**. He could have turned the situation around but didn't. He would have needed to be willing to look at himself first. This wasn't a step he could take at the time.

COERCION

Coercion is one of the most powerful and gratifying of defensive strategies and with few exceptions is associated with abuse of power. It occurs when force or intimidation is used to generate compliance.

Coercion can be blatant or subtle, but it always uses a threat of some kind. Although coercion, intimidation, or force can be used to ensure control, these strategies disregard and undermine free choice, clear thinking, and creativity.

Coercion deserves special consideration by anyone in a leadership position or with power over others. When you have power over someone else, and use power coercively, that person becomes justifiably frightened and often compliant. Fear is powerfully motivating. And it has advantages, mainly for the person who is doing the coercing. But the impact of coercive leadership and the use of fear as a motivator tend to be destructive.

You could think of coercion as a primitive solution to a complex problem. As a strategy for addressing complex business problems, it is extremely ineffective. This is especially so with cross-cultural and global challenges, which require respect for differences and an ability to collaborate for innovative solutions.

Even though a leader can motivate others through fear, it is at best a short-term strategy. Relationships formed under conditions of fear tend to break down over time. There are much more effective means to influence and motivate people, especially if the goal is long-term stability and viability for the relationship.

If you are to create long-term, relational solutions to complex issues and challenges, you need to give up coercion as a strategy. This is easier once you realize that full control of others is a fantasy. As you relinquish the illusion of control, the door opens up to a more complete understanding of the needs of another person or group. This supports the emergence of creative, collaborative, and elegant ways to respond to what is needed. We will discuss how to do this in the last few chapters of the book.

DEFENSIVE STRATEGIES IN THE WORKPLACE

To fill out your picture of defensive strategies, it's useful to see how these behaviors can do damage in the workplace. When reactivity and defensive strategies dominate, work usually grinds to a halt. If you as a leader get bound up in reactivity and act from the **Limited You**, both your work and the work of others will be significantly impaired. This is especially so with creative or innovative work.

Reactivity in the leader inhibits the work of others.

The following list highlights some of the ways that defensive strategies can show up at work:

- ◆ Bypassing personal responsibility, making excuses
- ◆ Blaming, devaluing, or sabotaging others

♦ Inability to focus on common goals
♦ Antagonizing or inflammatory communication
♦ Excessive compliance, accommodation, or apology
♦ Inefficient or sluggish performance
♦ Unspoken, unclear expectations
♦ Avoiding conflict, not holding others accountable
♦ Micromanaging, excessive control, perfectionism, rigidity
♦ Too little loyalty or blind loyalty

When a leader in a position of power engages in any of the above behaviors, that action tends to be amplified and then transmitted to the overall organization. This can generate many fearful reactions that also permeate the organization. The result is a general state of reactivity that leads to poor performance, lost revenue, and a potentially failing business or organization.

Alternatively, a leader can set the tone and act as a role model for others by finding alternatives to these reactive behaviors.

You have a lot of information about the **Limited You** with its core insecurity and the extensive array of possible defensive strategies. It's time now to pinpoint the defensive strategies that are most significant to the **Limited You**.

The following exercise asks you to draw on the wisdom of someone who knows you well and whom you can trust to give you objective feedback. If you do this exercise two or three times, with different people, it will be even more beneficial. You will probably glean extremely valuable information. This will help you further define your core insecurity and recognize how you insulate yourself against it.

If your defensive strategies are very strong and you aren't used to looking at yourself, it may be difficult to admit that there is a **Limited You** or that you have any insecurity. Examining personal limitations is especially challenging for those who have significant status or power through the position they hold. It's a learned behavior to not admit weakness, especially if you need to be very powerful in your role. Remember, though, the goal here is to make you even more effective, positive, and resilient in the long run.

If you haven't done the previous exercise in which you identify your core insecurity, please do it now. Even if you're not sure exactly what your core insecurity is, describe it as best you can. Then go ahead with the following exercise and see if you can learn something new and useful.

Exercise: Your Defensive Strategies

Identify one person you can share deeply with and whom you can trust to be honest with you.

Describe your core insecurity to this person. Verify that this person understands what you are sharing and that it makes sense to him or her.

Then ask this person the following question: Can you tell me five to ten ways you see me react when:

> ► My insecurity is operating?
> ► When I'm trying to avoid, not acknowledge, or not feel my insecurity?

Listen carefully. Don't argue or defend yourself. Write the answers below.

1. _____
2. _____
3. _____
4. _____
5. _____
6. _____
7. _____
8. _____
9. _____
10. _____

Did you learn anything new about yourself from this exercise? If the person who gave you feedback was on track, then it's a good bet that the above issues, behaviors, and tendencies are protecting you in some way.

You can combine the feedback from the previous exercise with information from other sources to help you define your defensive strategies. It would also be useful to think about how these strategies insulate you from your core insecurity.

At this point, you probably have a working idea of your core insecurity and some of your defensive strategies, including some juicy forms of Shadow Gratification™. The **Limited You** and some overall patterns of reactivity should be coming into focus.

> ◆ *Are you finding it helpful to be aware of your core insecurity?*
> ◆ *Can you identify two or three instances in which you used Shadow Gratification™?*
> ◆ *If you have a significant position of power or authority, can you think of any times when you used your power coercively?*
> ◆ *How did this play out over time?*

In this chapter, we've looked at many of the underpinnings of the **Limited You.** You've also seen some of the pervasive consequences of general reactivity and workplace craziness. Hopefully, you have some valuable insights into who you are and feel optimistic about your ability to work with this new information.

The next chapter may come as a welcome shift of focus to the **Essential You** and what you can do to offset and transform the **Limited You.**

4

THE ESSENTIAL YOU: CORE TRUTHS & ANCHORS

*The art of archery is...a skill with its origin in mental
exercise and with its object consisting in mentally hitting
the mark. Therefore, the archer is basically aiming for
himself. Through this, perhaps, he will succeed in hitting
the target—his essential self.*

EUGEN HERRIGEL, philosopher

ONCE you have the **Limited You** in clearer focus, your next step is to activate the **Essential You**. This requires you to bring the **Essential You**, which is embedded as a potential within you, to the surface and into expression. The **Essential You** is a mix of:

- ◆ Potential
- ◆ Anchors for your potential
- ◆ Processes and skills that can transform your potential into reality

The challenge here is that while the **Limited You** is already built and well established, the **Essential You** needs further development. The **Limited You** has its defensive strategies already built and ready to be launched automatically. It has an array of seductive illusions such as Shadow Gratification™, addictions, and reactive patterns that are compelling and sometimes gratifying or pleasurable.

You need the clarity of the **Essential You** to cut through this illusion and reveal what is true. Integrative anchors ground and reinforce this clarity so the essence of who you really are can ignite and shine visibly.

> *You don't have to control your thoughts, you just have to stop letting them control you.*
>
> DAN MILLMAN, athlete and educator

Recall that integrative anchors are those behaviors, processes, and skills that anchor your potential in specific, actionable ways. They are not automatic; you need to build and practice them in order to yield powerful results.

Most people have a few integrative anchors but far more defensive strategies. The result is that the core insecurity prevails more of the time. You can change this. First, you reveal the core truth and then put the integrative anchors in place and act upon them.

CORE TRUTH

Your *core truth* offsets your *core insecurity* and holds the **Essential You** in place. You recognize the core truth when your head is clear, you feel emotionally open, and you are willing to accept and work with reality.

Just as you saw that core insecurities follow a common pattern, core truths also have similarities. Core truths usually:

- ◆ **Accept the reality** of how things are in the here and now, facing it head-on and addressing it in a non-violent way.
- ◆ **Are truthful** about what is going on, making sure information and conclusions are accurate.
- ◆ **Honor the potential** for growth in yourself and others, by aligning with integrity and providing a long-term perspective that is also broad and deep.
- ◆ **Are relational** toward self and others, giving you a way to consider the impact of your actions and offering an inclusive alternative to reactive, polarized responses.

Core truths can't represent the *whole* truth, given the limits of human language. But they can represent the truth more completely than core insecurities. Core truths fill in information and acknowledge a wider range of experiences, and thus offset the often colorful but limiting stories told by core insecurities.

> *Core truths represent what is accurate, complete, and MORE TRUE.*

They are the product of adult thinking and a mature mind. Because they are more complete and accurate, core truths can effectively challenge black-white thinking[2] and the primitive beliefs of the **Limited Self**. As your core truth comes into focus, you can use it to challenge your core insecurity so it doesn't rule your life.

Let's return to Shirley and see how she brought her core truth into focus and started to build her integrative anchors.

Shirley, continued from page 32

Recall that Shirley, a director of nursing, had a pattern of overworking and caretaking when her core insecurity *("I am incompetent and can't make a difference.")* was triggered. She recognized, over a period of time, that these behaviors were rooted in anxiety around her competence.

Shirley was very committed to grappling with the anxiety that was plaguing her. She worked steadily to bring her **Limited Self** into focus and began to see more clearly where she had control and where she didn't.

One day while driving to work in heavy traffic, she had a very obvious thought: "I can't solve every problem." This was a simple but radical realization for her. She began to see clearly where she could make a difference and where she made herself crazy trying to do what was truly impossible. As she continued to reflect, a more complete truth came into focus:

> *"I am capable of solving some problems but not all of them."*

Shirley decided to make a list of the problems she could and could not solve. This helped her to think and feel clearly in areas that had been confusing. The list acted as an anchor to help her remember where she had control and where she didn't, so she could behave accordingly.

She established a series of integrative anchors. The following diagram illustrates the core truth and some of these anchors.

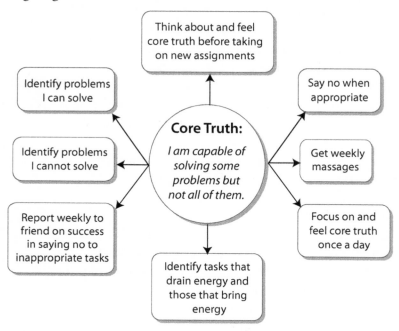

One of the anchors at work consisted of reflecting on her core truth for at least twenty-four hours before agreeing to any new optional assignments. This made a huge difference in her ability to be truly effective with her current responsibilities, which in turn reinforced a deep feeling of satisfaction and competence.

Because she had a hard time sleeping when she was stressed, she decided to get weekly massages to help her release tension and sleep better. During the quiet moments while being massaged she gained insight into what energized her in a positive way and what drained her of energy. She also developed a practice of focusing on her core truth for at least two minutes a day while driving to work.

Shirley took another courageous step in creating an anchor with a friend who was more than happy to support her. This consisted of reporting to her friend on a weekly basis her success in saying no to inappropriate tasks, assignments, and urges to rescue other people. This reporting process was highly effective in supporting most of her other anchors.

Do you see how Shirley's core insecurity (*"I am incompetent and can't make a difference."*) meets the following criteria?

- Dismisses or defies reality in some way
- Bypasses truth
- Limits growth in self or others
- Attacks and is reactive with self or others

Alternatively, do you see how her core truth (*"I am capable of solving some problems but not all of them."*) meets the following criteria in some way?

- Accepts reality as it is
- Is truthful
- Honors the potential for growth in self and others
- Is relational toward self and others

You'll use the above criteria when you identify your own core truth later on in this chapter. As you bring your core truth into focus, each point can act as a guideline to keep you on solid ground.

In the following example, you'll see how Donald went through a coaching process that helped him identify his core truth.

Donald

Donald was part of a non-profit organization that was committed to caring for the environment. After successfully contributing for a couple of years, he was promoted to executive director and found himself in over his head. He had the following core insecurity:

"I am a fraud and bound to fail."

Yes, he was being stretched to his capacity and was making some mistakes along the way. And while he wasn't masterful with everything, he was still competent overall. He was not failing. His peers and managers were less critical of him than he was of himself.

Nonetheless, he was riveted to his core insecurity, especially at three o'clock in the morning, when he woke up worrying about his performance and being "found out." His core insecurity was operating in all its glory at that vulnerable time of night. It was distorting many things and tangling truth with fiction in a very nasty emotional trap.

Donald had successfully worked with his coach to identify his core insecurity. As a next step in the process, she asked him to think differently about his core insecurity. The goal was to extract the kernel of truth in the core insecurity and build upon it.

He was asked to identify *three negative things that were true* regarding the core insecurity (*"I am a fraud and bound to fail."*). This seemed perplexing at first, but after he wrapped his head around it, this is what he came up with:

1. "I have lost some important competitions in the past."
2. "I was called a loser by my father and failed to meet the expectations of several people I admired."
3. "I wasn't given the tools I needed to succeed at an early age."

As Donald continued with his coach, they looked for three *positive and true things* that were related to his core insecurity. This is what they identified:

1. "I have won some very important competitions, especially the ones that I really put my heart and soul into."
2. "My father was very proud of me at times and wanted me to succeed."
3. "Deep down inside, I know I could do better if I had the tools and wasn't so scared."

When Donald looked at the negative and positive lists together, he noticed the interesting mix! He double-checked. Yes, all the statements were true. His coach pointed out how much more complete and complex the picture really was when compared with the simplistic core insecurity.

Donald was then asked to write down what linked the positive and negative aspects of what was true. He came up with the following core truth:

"When I put my heart into it and have the
right tools and support, I can succeed."

Notice how different the core truth is from the core insecurity, how it acknowledges Donald's potential, and is rooted in reality.

Let's look at some more examples of core insecurities and core truths that might correspond to them. The following list came from years of work with many different clients. None of these are unique to one person. When it comes to insecurities, even highly unique individuals have a great deal in common.

CORE INSECURITY	CORE TRUTH
I am a fraud and bound to fail.	I have or can find the tools to succeed. The more often I learn from mistakes, the greater my success.
I am unlovable.	I am essentially lovable. However, some people will love me and others won't. And those who do love me may not be able to do so absolutely or in exactly the way I want, due to their own limitations.
I will be abandoned and alone.	I am not alone. Help is available if I seek it. It may not be in the precise form I want, but it is there.
I am different and wrong.	I am different and that's a good thing. Some people may be threatened but other people will enjoy my differences.

I am worthless, with no value.	I have intrinsic value. Some people will recognize my value and others won't. No one will be able to appreciate my full value all the time.
Expressing myself is too dangerous.	I can take well-calculated risks and enjoy myself. I can also recover from most injuries.
I'll never be good enough to get it right.	I am good enough right now. I can't please everyone or be perfect, but I can please some people, some of the time. And I can fulfill my potential.

As you can see, arriving at the core truth is not a matter of just saying the opposite of the core insecurity. The core truth provides a more complete alternative, filling in the picture more thoroughly.

Notice how the core truths are anchored in what is currently true and what is possible. This is part of what makes them unifying and integrative.

This balance between accepting reality and placing faith in potential helps drive creative development. Your core truth does precisely this: it acts as a catalyst for your development as a person and as a leader.

Let's return to James, who lost his illusion of control but discovered his core truth.

James, continued from page 47

James would never have admitted to any insecurity if circumstances hadn't converged in a crisis. His defensive strategies had, in their peculiar fashion, protected him from feeling powerless and, paradoxically, put him in a position of being *very* powerless. He lost the trust of his customer base, his peers, and both the CEO and human resources department of his parent company. His career momentum was going in the wrong direction and he was on the verge of losing his job.

When he did start looking at himself, he lost his confidence for a while and really struggled to accept what he saw. His fear of being powerless was almost intolerable for him, but he came to accept that he would feel dependent at times (because he was dependent at times!) and learned that he could survive it.

With the deeper admission and acceptance of his basic insecurity, he didn't need to strike out at others so much or so often. Simply accepting that he did not have total power or control relieved much of what fueled his aggression. This was the beginning of identifying his core truth, which was:

"I often (not always) have the power to get
what I need from others and can participate
in successful relationships that support me."

As James accepted the loss of his fantasy of total power and control, he started to notice where he had control and where he didn't. This was crucial because he still needed to find a practical way to recover from the crisis he was in.

He realized that he did not have control over the behaviors, reactions, and perceptions of others, but he did have some control over his own behaviors and reactions. He could also start to manage the interface between himself and others. James needed to give some serious attention to his:

1. Customer base
2. Parent company
3. Direct staff
4. Peers

We'll return to James again to see how he addressed the above challenges. For now, we'll look at how you can identify your own core truth.

YOUR CORE TRUTH

As you think about the **Essential You**, you'll probably see that there are some well-developed areas and some places that need attention. When the **Essential You** is in focus, it acts like scaffolding, holding things in place. The following exercise is a first, specific step in defining your potential so you can see it more clearly.

The next exercise will help you see where you need to fill in gaps. It will ask you to look at some of the same issues that were raised in the "Identify Your Core Insecurity" exercise, but from a different angle. If you haven't done that exercise yet, please do it now and then follow up with this one.

Exercise: Identify Your Core Truth

PART 1: Explore
Breathe deeply and allow any tension in your body to soften and relax. Let your attention rest especially on the places of ease within your body. Notice the areas of your body where you feel relaxed, open, and at peace.

Section A
Breathe into your body and think about:
- ▸ Areas of your life where you have succeeded
- ▸ Qualities in yourself that you are grateful for
- ▸ Anything else about you that you are proud of

Write down the three things that bring you the greatest sense of joy.

1. _____

2. _____

3. _____

Section B
Keep breathing and relaxing into your body. What would be the most encouraging, supportive, and empowering thing someone could say about you? Write down three things they might say.

1. _____

2. _____

3. _____

Section C
Continue to breathe deeply. Imagine you are feeling open and accepting of yourself and others. You have access to all of your intelligence and wisdom. From this place of acceptance and wisdom, take a look at yourself. What do you see?

Write down three things that are true and positive about you, such as I care deeply about others, I want to contribute something of value, or I have excellent intuition.

1. _____

2. _____

3. _____

Section D

If someone gave you the highest compliment possible regarding your character and you were completely open to receiving it, how do you imagine you might feel about yourself? Write down three things you might feel.

1. _____

2. _____

3. _____

PART 2: Identify Your Core Truth

Recall that your core truth will address your core insecurity by bridging both the positive and negative aspects of what is true. It will:

- ► Accept reality as it is
- ► Be truthful
- ► Honor the potential for growth in yourself and others
- ► Be relational toward yourself and others

Finally, breathe deeply, expand, and write down what you see as the essential truth about yourself. Make sure it fits the above criteria.

My core truth is:

_____

_____

_____

Congratulations on completing the exercise. You have identified a source of real power! If you weren't able to complete it, consider trying the process Donald used on page 61, or come back to this exercise at another time. If you tried and are feeling frustrated, don't push it. You may need more background work or further support.

You should have some very encouraging things written down. If you don't, your **Limited Self** may be getting in the way. Remember that this is deep territory and some people find it easier to do it with a supportive friend or a professional coach.

INTEGRATIVE ANCHORS

Just as there are defensive strategies that reinforce and bind you to the **Limited You**, there are integrative anchors that reinforce and connect you to the **Essential You**.

Integrative anchors reinforce your core truth and assist you in staying strong, clear, and connected. They pull diverse elements together to keep you functioning in a whole, life-giving way that has integrity.

Integrative anchors also support creative thinking and the ability to connect with others in new ways. As the **Essential You** becomes more grounded and the integrative anchors more stable, the world is more often seen as an intricate web of relationships and interdependencies. Complex dynamics and relationships become easier to comprehend and respond to creatively.

Without solid integrative anchors, the forceful nature of your core insecurity and defensive strategies can temporarily wash away the Essential You. To become powerful in the world, the **Essential You** needs shape and substance.

Integrative anchors hold the ESSENTIAL YOU in place.

With strategic integrative anchors in place, you'll find it much easier to relinquish familiar and reliable defensive strategies. The power of the core insecurity will start to dissipate as you identify the core truth and put integrative anchors into action.

Earlier in this chapter, you read about some of the integrative anchors Shirley developed. Remember, her core truth was that she was adequate to solve some problems, but not all of them. She created the following integrative anchors:

♦ Identify problems she could and could *not* solve
♦ Reflect on her core truth before taking on new assignments
♦ Say no when appropriate
♦ Identify tasks that drain energy and those that bring energy

Notice how practical these anchors are. They point to specific, strategic actions that help her to bypass and supplant many of her defensive strategies. They also directly reinforce her core truth.

Shirley also reflected often on the following well-known quotation, which was especially useful as a reminder of her core truth. It's an example of how simple an integrative anchor can be.

Grant me the serenity
To accept the things I cannot change;
Courage to change the things I can;
And wisdom to know the difference.

ADAPTED FROM REINHOLD NIEBUHR, theologian

Integrative anchors act as mechanisms for bringing about positive change and allowing the core truth to shine. Imagine a crystal with many facets. The crystal can only reflect the light and color with full brilliance if the facets of the crystal are smooth and cut properly. The crystal is like the core truth, and the integrative anchors are the clear facets that give full expression to the potential of the crystal.

You can create integrative anchors from almost anything that has meaning to you and helps you act from your essence and core truth. Use the same criteria to identify integrative anchors as you use to identify core truths: accept reality, be truthful, honor potential, and be relational. We'll discuss many specific options for integrative anchors in Chapters 4 and 6 and all of Part Two.

Now let's get back to James and some of the courageous choices he made. As he focused on his core truth, he created and implemented several integrative anchors. His core truth, like a crystal, became much more lively in his life as he cut, sanded, and polished several of its facets.

James, continued from page 64

James acknowledged significant relationship challenges with his customers, parent company, staff, and peers. He went to work.

He identified his biggest, best, and most strategic customers and created a plan to repair the damage done when the last product delivery was mishandled. While making personal contact with several of these customers, he listened to their complaints. He was still defensive at times but was able to manage his irritability well enough to listen and take notes. At the end of the meetings, he and his customers agreed on specific action and assurances to address the customers' concerns.

James also talked to human resources and sincerely asked them for feedback on what he needed to do to become a better leader. Because he was inclined to dismiss feedback, he had to make a real effort to stay open. Afterward, he discussed their suggestions, along with his own objections, with his executive coach. They then sorted out the feedback and converted it into what James could wholeheartedly work on. He began to do the needed work that surfaced through the coaching.

He reassessed the capacity of his group of VPs. This required him to set aside his unreasonable demands and instead observe and accurately assess the capacity of those who worked for him. He saw that he had significantly underestimated some people and overestimated others.

James found some pockets of brilliance on his team that he hadn't seen before. He reinforced these people and their ideas with verbal support and financial incentives. He adjusted his expectations so they were more realistic and looked for ways to creatively respond to the strengths and limitations of each member of the team.

Then James began the long-term process of building his team with the goal of minimizing turnover of valued members, and ensuring that they were working together to respond to the customer base. This required him to rein in his own snap judgments and tolerate different points of view.

He identified his key peer relationships and talked with each of them to determine where he needed to strengthen or repair the relationship. This was especially difficult because he didn't respect several of these people.

His efforts at becoming more relational started to pay off as others responded to him more favorably and began to trust that he would be sensible and respectful. Not everyone was responsive, though. Several key people continued to distrust and dislike him. It was going to be a long-term effort.

Internally, James was also gradually changing. He was less propelled by unconscious fears and was learning to trust something more expansive than his powerful array of defensive strategies. He was relying more on his **Essential Self.**

James was increasingly able to recognize and work with his fears and give up some significant areas of Shadow Gratification™. He was learning to rely less on the questionable control of his **Limited Self.**

The following diagram outlines James's core truth and some of his integrative anchors.

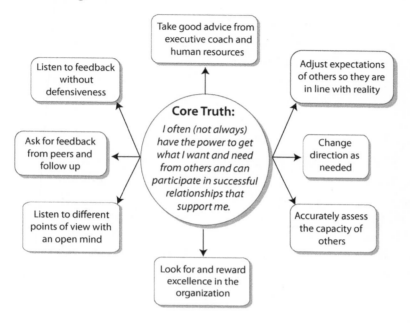

Take good advice from executive coach and human resources

Listen to feedback without defensiveness

Adjust expectations of others so they are in line with reality

Core Truth:

I often (not always) have the power to get what I want and need from others and can participate in successful relationships that support me.

Ask for feedback from peers and follow up

Change direction as needed

Listen to different points of view with an open mind

Accurately assess the capacity of others

Look for and reward excellence in the organization

James demonstrated enormous inner strength as he initiated the shift from the **Limited You** to the **Essential You**. The above cluster of integrative anchors continued to evolve over time as he made them even more practical and specific. But this was his working list; it was the starting point for becoming a far more powerful and effective leader.

INTEGRATIVE ANCHORS IN THE WORKPLACE

When integrative anchors replace defensive strategies, the picture changes drastically. This is very obvious in the workplace, where the organizational climate can make work a living hell or a lively, creative place to contribute and thrive. When reactivity subsides, more relational behaviors can come into play. The focus is then on addressing what is true rather than resisting what is feared.

The following list shows some of the ways that integrative anchors can show up in the workplace.

+ Taking responsibility for strengths, weaknesses, contributions, and mistakes
+ Giving and receiving credit and constructive feedback
+ Valuing unique contributions and diverse strengths
+ Influencing with integrity and being open to change
+ Sharing valued information when appropriate
+ Respecting organizational roles and agreed-upon policies
+ Focusing on common purposes, goals, and organizational mission
+ Collaborating in design and execution of strategic projects

An organization will come alive with more of the above behaviors if you, as a leader, are modeling them. Your leadership presence and impact will ripple through the organization, for better or worse. Be sure that you set an example you want emulated. Choose a vision, make decisions, and forge relationships that support your core truth and the core truths of others. Your efforts will come back to you in immeasurable ways.

CHOICE

Between stimulus and response, there is a space. In that space lies our freedom and power to choose our response. In those choices lie our growth and our happiness.

UNKNOWN SOURCE, often attributed to Viktor Frankl, psychiatrist and Holocaust survivor

Integrative anchors will remain great ideas or just intellectual constructs unless you choose to implement them at critical moments. Once you are aware of your core insecurity and core truth, you have the option to gather up your courage and make repeated choices to act on your integrative anchors.

Choice is that mysterious ingredient that liberates some people and keeps others mired in what is painful but still familiar. You can have all the awareness in the world and a deep desire to change, but if at your core you haven't made the choice to act, not much change will take place.

As is often the case, things have to get worse before a person has enough momentum to make a tough choice. This is because of the human tendency to stubbornly refuse to change until pain forces us to do so. You can be more proactive than this.

When you choose, the decision needs to be more than intellectual. Life-altering choices come from your gut, heart, and head all coming together and saying, "Yes, I'll do it."

The following exercise will give you a chance to gather your own best ideas for integrative anchors. These will help the **Essential You** gain more traction in your life. You'll work once again with someone you trust. This could be the same person who helped you identify your defensive strategies in Chapter 2, or it could be someone else.

Exercise: Your Integrative Anchors

Identify one person you can share deeply with and whom you can trust to be honest with you.

Describe your core insecurity and your defensive strategies to this person. Your description doesn't have to demonstrate perfect understanding. Just do the best you can. Verify that this person understands what you are sharing and that it makes sense to him or her.

Then ask this person the following question: "Can you identify and describe to me five healthy and empowering ways that I could shift out of these limiting or defensive patterns?" Tell the person you'd like to hear about strategies you may already be using as well as new ones you could try.

Listen carefully. Clarify to make sure you understand. Write the answers below.

1. _____
2. _____
3. _____
4. _____
5. _____

Reflect on the relevance of what the person suggested. Check to see if the suggestions resonate with your core truth.

Now link the feedback with your own ideas and write down five healthy and empowering ways you could shift out of these patterns.

1. _____
2. _____
3. _____
4. _____
5. _____

> ♦ *Did the feedback you received through this exercise give you some new information or insight?*
> ♦ *Does it feel freeing or liberating in any way?*
> ♦ *Would it be useful to go through the same process with another person?*

At this point you probably have some new ideas for integrative anchors as well as some that are already effective. Make sure you write these down. Then highlight two or three that you think would be strategic in order to achieve your goals. As you practice your new integrative anchors, they will get stronger. And the longer you put them into practice, the more accessible they'll be when you need them.

You now have foundational information regarding both the **Limited You** and the **Essential You**. You have a working knowledge of core insecurities and core truths, of defensive strategies and integrative anchors. You also are familiar with some of the attitudes and behaviors that reinforce the **Limited You** and the **Essential You**.

> ♦ *Do you see how the model of the **Limited You** and the **Essential You** applies to you?*
> ♦ *Refer to the leadership goal you identified in Chapter 1.*
> ♦ *How could the **Limited You** prevent you from achieving it?*
> ♦ *How could the **Essential You** support you in achieving the goal?*

Remember to consider getting professional help if you get stuck here. A therapist can help you sort out territory that may be linked with painful experiences that still need to be processed. A coach could help you gather and sort through feedback and patterns and convert that information into action.

The next chapter will bring you back to the **Limited You** and its defensive strategies with an in-depth look at four of its most widely used reactive patterns. In the chapter following that, we'll return to the **Essential You** and the integrative anchors that can serve as relational alternatives to defensive strategies.

5

REACTIVE PATTERNS

*Finish each day and be done with it. You have
done what you could. Some blunders and absurdi-
ties no doubt crept in; forget them as soon as you
can. Tomorrow is a new day; begin it well and
serenely and with too high a spirit to be cumbered
with your old nonsense.*

RALPH WALDO EMERSON, philosopher and poet

YOU now have a basic working understanding of the **Limited
You** and the **Essential You**. This chapter and the next will help
you fill in some specific pieces of this foundational model. In
this chapter, you'll expand your knowledge by learning how to spot
four very common patterns that define the **Limited You**. In the next
chapter, you'll learn about four alternative patterns that can help to
anchor and more securely establish the **Essential You**.

These universal patterns provide a reliable tool for understanding
and managing your own behaviors and those of others. The reactive
patterns are the basis for being agonizingly stuck, and the relational
patterns will show you how to get unstuck. You'll see how you block
your success with reactivity or enhance it through relational behaviors.

The **Limited You** draws heavily on the four reactive patterns listed
in the following table. These four reactive patterns are thoroughly

bound up with power, and as a result, highlight the most pervasive and prevalent ways people use and abuse power.

The **Essential You** draws on four relational patterns, which provide precise alternatives to each reactive pattern.

REACTIVE PATTERNS SUPPORT THE LIMITED SELF	RELATIONAL PATTERNS SUPPORT THE ESSENTIAL SELF
Dominate-Punish	Respect-Accept
Rescue-Control	Define-Release
Defy-Subvert	Contain-Collaborate
Comply-Complain	Risk-Reveal

These terms and categories are a synthesis of many years of study and observation and have been tested and demonstrated with hundreds of individual clients. They cover a wide range of complex mindsets and behaviors that will be discussed in detail in this chapter and the next. These patterns distill the essence of persistent, recurring power themes and provide a prescription for using power in a relational way.

The reactive patterns above the bold line (*dominate-punish* and *rescue-control*) are most often found when the person has some kind of authority or position of power, as is the case with managers, teachers, parents, law enforcement, clergy, and health care professionals.

The reactive patterns below the bold line (*defy-subvert* and *comply-complain*) are associated with *reactions to* that authority or the person with overt power. Often these patterns are found in people who are in a subordinate position.

The reactive patterns are very easy to spot, once you know what to look for. The relational ones are not as easy to see, partly because they aren't as developed in most people. Even when the relational patterns are well developed and events are going smoothly, they don't capture our attention the way reactive ones do. But if you pay attention, you'll be able to recognize the relational patterns, once you know what you're looking for.

Relational patterns can be used as powerful tools to more firmly ground the **Essential You**. A relational pattern can bring you to your enlightened edge when you use it to transform a reactive pattern. Each relational pattern is designed to act as a precise antidote to its toxic, reactive counterpart. Because the relational patterns are rooted in specific behaviors and attitudes that challenge the **Limited You** and support the **Essential You**, they serve as excellent integrative anchors.

Each of the reactive and relational patterns will be explained in more detail in this chapter and the next. But first we'll discuss the instinctive basis for reactivity and why it's so difficult to manage.

FIGHT OR FLIGHT

Most people don't start out trying to be reactive, aggressive, or annoying; yet, the emotionally pressed and stressed person tends to lose perspective and move into survival mode. When the core insecurity of the **Limited You** is triggered, it creates an internal state of alarm that sets up an automatic and instinctive chain of physiological and psychological events.[1]

These events are rooted in the drive to survive, and as such, are designed to help you in the short term. But the result is a reactive state. As we've discussed, reactivity can create an enormous gap in the ability to process information, make decisions, exercise good judgment, and regulate emotional impact on others. A person in a reactive state is too busy surviving in the moment to think about long-term survival or impact on others. Healthy contact with others is lost when survival reactions supplant a respectful relationship with self or others.

Fight-or-flight impulses lead to the tendency to attack, defend, withdraw, submit, or camouflage. These states inhibit effective leadership. Managing them in order to prevent needless harm, especially when power differences are involved, is part of the work of enlightened leadership.

> *Fight or flight reactions work against effective leadership.*

POWER DIFFERENCES

Reactivity and specific reactive patterns are especially visible when there is a power difference operating between people. With greater understanding and conscious awareness of how power operates, you can be far more effective as a leader. This is especially so if you have formal power over others, a position of authority, or an executive position in an organization.

Reactive patterns are often triggered by power differences

Any time you use power coercively, you can count on others to react in a less than desirable way. When they do, this can trigger the tendency to further react in coercive ways. This, of course, may trigger others into reacting even more intensely to you, and so on. Reactivity begets reactivity, and once the escalation gains enough momentum, it's very difficult to contain.

You can prevent the situation from escalating by recognizing and managing your own reactivity. Doing so will be easier when you can identify your own your preferred reactive patterns.

PREFERRED PATTERNS

No one uses just one reactive pattern in his or her repertoire of defensive strategies. You can safely assume that everyone uses every reactive pattern at least some of the time, in some setting.

This is the very perfection of a man, to find his own imperfection.

SAINT AUGUSTINE,
philosopher and
theologian

Most people have an obvious preferred reactive pattern. The patterns you use less often may be harder to recognize. While it's best to give full attention to the preferred pattern, don't forget the other patterns. Look for yourself in *each* pattern.

It is especially important to be aware of your patterns as a leader, because they will trigger predictable reactions in those you lead. Pay attention to your preferred pattern and notice what setting it operates in. Then notice if you switch to an alternate pattern in different settings. Also, be aware that sometimes more than one pattern will be operating at the same time.

REACTIVE PATTERNS: WITH USE OF AUTHORITY

We'll start by examining in depth the *dominate-punish* pattern, which is the one most obviously linked with misuse of power.

Dominate-Punish

The *dominate-punish* pattern is very frequently found in tyrannical political figures, corporate executives, and people who hold a great deal of power associated with position or authority. In this pattern, ego needs can dominate forcefully, blatantly disregarding or devaluing the significance of others.

This pattern tends to be overly critical and rigid, controlling through fear and intimidation. When things don't go the "right" way, this person can be punishing and very harsh. The punishment can take the form of ridicule, personal attacks, and making a public example of someone who has made a mistake. The following quotation from a threatened employee illustrates the point:

> "My manager is someone who leads by intimidation. She yells at staff, talks down to people. She makes blatantly discriminating comments.... She has no time for people. When you approach her, all you get are short, sharp answers."[2]

The *dominate-punish* pattern is not reasonable or respectful of limits. A person operating from this pattern may announce new policies unilaterally, with no room for discussion. Decisions may be harsh, restrictive, and lacking sensitivity about their impact.

The Shadow Gratification™ that comes from having power over others and being in control can make it very difficult for the person in power to listen to different points of view. This person often won't tolerate differences and disagreements. He or she can then easily dismiss or devalue the contributions of others.

When a person in a position of authority is acting largely from this pattern, no one is safe. The most dramatic examples of this are notorious dictators and tyrants like Joseph Stalin and Adolf Hitler. On an everyday basis, the petty tyrants found in bureaucracies also exemplify the pattern.

The following diagram summarizes some of the behaviors found with the *dominate-punish* pattern. As you look at the behaviors associated with the *dominate-punish* pattern, be sure to check the ones that apply to you, then think about how they might function as defensive strategies for a deeper insecurity.

DOMINATE-PUNISH

Exerts excessive control and uses force	Fixates on flaws and imperfections
Makes unreasonable demands	Criticizes harshly
Intimidates, threatens	Punishes others when displeased
Discounts the rights of others	Has to be right or superior
Doesn't respect the efforts of others	Humiliates others with sarcasm or ridicule

Underneath the facade of control and power, this person often feels insecure, anxious, and powerless. But you'd never know it. People with this pattern are very careful to mask their core insecurity—as in the case of James, the CEO from previous chapters.

James, continued from page 69

Before he began to work with his leadership challenges, James was disconnected from others and consistently forced his agenda. He was passionate about what was important to him but couldn't validate what was important to others. He used other people and organizational systems primarily to serve his agenda.

James was driven by his own survival needs, which were tied up in the success of his business. He was so fixated on his own vision of survival that he couldn't tolerate input from others. This limited his ability to consider creative options.

Although James had very high standards, he was forceful and even brutal in how he implemented them. He didn't want to hear excuses or discuss reasons when his deliverables were at risk for not coming in on time. He mismanaged the talent in his organization through blaming, bullying, and not listening. This was part of what led to the product delivery crisis that threatened his business.

But under it all, James was trying to do what he thought was best, given the circumstances. He was also trying his best to create a powerful personal presence. The fatal flaw in his strategy is that it was built on the defensive strategies of his **Limited Self** rather than the core truth of his **Essential Self**.

As James worked with his *dominate-punish* pattern and made the shift to his **Essential Self**, he drew upon the *respect-accept* behaviors (to be discussed in the next chapter). This helped to neutralize his reactivity and anchor many of the changes he was making.

♦ *Everyone has a little of James in them. Do you see any evidence of the **dominate-punish** pattern in yourself?*

♦ *Can you find a place inside where you are able to understand or empathize with this aspect of James or of yourself?*

Rescue-Control

The *rescue-control* pattern shares some features with the *dominate-punish* pattern. If *dominate-punish* acts like the "bad cop," *rescue-control* is more like the "good cop." The *rescue-control* pattern does almost as much damage as *dominate-punish*, but looks nicer and is harder to detect. Both patterns are coercive.

The *rescue-control* pattern can be very sensitive to the needs of others. However, concentrating on others can also be a ploy to avoid taking personal responsibility. It's almost always easier to try to fix others than to fix yourself.

The focus of this pattern is controlling others through caretaking, protecting, rescuing, and being indispensable. This generates dependencies in others that provide a significant degree of power for the *rescue-control* person. People with this pattern need to be needed, even if it is at the expense of others and even if they burn out in the process.

The person using the *rescue-control* pattern can appear "nice," but the tendency to control through caretaking can be quite intrusive and unwelcome to others. This is especially evident under conditions of stress. An example of this is micromanaging.

The *rescue-control* person tends to overfunction for others. This occurs when you take on responsibility that isn't yours or belongs to someone else. The more you overfunction, the more you enable others to underfunction. This sets up a dysfunctional dynamic in which others become too dependent on you and your expertise and bypass their own development.

The *rescue-control* person's tendency to cultivate inappropriate dependencies makes it difficult for the dependent person to be empowered and to grow. Other people can also feel systematically disempowered and manipulated by the *rescue-control* person's often unspoken but deeply entrenched expectations.

Many subordinates really want honest, accurate feedback about their performance and potential for advancement. They also want to be able to give feedback to their manager. Neither option takes place when the leader of a group is defined by the *rescue-control* pattern.

The *rescue-control* person will often demand that compliance or some kind of payback be returned at critical junctures. If the other person doesn't comply, he or she may be subjected to a series of maneuvers designed to generate guilt. It's very difficult to refuse a *rescue-control* person who has been so "nice."

People who have been "helped" by the *rescue-control* person may feel a binding loyalty and obligation to return some favor. Often, the result is a growing resentment and anger that creates deep confusion and more guilt.

A leader who is stuck in the *rescue-control* pattern usually has poor self-care and may feel like a martyr. Being supportive of others takes the place of defining clear accountability to oneself and others. Important issues are neglected, and feedback is often not received well or acted upon. Mistakes and poor performance can be hidden at multiple levels.

The *rescue-control* pattern is masterful at camouflage. It exerts its control largely in the shadows, where activities and motives are covert and hidden from awareness. The *rescue-control* person's agenda is often hard to identify. Murky agreements and unspoken, unclear expectations exacerbate the problem. One very frustrated client stated it like this:

> "He runs from one crisis to another but when I try to get clarity from him or nail him down, he's like Jell-O. He always squirms and slips away."

Much of the vagueness of the *rescue-control* pattern is due to a lack of honesty about the nature of the emotional exchanges that are taking place. The outward impulse to take care of others can mask an inner need to control others or to avoid having to define and take responsibility for personal needs.

There is often a firefighting approach to problems that keeps this pattern energized. Running from fire to fire also creates a feeling of being heroic. The Shadow Gratification™ that goes with being a martyr, "saving" others, feeling needed, and feeling benevolent, makes it very difficult for this person to see the damage he or she is doing.

Lynette exemplifies the *rescue-control* pattern.

Lynette

Lynette was VP of human resources in a mid-size health services company. She was soft spoken, listened carefully, and reflected back what she heard with astounding accuracy. She was a great mediator and kept her company out of litigation and negative media publicity many times, thanks to her careful intervention.

However, within her department and at a personal level, it was a different story. She was burned out, exhausted most of the time, and felt much older than her forty years. She had an open-door policy, which supported a constant stream of people who needed to talk. This kept her off-schedule, so she stayed up late to get her work done. At home, her husband and kids felt resentful and neglected.

She hired a new director, Dan, about whom she was very enthusiastic. He seemed great for the position. But within a month, a powerful tension began to develop between them that Lynette didn't understand. What Dan knew that Lynette didn't is that she was driving people around her crazy. They were bubbling with unspoken resentment.

Lynette was so intent on taking care of others that she intruded with personal and technical information that clearly was not asked for or welcome. She micromanaged the most mundane tasks but didn't have time to address pressing strategic issues. She offered emotional support ad nauseam but wasn't actually supporting the development of her staff. She empathized with her staff's problems but didn't create accountability. She was great in a crisis but didn't see the crisis brewing in her own department.

Dan, being new to the organization, was flooded with this information. He didn't know how to give Lynette feedback, nor did he feel empowered to do so.

A pervasive atmosphere of misplaced guilt or resentment in the workplace (or anywhere else) is an indicator that someone with authority is using the *rescue-control* pattern. The climate of resentment in Lynette's group was a clue that something was off, but it was invisible to her. Dan, as a newcomer, saw it clearly as a big red flag.

Lynette was caretaking others to avoid taking care of something within herself. She was operating from the illusion that caretaking others would make up for something in herself that she feared she could not fix. Her **Limited Self** was in full force.

The *rescue-control* pattern is harder to recognize than the *dominate-punish* pattern because the *rescue-control* person appears to be relational. But Lynette used other people through the *rescue-control* pattern just as surely as James did with the *dominate-punish* pattern. The difference is that everyone knew James's agenda, while Lynette's was hidden, even from herself. We'll return to Lynette in Chapter 8, where you'll see how she worked with her pattern.

Respect for individuals, groups, and organizations is impaired in the *dominate-punish* and *rescue-control* patterns. In both cases, the person acting from this pattern isn't making effective contact. While the *dominate-punish* pattern is oblivious to the needs of others, the *rescue-control* pattern can have intense but spotty awareness of what others need.

The next diagram summarizes some of the themes found with the *rescue-control* pattern. As you look at the behaviors associated with the *rescue-control* pattern, be sure to make note of those that apply to you.

RESCUE-CONTROL

Overprotects others	Avoids responsibility for self while rescuing others
Needs to be needed and to be indispensable	Controls through guilt and obligation
Avoids holding others accountable	Undermines through excessive caretaking
Is emotionally dishonest, too "nice"	Holds unspoken or unclear expectations
Micromanages others	Acts like a martyr

- *Do you see how any of the **rescue-control** behaviors could act as defensive strategies for your own core insecurity?*
- *Can you think of a time when you were on the receiving end of this pattern and it undermined your potential?*

Since almost everyone falls into the *dominate-punish* or *rescue-control* pattern (or both) some of the time, it's worth learning about how they apply to you. The following exercise will help identify the pattern you rely on most often.

Exercise: Dominate-Punish & Rescue-Control

Place a √ beside those statements that most closely describe you. Consider not just how you see yourself, but how others may see you.

Dominate-Punish

☐ Harsh and critical with yourself and others

☐ Intimidating or threatening to others

☐ Forceful, demanding

☐ Diminishing or devaluing of others

☐ Needing to be right or superior

Rescue-Control

☐ Needing to be the nice guy

☐ Overprotective

☐ Micromanaging others

☐ Generating guilt in others

☐ Overfunctioning for others

If you checked a couple in each group, you're not alone.

If you checked one group more than the other, your tendency is clear.

If you checked nothing, then ask three people who won't be threatened by speaking honestly to you, and who will give you candid feedback, to go through the checklist with you.

Both the *dominate-punish* and *rescue-control* patterns will limit your personal power and leadership effectiveness. Fortunately, there are clear alternatives, which we will look at in the next chapter.

REACTIVE PATTERNS: TOWARD AUTHORITY

There are two other reactive patterns to look at: *defy-subvert* and *comply-complain*. These are especially relevant for the person who has *less* power or authority through his or her position. They almost always occur in response to an authority figure or symbol of authority. As you examine these patterns, think about how you respond to your manager or other people in positions of authority. Consider also, how your subordinates respond to you.

Defy-Subvert

You'll recognize the *defy-subvert* pattern in most adolescents, but it is a powerful pattern in adults as well. This rebellious, defiant reaction to authority is volatile when visible. When operating behind the scenes, it is subversive.

At the core of the *defy-subvert* pattern, there is a refusal to take personal responsibility. The tendency is to blame others, make excuses, refuse to be accountable, and sabotage authority. This pattern is exacerbated when someone with power attempts to dominate or control.

You can count on people with the *defy-subvert* pattern to take an automatic position against management, policies, and rules that they don't like. They can become very self-righteous and even smug along the way and act as though they are speaking for the greater good. They may indeed be speaking some truth, but the context is a destructive one.

For example, a cynical joke about the company's leadership can point to an existing problem that really does need attention. But when used as a subversive tactic, the humor lowers morale even further. Nothing is lifted up or improved.

Anger, blame, and negativity can be overt or covert. When the aggression is overt and explosive, the result can be workplace violence and "going postal." This dramatic acting out, however, usually doesn't happen unless the person has exhausted his or her options.

More commonly, the aggression is played out behind the scenes through subversive activity like lying, stealing, distorting information, and cheating. Petty grievances and nuisance lawsuits can be a result of this pattern and are often symbolic ways to "get back" or to express hostility.

The *defy-subvert* pattern gets energy from being oppositional and defiant. It can enjoy a fight and engage in reckless risk taking. Shadow Gratification™ can also be found in the "fun" of taking something apart and in the pleasure of extracting revenge.

Sabotage, which is an expression of this pattern, can show up in many ways. It can be relatively minor, such as spreading gossip about a manager, or quite serious, as in giving sensitive information about the organization to the competition or the media.

The subversive, angry aspect of the *defy-subvert* pattern is found in the following comment from an angry but passive employee speaking about her boss:

> "I become less communicative—the thing he likes the least.
> I won't jump in and pick up the pieces. I take the attitude,
> 'I'm not going to help you out.'"[3]

The following diagram summarizes the *defy-subvert* pattern.

DEFY-SUBVERT

Shows overt and passive aggression	Displays overt and passive resistance
Becomes defiant and rebellious	Undermines authority, sabotages
Opposes and negates others	Gets angry, blames, threatens
Is defensive, avoids responsibility	Subverts the efforts of others
Uses humor cynically	Engages in reckless, self-destructive actions

Be sure to make note of any of the *defy-subvert* behaviors that you identify with.

> ◆ *Can you think of some time in your life when you played out some of the **defy-subvert** behaviors?*
> ◆ *As a leader, are you aware of anything you have done that could trigger **defy-subvert** behaviors in your subordinates or staff?*

The *defy-subvert* person is invested in doing hidden or obvious damage to what he or she sees as oppressive. In the process, the person may become willingly self-destructive. Suicide bombers are a dramatic example of this. A more ordinary example is the naysayer in a group who blocks forward movement through objections, negativity, and passive resistance and doesn't mind being labeled a troublemaker. You'll see other examples of how the *defy-subvert* pattern operates when we talk about Edward later in this chapter.

In established organizations, people who are caught in a *defy-subvert* reaction are often seen as immature, unreliable, politically subversive, and dangerous. Because of the instability associated with the *defy-subvert* pattern, it doesn't remain visible for long in a stable organization. Usually it goes undercover, operating behind the scenes.

The *defy-subvert* pattern is fueled and made worse by coercive leaders who demand compliance. The person locked into this pattern will not comply. He or she will defy, push back, and meet force with force. It's very difficult to defuse the charge behind this pattern once it is activated. A leader who responds to the *defy-subvert* pattern with a *dominate-punish* reaction will be in trouble. This is a highly toxic combination, with huge potential for damage.

Responding to the *defy-subvert* pattern with a *rescue-control* reaction doesn't solve the problem, either. In fact, a *rescue-control* response can reinforce the *defy-subvert* pattern. This happens when the *rescue-control* person acts nice and fails to hold people accountable for unacceptable behavior. This sends a "no problem" signal to the *defy-subvert* person, who can easily interpret it as a sanction for behavior that is actually not okay. The *defy-subvert* person can also feel an unfounded sense of entitlement to do as he or she wishes because of the lack of appropriate feedback.

The *defy-subvert* pattern needs to be contained in kind, firm, and fair ways. The next chapter, on relational patterns, will give you information on how to do this.

Comply-Complain

The final reactive pattern is called *comply-complain*. This is the pervasive pattern driving most of the corporate workforce. It is an accommodating pattern, designed to please authority and stay out of trouble.

The downside of this pattern is that it severely limits innovation, collaboration, and personal power. It creates a roadblock to highly creative, committed teams because it can't expose differences or take necessary risks.

Leaders who use this pattern with those more senior invariably lack presence and impact. The same compliant and accommodating behaviors that are rewarded at more junior levels may be undesirable at more senior levels.

> I can't give you a formula for success, but I can give you a formula for failure: try to please everybody all the time.
>
> HERBERT BAYARD SWOPE, journalist and first recipient of the Pulitzer Prize

The *comply-complain* person plays it safe, but the safety is at the expense of individuality and creative expression. The person with this pattern tries to avoid conflict and get the approval and validation of others, especially those who are in positions of authority. The result is a loss of authenticity.

The tendency to defer to others and to please them at one's own expense leads to self-doubt, confusion about personal and professional worth, and loss of personal integrity. Self-esteem suffers.

Since the *comply-complain* person isn't fully engaged, the quality of his or her work also suffers. As one supervisor described the climate in the company he worked for:

"When people come in the door, it's almost like they lose their competence and become people who say, 'Just tell me what to do.'"[4]

The person in the *comply-complain* pattern stays in the background and doesn't come forward with opinions that might be objectionable or cause a "problem." This includes a failure to speak up on one's own behalf.

Because of the difficulty in saying no or creating self-respecting limits, this person can be overworked and feel quite resentful about it. Poor self-care, accommodating others at the expense of self, and low energy all tend to reinforce each other. The result can be chronic but manageable depression.

The person with this pattern may feel taken advantage of but will turn anger inward. The anger and powerlessness leak out, though, in the form of complaining or whining. If enough anger builds up, it can act as a trigger for the *defy-subvert* pattern.

The following diagram provides a summary of the *comply-complain* pattern.

COMPLY-COMPLAIN

Shuts down to avoid risk, plays safe	Gives up, withdraws into passivity
Doesn't take a stand or speak one's mind	Complains and whines
Relies too much on others for reassurance and validation	Avoids conflict whenever possible
Turns anger inward	Engages in excessive self-doubt and questioning
Tries too hard to please and accommodate	Minimizes one's value to others

The *comply-complain* pattern is designed to ensure self-preservation and safety in a relationship with someone more powerful. This makes sense if you are a child or are threatened by a coercive tyrant. But it is greatly overused in the workplace and in many stable, seemingly healthy relationships.

The submissive emotional tone of this pattern points to the Shadow Gratification™ that comes from being safely hidden and sheltered by the approval of someone more powerful. This pattern is widely used as a way to hide from the challenges of personal development.

Shirley, from Chapters 2 and 4, played out both the *comply-complain* and *rescue-control* patterns. Her tendency to be too nice and to overwork in order to please others was part of the *comply-complain* pattern. Her need to be needed and to take care of others was part of the *rescue-control* pattern. These two reactive patterns are often found together, especially among people in the helping professions.

Coercive leadership aggravates both the *comply-complain* and the *defy-subvert* pattern. However, the *comply-complain* person makes little trouble. He or she just plugs away in a lackluster fashion that drains energy.

People who are stuck in the *defy-subvert* and the *comply-complain* patterns feel powerless and victimized in some way. The person in the *defy-subvert* pattern is more aggressive about his or her situation, while the *comply-complain* person is more passive. You can expect both of them to show up in reaction to the *dominate-punish* and *rescue-control* patterns.

As a leader, you may notice the *defy-subvert* and *comply-complain* patterns in others, even if you are using your power in healthy, clear, positive ways. You can't control what other people bring to the table; you can only control what you bring. If you do your best to stay out of your own reactive patterns, it will help others do the same. But other people will still react in ways that have nothing to do with you. We'll work more with the issue of who is responsible for what in Chapter 9.

MORE THAN ONE PATTERN

As we said before, you can expect everyone to play out each pattern to some extent in one setting or another at one time or another.

Edward is an example of someone who alternated especially between the *dominate-punish* and *rescue-control* behaviors. His staff played out the *comply-complain* and *defy-subvert* patterns at great expense to his business.

Edward

Edward was a feisty, energetic, and warmhearted man in his late forties. He was the president and owner of a successful technical service business that had been operating for about fifteen years with about forty employees.

Edward had a long-standing pattern of hiring people he felt sorry for. Because of his own disadvantaged upbringing, he wanted to give others a chance. He expected that others would rise to the challenge (as he had done) and return the favor in the form of loyalty and high performance. He didn't clarify expectations or hold his staff accountable. The *rescue-control* pattern was in full swing.

Many of his employees felt quite entitled to both underperform and reap the benefits of his generous compensation plan, which was not based on merit. He had created a dismal team of complaining, whining, and seemingly loyal workers. The *comply-complain* pattern was well established.

Edward reacted to the inadequate performance of those around him with increasing outbursts of exasperation and barely concealed rage. He felt bad about "losing it" and knew his staff was afraid of him at times, but he also felt helpless to neutralize his contempt. He alternated between reactive spikes of the *dominate-punish* pattern and the ongoing, more even-tempered *rescue-control* pattern.

He was, with good reason, concerned about his business, which was not responding to a changing competitive landscape and was losing ground. As he began to delve into the details of what was going wrong with his business, he was horrified to see how systematic and deep the dysfunction was.

Edward discovered considerable theft of equipment, several counts of embezzlement, and pervasive deceit. The *defy-subvert* pattern had been operating without his awareness for some time. He was disgusted by it and reluctant to dig into the mess he knew needed to be cleaned up. It was a crisis of leadership for the company and for him personally.

Edward needed to look at his defensive strategies. As he did so, it became clear that even though he operated out of the *dominate-punish* and *rescue-control* patterns as a business leader, he played out the *defy-subvert* and *comply-complain* patterns at home and especially with his wife. All four patterns were operating at once!

This variability in the use of reactive patterns is not uncommon. It is, in fact, very common to have different patterns operating at work than at home. There is no field of human activity where they are exempt.

The four patterns just described are at the center of most human drama. *Dominate-punish, rescue-control, defy-subvert,* and *comply-complain* weave together in complex ways. They also hold the **Limited You** in place with remarkable effectiveness. The goal is to see how each one operates to reinforce the **Limited You**.

- ◆ *What do you see as your primary pattern at work?*
- ◆ *What about at home?*
- ◆ *When challenged by an authority?*
- ◆ *When challenged by a subordinate?*

PATTERNS EVERYWHERE

Whole organizations, political parties, social causes, and religious agendas can be built upon a reactive pattern. The reactive patterns just described can be found in any relationship at any level where power is operating. That includes relationships between:

- ◆ Individuals
- ◆ Groups, organizations, factions
- ◆ Different parts of your own psyche

Here, we're focusing especially on the relationships between individuals. We won't discuss in this book how these patterns play out between groups or different parts of your psyche, but it is fascinating territory and worth considerable attention.

As you observe and develop skill in knowing what to look for, you'll see reactive patterns everywhere. Fortunately, there are strategic alternatives.

In the next exercise, you'll be able to summarize what you believe to be your main defensive strategies. As you consider your own reactive behaviors, remember that Shadow Gratification™, addictions, and reactive patterns all work together to push away awareness of your core insecurity. Don't underestimate how seductive and gratifying this constellation of defensive strategies can be.

Please don't skip this next exercise. It is one of the most useful references you can have when you're trying to sort out what is going on in times of stress and distress and are looking for perspective.

Exercise: Sketch the Limited You

In the center box of the diagram that follows, fill in your core insecurity. (Refer to page 37.)

Now refer to the following sources of information that could provide clues about your defensive strategies:

- ► Feedback received from others
- ► Insights and notes you may have collected
- ► Defensive strategies identified from the exercise in Chapter 3.
- ► Examples of Shadow Gratification™ from Chapter 3 and possible addictions
- ► The four reactive patterns and associated behaviors
- ► Examples from this book or from your life that you identify with

In the surrounding boxes, write down your strategies for defending yourself against your core insecurity. To review some examples, refer to page 29 for the defensive strategies used by James and page 33 for those used by Shirley.

Create additional boxes and add to this diagram when you recognize another defensive strategy.

The LIMITED YOU

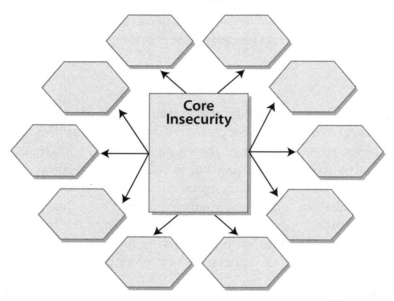

Now that the **Limited You** is gathered into a coherent pattern, do you see the possibility of releasing yourself from its control? Whatever your pattern, it does not have to stand in the way of what you know in your heart is a higher potential.

Whether it seems like it or not, your awareness of the **Limited You** has the potential to make you a better leader! This is your enlightened edge, where you can grow enormously as a leader and as a human being.

For some people, this awareness can be very challenging and even discouraging. If you feel stuck or defeated, get some help. If you need to see a therapist, do so. If you require a support group for a certain issue, find one. If you need an executive coach who is trained to work in the areas we have been discussing, refer to the resources at the end of the book.

This is not the time to stop reading. The pathway through this territory will become clearer. We'll now turn to the relational antidotes to the four reactive patterns. This will give you some excellent ideas for building strategic integrative anchors.

6

RELATIONAL PATTERNS

Good leaders make people feel that they're at the very heart of things, not at the periphery. Everyone feels that he or she makes a difference to the success of the organization. When that happens people feel centered and that gives their work meaning.

WARREN BENNIS, scholar and author

THE awareness of the interrelatedness of all things and the capacity to be relational are at the center of the **Essential You**. This relational approach is one of the main criteria for a core truth. It is fundamental to healthy human relationships because it is rooted in respect for others. The capacity to be relational isn't just an attitude. It is a set of behaviors that you can practice in the middle of a stressful life when triggers for reactivity are abundant.

The ability to be relational is tested in trying circumstances, such as when profits are threatened, when a project isn't successful, when being critically evaluated, or when feeling personally threatened. If at times like these, a leader can continue to treat other people with respect and as valuable, those people are more likely to respond in creative, constructive, and collaborative ways. It is possible to be a gracious and positive leader, even in the worst of circumstances. This ability to demonstrate grace under pressure hinges on managing reactive and polarized states and developing relational practices.

This chapter will focus on four relational patterns that act as specific antidotes to the four reactive patterns we looked at in the previous chapter. The following table is a reminder.

REACTIVE PATTERNS SUPPORT THE LIMITED SELF	RELATIONAL PATTERNS SUPPORT THE ESSENTIAL SELF
Dominate-Punish	Respect-Accept
Rescue-Control	Define-Release
Defy-Subvert	Contain-Collaborate
Comply-Complain	Risk-Reveal

Relational patterns show you behavioral ways to work with your enlightened edge as a leader. They are antidotes to reactive patterns and will neutralize the corresponding pattern, but they need to be applied on a regular basis. By practicing these behaviors in a disciplined way, you'll strengthen your integrity. Greater integrity will bring its own rewards: stability, clarity, confidence, leadership presence, and the ability to inspire trust in others.

Reactive patterns can be neutralized with the correct antidote.

Once you have identified the reactive pattern that needs special attention, work with the relational antidotes for that pattern. This is a streamlined way to shift from the **Limited You** to the **Essential You**.

RELATIONAL PATTERNS: WITH USE OF AUTHORITY

The *respect-accept* and *define-release* relational patterns are especially important for leaders and those in positions of power. We'll start with *respect-accept*, the relational antidote that will transform the *dominate-punish* behaviors.

Respect-Accept

When a leader shifts from *dominate-punish* to *respect-accept*, he or she takes other people into consideration in a respectful way. The leader finds a creative balance between respecting reasonable human limits and challenging those limitations that inhibit growth of the individual, group or organization.

The leader recognizes when it's possible to have control and when it isn't. More importantly, he or she can let go of futile attempts to establish control. This greatly reduces the tendency to use force. This person uses force very sparingly and only when absolutely necessary.

The *respect-accept* leader accurately assesses the needs and limitations of others and creates expectations that are both reasonable and respectful. Expectations of others are firm but not rigid. People are expected to perform to their capacity, not below or beyond it.

By seeking out diverse opinions and listening carefully, the leader can clearly assess what is reasonable and possible. One executive who was committed to staying connected with reality and needed information from one of his managers said it this way:

> "Honestly, I want the good news and the bad. Give it to me straight. I don't want any surprises later on."

With the *respect-accept* pattern, listening is linked with true receptivity to new information and ideas. Differences are appreciated and even encouraged. With new input, strategic changes in priorities and direction can occur as necessary. There is much greater resilience.

The *respect-accept* leader is sensitive to how he or she affects the well-being of others. That leader respects, appreciates, and supports the strengths, gifts, and achievements of others. Here are two examples of how this could be expressed:

> "You look a little confused. Before we go on, is there anything you'd like me to clarify?"

> "What kind of support do you need from me? What about from others in the organization?"

When leaders use the *respect-accept* pattern, they empower their organizations. This gives the organization a better chance of achieving long-term viability.

The following diagram outlines the behaviors that will offset the *dominate-punish* pattern. Reading from left to right, note that the behavior on the right is an antidote to the one on the left.

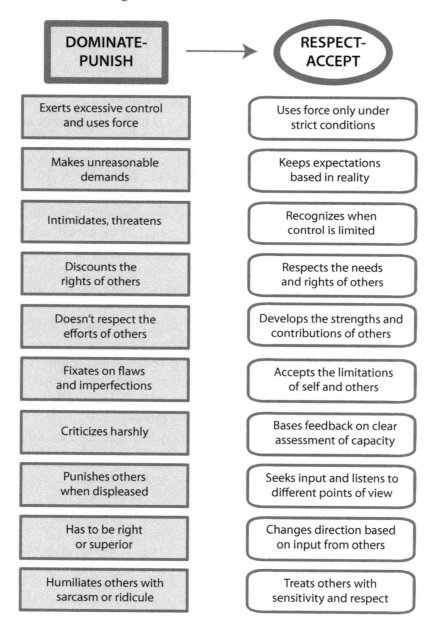

DOMINATE-PUNISH	RESPECT-ACCEPT
Exerts excessive control and uses force	Uses force only under strict conditions
Makes unreasonable demands	Keeps expectations based in reality
Intimidates, threatens	Recognizes when control is limited
Discounts the rights of others	Respects the needs and rights of others
Doesn't respect the efforts of others	Develops the strengths and contributions of others
Fixates on flaws and imperfections	Accepts the limitations of self and others
Criticizes harshly	Bases feedback on clear assessment of capacity
Punishes others when displeased	Seeks input and listens to different points of view
Has to be right or superior	Changes direction based on input from others
Humiliates others with sarcasm or ridicule	Treats others with sensitivity and respect

These behaviors anchor the ability to respect and accept yourself and others. You can use this list as an outline for initial understanding and for future reference. Don't worry about trying to remember each item. But do try to get a feel for the pattern as a whole. The behaviors tend to link together naturally.

> ◆ Are there two or three items from the **respect-accept** pattern that could serve as strategic integrative anchors?
>
> ◆ Is the **Limited You** raising any objections to the **respect-accept** behaviors? If so, how will you address this?

Respect-accept behaviors actively neutralize the *dominate-punish* pattern by requiring you to be aware of others, respect them, and restrain the use of force. Through the *respect-accept* behaviors, you'll be better able to assess and serve the real needs of your business or organization. These behavioral antidotes reinforce the ability to trust in something that extends beyond your immediate control.

James, whom we discussed in detail in previous chapters, is a straightforward example of how a leader can shift from the *dominate-punish* pattern to the *respect-accept* leader. To refresh yourself on how he applied the *respect-accept* antidotes, refer back to Chapter 4, especially starting on page 69.

Under the influence of the *respect-accept* antidotes, other people, especially subordinates, can flourish rather than shrink in fear. They can respond to reasonable expectations rather than unpredictable blaming or ridicule.

As we discuss the relational patterns, you'll learn more about Edward, who was introduced in the last chapter. You'll see how he created integrative anchors to offset some of his limiting patterns. He is an example of how complex and interwoven the reactive and relational patterns can be.

Dominate-punish wasn't Edward's main pattern, but he dropped into it at times, as most of us do. It was a challenge for him to accept his own limitations as well as those of others, and when he was angry or exasperated, he found it difficult to be respectful.

Edward, continued from page 93

Recall that Edward alternated between the *dominate-punish* and *rescue-control* patterns at work. At home with his wife and kids, he displayed more of the *defy-subvert* and *comply-complain* patterns. His employees participated heavily in the *defy-subvert* and *comply-complain* patterns.

His frequent bouts of exasperation and his seeming inability to control these flares brought Edward to seek an executive coach. Since his main pattern was *rescue-control* and he saw himself as a good-hearted liberal, he was disturbed to find the *dominate-punish* pattern in himself. But he couldn't ignore the contempt that he displayed toward others when he was angry.

Edward's first step was to honestly admit that he did feel contempt, and that he was intimidating when he rolled his eyes, pounded his hand against his fist, and pulled at his hair. He also began to see that his demands really were unreasonable if he didn't communicate them in the first place.

As Edward built his repertoire of integrative behaviors, he began by accepting his own limitations. He knew all too well that he was far from perfect, and it was a big step to not berate himself. As he accepted himself with more kindness, he opened up the space to observe others more clearly and to assess his impact on them.

He saw that others took him more seriously than he took himself. Edward was quite surprised to see how scared some of his best employees were when his temper flared. He realized he was getting their attention but wasn't creating the accountability that was needed.

The problem with accountability was rooted in his tendency to be very *unclear* about his standards and expectations. Even though his expectations theoretically were reasonable, his lack of clear communication made it *unreasonable* to expect that others would fulfill those expectations. Edward built an additional integrative anchor, which was to verify that his expectations were communicated and agreed upon.

We'll continue to discuss Edward and his challenges as we look at the three remaining relational antidotes: *define-release, contain-collaborate,* and *risk-reveal*. Since Edward's biggest challenge was his *rescue-control* pattern, *define-release* antidotes were especially important for him.

> ◆ *Do you struggle with accepting your own imperfections and limitations?*
> ◆ *Have you had moment when you could feel acceptance? What was that like? What helped you get to this state?*

Define-Release

Our discussion of Edward illustrates one of the important features of the *rescue-control* reactive pattern: creating clear expectations and agreements. Leaders who have given up the need to have others be dependent upon them are free to create clearer accountability.

Vagueness gives way to increased clarity and crispness. Roles are clearer, and feedback regarding performance is specific. Expectations are based on verified understanding of the task. People then know where they stand and don't need to guess or swim in confusion. The following is an example of how this might be expressed:

"Can you tell me your understanding of what we agreed on?"

Establishing accountability is a point of focus with the *define-release* pattern. The leader who embodies this pattern provides clear expectations that have "teeth." He or she expects that people will perform to capacity and not underfunction. If they don't perform according to agreement, there is clear, consistent follow-through based on an agreed-upon understanding. This could be communicated as follows:

"What action will you be taking after this meeting? When? How will we both know it's been handled successfully?"

Providing clear performance feedback means addressing difficult issues and not avoiding them. Others are likely to perform better when they know what they are responsible for and what is expected of them.

The following diagram summarizes the *define-release* antidote. It shows specific action to take in order to define what is expected and release the insidious impact of the *rescue-control* pattern.

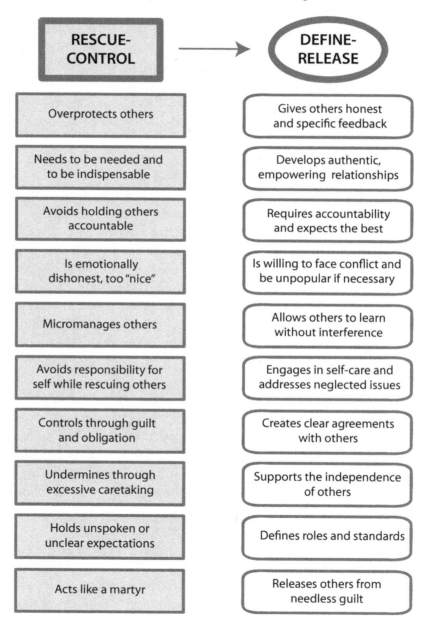

RESCUE-CONTROL	DEFINE-RELEASE
Overprotects others	Gives others honest and specific feedback
Needs to be needed and to be indispensable	Develops authentic, empowering relationships
Avoids holding others accountable	Requires accountability and expects the best
Is emotionally dishonest, too "nice"	Is willing to face conflict and be unpopular if necessary
Micromanages others	Allows others to learn without interference
Avoids responsibility for self while rescuing others	Engages in self-care and addresses neglected issues
Controls through guilt and obligation	Creates clear agreements with others
Undermines through excessive caretaking	Supports the independence of others
Holds unspoken or unclear expectations	Defines roles and standards
Acts like a martyr	Releases others from needless guilt

These behaviors will neutralize the tendency to *rescue-control* by making expectations clear and requiring accountability. The focus on definition of roles and responsibilities addresses the blurry personal boundaries found in the *rescue-control* pattern.

> ◆ Do you see a need to apply the **define-release** pattern at work? What about at home?
> ◆ What behaviors would be most strategic in accomplishing this?

The *define-release* antidotes require you to release others and to face conflict directly rather than escaping into *rescue-control* "niceness" or flipping into the *dominate-punish* angry outbursts, as Edward did. This often means getting more comfortable with directness and confrontation, and developing the skill to do so.

Define-release leaders are not hardened to their impact on others; they are just more honest about what is really needed and are willing to risk not being liked in order to empower others at a much deeper level. As a result, their teams are stronger, swifter, and higher-performing. Sometimes a tough or unpopular judgment must be made, and the *define-release* leader is willing to do so, if necessary for the greater good.

As expectations and agreements become clearer, these leaders can let go of misplaced control. They make the independence of others a priority, and this releases inappropriate dependency. They allow others to learn and make mistakes at acceptable levels without interference. Perhaps most significantly, they release others from excessive obligation or guilt.

Define-release leaders shift the focus of "fixing" back to themselves. They establish self-care and address gaps in personal responsibility. With healthy self-acceptance they have less need to be needed by others. This firm personal foundation helps them support clear definition in relationships with others.

Once you release others, you're also more free to develop who *you* are, pay attention to your own needs, and tend to the areas you may have neglected while you were caretaking others.

Edward had a lot of work to do in this area.

Edward, continued from page 104

The biggest challenges for Edward were to define himself and his expectations as a leader and to create systems of accountability that would support the development of his team and his business. This was a huge undertaking because his company had grown due to his singular efforts. Edward's instinct for business, his ability to do almost anything he put his mind to, and his self-sufficiency made it difficult for him to rely on others and build a team.

Edward's business, like many successful businesses, had outgrown his entrepreneurial style of leadership, which was to take over a task and do it himself when he became too frustrated. His *rescue-control* pattern was severely limiting the success of his business.

His first efforts at creating accountability began with Liz, the woman who managed the front desk. She was the first point of contact for customers. Liz was in her late fifties, had worked for him for fifteen years, and was paid a full-time salary, but was doing only about ten to fifteen hours of real work per week.

He was very reluctant to speak to her about his expectations, but knew this was a strategic entry point into shifting his pattern. He felt that if he failed to hold her accountable, when the facts were so obvious, he would find it almost impossible to confront less blatant problems.

Edward was embarrassed to finally speak up, after letting her poor performance go on for so many years. He anticipated that Liz would feel entitled to continue as before, and he was right. There was considerable push back from her. Not only did her performance not improve, but she also began to exert a subversive toxic influence on her fellow employees.

At this point, Edward was just scratching the surface of the dysfunction operating in his company. After about three months, he fired Liz. She filed a lawsuit, and even though it had no legal basis, it taxed his time, energy, and resources.

He felt very discouraged, and despite being committed to defining his expectations and agreements, he wondered when and if his efforts would ever pay off. Then he met an energetic, competent young man at a trade show.

He saw such potential in this young man that he hired him with the idea that he might eventually run the business. Edward started to develop and rely on someone he believed in. This excellent hire was the silver lining on a fairly dark cloud.

Edward continued to dig into the systems in his company, creating clear roles and standards. He communicated these as well as he could. He stopped occasionally to verify that others understood and were buying into what he was communicating. The feedback was helpful in showing him how to be even clearer.

He learned what clear feedback was and how to give it. He learned the hard way, by doing it awkwardly the first and even the second time, but he *did* learn and became skillful. And as he continued his efforts, his business started to claim ground. The learning was painful at times, but it was paying off.

Edward was beginning to come into his real power as a strategic thinker and visionary for a company that had some new choices to make.

- ◆ *Is holding others accountable a challenge for you at times?*
- ◆ *Can you remember a time or two when you did it well (kindly and firmly)?*
- ◆ *When you did it well, what was the long-term impact on the other person? On yourself? On the organization?*

Implementing relational antidotes is not always easy, but it is rewarding. You'll find your enlightened edge, and like Edward, see the results of your effort as you practice these antidotes.

RELATIONAL PATTERNS: TOWARD AUTHORITY

We'll turn now to the last two relational patterns: *contain-collaborate* and *risk-reveal*. These antidotes are especially important when you are in a subordinate position, dealing with someone with authority or greater power than you. You could also think about how to encourage and support these behaviors in those who follow you, report to you, or are in your chain of command.

Contain-Collaborate

The *contain-collaborate* behaviors act as an antidote to the *defy-subvert* pattern. This antidote requires containment of negative, angry, and defiant reactions. Volatility is regulated so it doesn't damage relationships or a larger team effort. Sometimes this can include taking a time-out if emotions are running too high.

As concerns arise, they are expressed respectfully and addressed through the appropriate channels. Interpersonal issues are taken directly to the person involved rather than being expressed passive-aggressively or subversively.

Conflict is managed in a way that leads to constructive discussion rather than a confrontational attack. This makes it possible to sort out areas of confusion and to clarify misunderstandings. Agreements can then be negotiated as needed to resolve issues as they emerge.

The *contain-collaborate* person interrupts and neutralizes the impulse to blame, while taking responsibility for the impact of his or her actions. People using this pattern are willing to be held accountable and to learn from mistakes, problems, and failures. In the spirit of collaboration, they engage constructively around solutions to even seemingly insurmountable problems. These people often use humor to lighten the load and lift morale rather than lower it.

The *contain-collaborate* person supports the development of true collaboration and teamwork. He or she sees others as a source of collaboration and potential connection rather than as a threat to autonomy. Instead of fighting for individuality and uniqueness at the expense of the whole, this person makes a commitment to collaborative goals and constructive problem solving.

This person values his or her unique contributions as well as those of others and makes an effort to identify mutual interests. This often includes an uplifting and positive view of what is possible, rather than the cynicism of the *defy-subvert* pattern.

The following diagram summarizes how the *contain-collaborate* pattern acts as an antidote to the *defy-subvert* reaction.

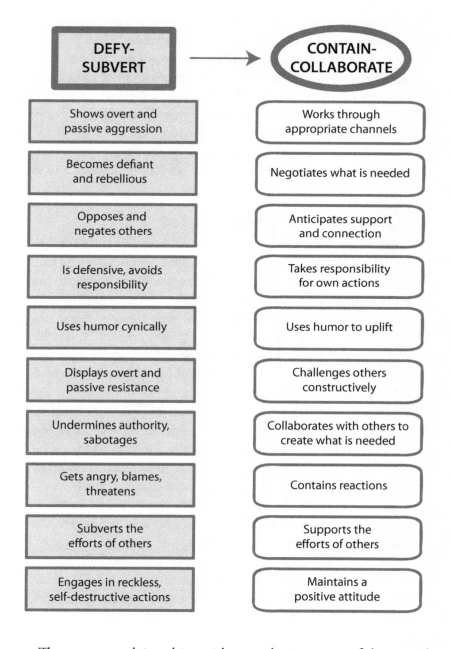

The person applying this antidote works in a respectful way with those who have authority. He or she works with and accepts the existing structure and rules. When encountering systems that don't support the common good, this person may become involved in changing them in a way that is still respectful and self-responsible.

Contain-collaborate behaviors help a person grow beyond defiant adolescent reactions. The *contain-collaborate* person moderates the adolescent need to strike back or get even and instead focuses on taking responsibility and negotiating constructively. This leads to emotional maturation in relationship with authority figures.

When Edward started to address the dysfunction in his business, his employees were involved in a lot of subversive activity and very little collaboration.

Edward, continued from page 108

As Edward started to create greater accountability and act more from the *define-release* pattern, he saw the extent to which he had neglected his business by being a "nice guy." When caught in his *rescue-control* pattern, he had not created a standard for many of the systems that supported his business. This was especially so with accounting, operations, and quality control. When he began creating standards and new systems, he ran into considerable resistance from many long-time employees who resented his new leadership presence.

When two of the new people he hired told him they "smelled a rat" and discovered that company supplies were being stolen regularly, Edward didn't want to face it. He had no idea how long the stealing had been going on or how much it had cost him over the years and wasn't sure he could face more disappointment in people he had trusted. His *rescue-control* tendency didn't want to face the harsh reality, but his commitment to the *define-release* anchors required him to take action.

As he dug deeper into the accounting department, he was extremely disturbed to find evidence of embezzlement. He hadn't provided any oversight of these employees and because there was no reliable system of checks and balances in place, he didn't know how much money had been siphoned off over the years. It was another crushing disappointment and pointed to a daunting task ahead. But he was fed up with the deceit and determined to address the *defy-subvert* dynamics in his employees.

Over a period of two years, Edward replaced over one-third of his employees. Those he replaced had responded to his new, clearly stated expectations (*define-release*) with threats, stony silence, further stealing, missing required meetings, lawsuits, and collusion to refuse to comply with quality-control requirements (*defy-subvert*).

The people who continued to work for him joined with the strong new core that was emerging in the new hires. They learned how to be part of a new *contain-collaborate* pattern rather than the established pattern of collusion. Most importantly, they stopped blaming others when something went wrong and began to take responsibility for their individual and collective actions. Regular meetings to address unresolved issues also helped to support a constructive and collaborative team process.

When subversive activity is contained, collaboration is much more likely because teamwork isn't being undermined. What is best for the team overall can then become the focus of work.

♦ *Are you currently in a situation that could benefit from greater **contain-collaborate** behaviors?*

♦ *What could you do to make it easier and safer for those you lead to engage in **contain-collaborate** activity?*

Risk-Reveal

Risk-reveal, the last relational pattern, challenges the accommodating tendencies of the *comply-complain* pattern. The person working with this antidote is willing to take personal risks in order to act with greater integrity.

At the core of this pattern is a willingness to articulate and stand behind what is truly important. This person raises issues and concerns visibly and clearly. He or she also offers opinions and holds others accountable. Fear may be present, but isn't disabling and doesn't prevent this person from speaking up. He or she has a bolder profile and is willing to take the heat that comes with greater visibility.

This person is willing to risk voicing disagreement that could be met with disapproval. He or she is also willing to risk disappointing someone else if core values, integrity, or self-respect are at stake.

People operating from the *risk-reveal* pattern are willing to engage in challenging conversations. They deal with conflict directly rather than avoiding it. They also handle anger in a clean, clear way rather than turning it inward or allowing it to leak into the *defy-subvert* pattern.

Risk-reveal people communicate self-respecting boundaries and limits. At times, this means appropriately and graciously saying no. Before they say yes and agree to a task, they consider how it will affect their self-care and work-life balance. By acting on behalf of healthy self-interest, they develop greater self-esteem.

> A 'No' uttered in deepest conviction is better and greater than a 'Yes' merely uttered to please, or what is worse, to avoid trouble.
>
> MOHANDAS GANDHI, non-violent resistance leader

The *risk-reveal* person acts from a base of self-acceptance and confidence, recognizing and validating his or her worth and value to others. This individual doesn't lose energy through needless self-doubt or a never-ending search for validation from others.

By bringing energy and creative edginess to problems and negotiations, the *risk-reveal* person participates fully. This pattern is in sharp contrast to the shut-down, disengaged attitude of the *comply-complain* person. The *risk-reveal* person is a fully empowered player who can think outside the box and offer creative solutions.

The next diagram outlines the *risk-reveal* pattern as it acts as an antidote to the *comply-complain* reaction.

Instead of remaining passive and meek, the *risk-reveal* behaviors require a person to actively represent his or her own personal interests. This, of course, means taking some risks and assuming a higher profile in relationship with others.

The *risk-reveal* behaviors support the shift from a person who makes childlike, compliant choices that are often designed to please authorities, to one who makes mature committed choices that have integrity. This shift to greater maturity requires self-esteem, self-respect, and a significant level of self-confidence.

With greater internal resilience in place, the *risk-reveal* person can afford to take risks and become more visible. The result is a high level of commitment and more abundant energy.

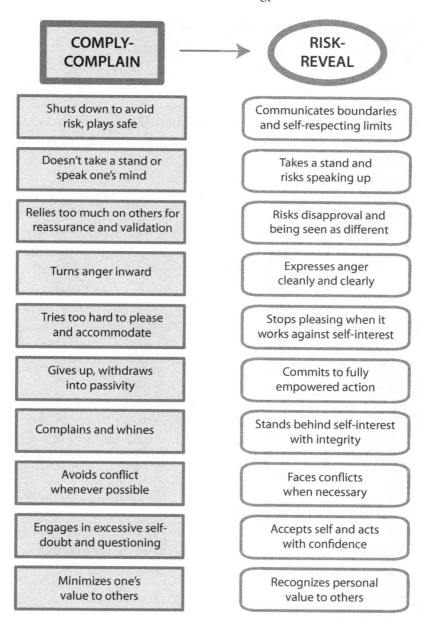

COMPLY-COMPLAIN	RISK-REVEAL
Shuts down to avoid risk, plays safe	Communicates boundaries and self-respecting limits
Doesn't take a stand or speak one's mind	Takes a stand and risks speaking up
Relies too much on others for reassurance and validation	Risks disapproval and being seen as different
Turns anger inward	Expresses anger cleanly and clearly
Tries too hard to please and accommodate	Stops pleasing when it works against self-interest
Gives up, withdraws into passivity	Commits to fully empowered action
Complains and whines	Stands behind self-interest with integrity
Avoids conflict whenever possible	Faces conflicts when necessary
Engages in excessive self-doubt and questioning	Accepts self and acts with confidence
Minimizes one's value to others	Recognizes personal value to others

Even though the *defy-subvert* pattern was most problematic in Edward's company, the *comply-complain* pattern was still evident. There was plenty of opportunity for the *risk-reveal* pattern to come into focus.

Edward, continued from page 112

For years, the *defy-subvert* and *comply-complain* patterns operated together in Edward's company. In the absence of clear expectations from Edward, his employees acted from a position of lethargy, compliance, and dependence.

Most of his employees assumed they would be taken care of and have jobs as long as they just showed up. It was only when Edward required a higher standard that many of them began to seriously complain. Some of his employees slid into the *defy-subvert* pattern; others simply continued to complain and underperform.

The people who eventually stayed with the company learned to use the *risk-reveal* behaviors. They found a way to speak up more clearly, ask for clarification, and negotiate what they needed in order to get the job done.

It was easier for Edward's employees to make the shift from *comply-complain* to *risk-reveal* when Edward was able to hear bad news in a centered way. As his lapses into *dominate-punish* outbursts of exasperation became less frequent, he created a safer environment for others to voice their concerns.

Edward hired a few key people who were very capable of speaking up and bringing difficult issues to the table in a constructive way. These "seed" people were already engaging in *risk-reveal* behaviors and helped set the tone for others. His business was starting to hum in a new way.

The investment Edward made in strengthening his business was rewarded financially, when he negotiated the sale of his company. The price was very gratifying to him and allowed him the option of retiring comfortably if he chose to do so. He didn't retire. In some ways, he was just getting started.

As Edward met his challenges as a leader, he worked consistently with his enlightened edge. He drew on one of his core values, his deep commitment to the people who worked for him. He didn't have an easy time of it, but by coming to grips with his reactive patterns and making tough decisions, he made it possible for his company to go through a transformation and come out much stronger on the other side.

♦ *How comfortable are you with being highly visible—when you aren't the one in charge?*

♦ *How could you make it safer for others to engage in risk-reveal behaviors?*

APPLY THE ANTIDOTE

With the information about the four reactive patterns and their relational antidotes, you have a clear strategy for offsetting your own reactions. The next time you're in a reactive state, try identifying which pattern or patterns you're operating from. Then look up the antidote and select the relational behaviors that seem most applicable to you and your situation. The most important step, of course, is to take action and build the new behaviors into solid integrative anchors.

> Bad times, hard times, this is what people keep saying; but let us live well, and times shall be good. We are the times: such as we are, such are the times.
>
> SAINT AUGUSTINE, philosopher and theologian

You can use all of the relational patterns and their associated behaviors as a resource for creating integrative anchors. It's now time to start identifying the integrative anchors that will be most effective for you.

Because the **Essential You** isn't delivered to you fully formed, you still need to build it. The goal is to create a tailored set of integrative anchors that can offset your defensive strategies and serve your unique needs.

The following exercise will help you see the **Essential You** more clearly and help you define and focus on your own enlightened edge.

Exercise: Sketch the Essential You

In the center oval of the diagram below, fill in your core truth. (Refer to page 67)

Pull your thoughts together regarding current or potential integrative anchors by considering the following sources of information:

- ► Feedback and suggestions received from others
- ► Insight and notes you may have collected
- ► Information you gathered from the exercise in Chapter 4
- ► The four relational patterns and associated behaviors
- ► Examples from this book or from your life that you identify with

In the surrounding boxes, write down your integrative anchors. These will be your most strategic ways to anchor your core truth and integrate the *Essential You*. For examples of this, refer to the case studies of Shirley on page 60 and James on page 71.

Create additional boxes and fill them in when you want to add more integrative anchors.

The ESSENTIAL YOU

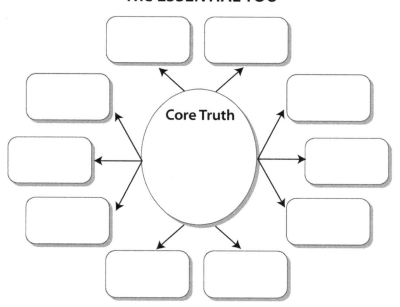

Refer to this diagram often! As you add to it, with ongoing work, it will become a powerful guide for your growth as a leader. Use it whenever you find yourself in the grips of your core insecurity or in a situation where you know you aren't at your best. Consistently acting on and developing your integrative anchors will ensure that you have the impact, presence, and effectiveness that you can be proud of as a leader.

> ♦ *Do you see the link between relational behaviors, integrative anchors, and your full potential?*
> ♦ *Can you think of a time when the power of your inner being and your leadership converged in a positive, high-impact event?*

If you are certain you need support in managing the **Limited You** and developing the **Essential You**, consider getting it right away. Don't delay in doing something this central to your success. Workshops, therapy, and coaching* could all be helpful.

If your organization needs support in shifting from reactive patterns to their relational antidotes, *The Contact Zone*™: *Power & Influence* board game and training can help. They focus in depth on the reactive and relational patterns.**

We now turn to Part Two of *The Enlightened Edge for Leaders*, where we will examine the attitudes, choices, processes, and skills needed to firmly establish the **Essential You** and bring your enlightened edge to your work and relationships.

---

* Go to **http://contactpointassoc.com/contact.html** for a referral.

** For more information on *The Contact Zone*™: *Power & Influence* board game and training, go to **http://contactpointassoc.com/boardgame.html**.

PART TWO:

HOW TO MAKE THE SHIFT

The second part of *The Enlightened Edge for Leaders* will help you deepen your understanding of the **Limited You** and show you how to create the indispensable integrative anchors that will ignite the **Essential You** and establish you as an enlightened leader.

You'll be provided with the strategic tools to shift from reactive to relational patterns and from the **Limited You** to the **Essential You**. Then you can collaborate and influence with skill, integrity, and grace, even with people who are difficult or frustrating. These tools include:

- Expanding your ability to learn from your life, mistakes, and pain
- Working with the reality of what is going on in the here and now rather than denying or defying it
- Containing, accepting, and caring for the **Limited You** as you challenge its limiting stories
- Holding creative tension so you can use it to ignite your power
- Working skillfully in the Contact Zone™ (the space where people connect and have significant impact)
- Increasing your leadership presence and vision

7

GATHER AWARENESS & LEARN

Live as if you were to die tomorrow.
Learn as if you were to live forever.

MOHANDAS GANDHI,
non-violent resistance leader

NO one is simply who they appear to be. Each person is a multi-layered and complex mix of dynamic forces that are always changing. If you assume there is always more to discover about yourself as well as others, you'll keep the door open to learning. It is a cornerstone in the shift from the **Limited You** to the **Essential You**. Ongoing curiosity is the key that opens the door to discovery and learning.

Curiosity can make even the unpalatable quite fascinating. Have you ever had the desire to learn about or watch a medical procedure that was being performed on you or someone you know? Or wanted to know more about an unfamiliar ritual you witnessed in a culture you were visiting? That kind of curiosity can offset what might otherwise be an unnerving experience.

> *Curious investigation is the catalyst for learning.*

When you approach learning with curiosity that is also kind and warm, the process will feel safer and you'll find it easier to stay open to learning. The kind, warm approach makes

123

learning about yourself less threatening. When your heart and your mind are engaged in this way, other people may also be more open to you. Kind, warm curiosity can make learning and discovery an enjoyable adventure.

> *I think if a mother could ask a fairy godmother to endow her child with the most useful gift, that gift would be curiosity.*
>
> ELEANOR ROOSEVELT, humanitarian

With greater awareness and a commitment to learning more about yourself, you'll discover a wider range of choices than you thought possible. Opportunities that you may have previously overlooked will become surprisingly and happily apparent, and you will be more skillful in managing the impact you have on others.

YOU ARE DYNAMIC

As you fill in areas of awareness about yourself, consider whether the new information belongs to the **Limited You** or the **Essential You**. If you notice a behavior that is a defensive strategy, remind yourself that it belongs to the **Limited You**. If you notice an integrative anchor, be sure to link it with the **Essential You**.

The diagram on the next page illustrates the **Limited You** and the **Essential You** as they co-exist within one person. The light and dark are mixed together in a dynamic relationship. The dark areas refer to the defensive strategies, and the light areas to integrative anchors.

Notice that there is no particular order to the arrangement. You can see that several of the areas are left blank and can still be filled in. There are also a few concepts like "unregulated tension," "creative tension," "defiance of reality," and "reality adjustment" that haven't been thoroughly discussed yet; they will be.

> *The LIMITED YOU and the ESSENTIAL YOU are in a fluid relationship that is always open to revision.*

This diagram is a bulky snapshot of what is actually a fluid relationship of psychological energy and behaviors. A huge number of dynamic forces operate simultaneously within one person.

Who you are and how you bring yourself to the challenges and opportunities in your life are completely open to revision. Greater awareness and learning, paired with wise choices and actions, will shift your profile over and over again. This profile will be more or less enlightened, depending on the extent of your awareness and the integrity of your choices.

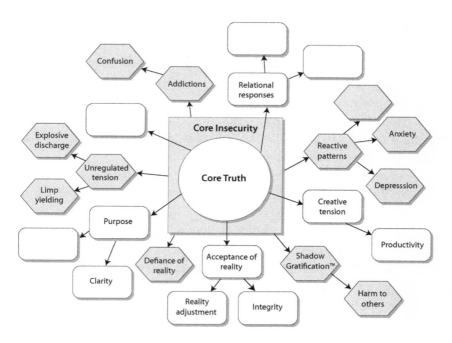

EXPAND SELF-AWARENESS

Think of someone you know who is in a position of power and has limited self-awareness. What kind of needless mistakes, unnecessary harm, and limited vision do you see being demonstrated? It doesn't have to be this way for you. The choice to continue to expand your self-awareness is the surest safeguard against obliviousness.

Self-awareness is the foundation for the enlightened edge. It draws on your unique capacity as a human to observe yourself and to consider what you are experiencing in a meaningful way. With observation comes awareness, and with greater awareness comes an enhanced capacity to choose.

There are some areas of self-awareness that are especially important. Observing and acknowledging your strengths, talents, and potential will help you expand the **Essential You**. Observing your limits and acknowledging your blind spots will help you manage the **Limited**

You. Paying attention to what you feel and then linking it with clear thinking is particularly important.

Be Honest About What You Feel

If you're willing to take an honest look, you can learn a great deal. Start by acknowledging the places in your body where you don't feel settled. Initially, you may just be aware of sensations like pressure, tightness, or heat. Think of the sensations as a gateway to emotions that you can feel within your body. Joy, sadness, tenderness, excitement, anger, jealousy, gratitude, and fear are just a few examples of feelings that you might find within your body.

The goal is to simply feel what you feel. Certain emotions are not comfortable, but after you acknowledge them and bring them into the light of your awareness, they suddenly become easier to deal with.

You may be tempted to bypass or cut off feelings like shame, fear, loss, embarrassment, powerlessness, aloneness, isolation, and helplessness. However, if you cut off awareness of these emotions, you lose access to vital information. This choice may be more comfortable, but you lose the opportunity to discover something about yourself. Try staying with uncomfortable feelings for limited periods of time and see what you can learn about yourself.[1]

Think-Feel

A mind all logic is like a knife all blade. It makes the hand bleed that uses it.

RABINDRANATH TAGORE, poet, Literature Nobel Prize winner

When you can tolerate and accept the difficult feelings that your insecurity triggers, you'll find it possible to *think and feel* at the same time.

In the following example, Alex was frustrated by his inability to think when he was very emotional. He wanted to change this in order to improve his communication. Alex's *think-feel* challenge was to:

◆ Allow space for his emotions
◆ Sort out what he was feeling
◆ Give his emotions an appropriate voice

Alex

Alex was a manager in his late twenties, working in a mid-size software company. He was responsible for ensuring that the software being created was aligned with customer needs. He tended to be intellectual and data-driven in his day-to-day work, but when faced with highly emotional disagreement in meetings, he lost his ability to think clearly.

Alex was so overwhelmed with frustration and felt so misunderstood that he often lost command of the facts and couldn't articulate his position. His reaction was to sit silently with arms crossed to hide his brain freeze and agitation. His very red face was a giveaway that he was upset, but most people had no idea what he was upset about. They assumed he was pouting.

Even though he found it difficult to admit his limitations, he was tired of not being as effective as he could be. Alex decided to work with a coach to "unpack" the bundle of emotions that were contributing to his overwhelming frustration. As he sorted out different emotions, he was able to give them accurate labels. Alex practiced linking thought with feeling, and this helped him to verbalize what he was feeling.

The next step was to articulate his emotions at work in ways that were appropriate to the situation. It was awkward at first, but he was determined. With practice he became more skilled. He was no longer completely caught off guard or disabled by his emotions.

The *think-feel* situation is different for each person, but in most cases, the steps are similar to Alex's—allow space to sort out feelings and give them appropriate expression.

You know that the *think-feel* alliance is operating when you can *feel your thoughts* and at the same time *think clearly about what you're feeling*. Thinking and feeling at the same time will increase your emotional intelligence and strengthen your participation in any activity.

The alliance of *thinking and feeling* also leads to meaningful reflection and questions such as: Is my insecurity telling the truth? Are its conclusions valid? Is this belief relevant in the present? These questions set the stage for further learning.

LEARN FROM LIFE

Life gives you feedback all the time. If you enter into a learning relationship with everything that comes your way, a great deal of informal, subtle but powerful learning can occur. This attitude can take you into a constant learning relationship with life.

What if you saw every circumstance you find yourself in as a perfectly designed opportunity to expand and deepen the **Essential You**? There is no better teacher than life. When you decide to learn from life, you take on a wise but challenging teacher.[2]

Life sometimes teaches more than you want to know, but with the passage of time, you often discover that you learned something profound in an area that was limiting you.

> When I hear somebody sigh, "Life is hard," I am always tempted to ask, "Compared to what?"
>
> SYDNEY J. HARRIS, journalist

All roads come back to the choice between the **Limited You** and the **Essential You**. Issues don't go away; they hang around to be recycled. How they are recycled depends upon how you deal with them.

You can choose to continue to learn and expand, or slip back into the comfort of the **Limited You**, where you can hold onto a fixed, solid, and safely insulated view of yourself and the world. The **Essential You**, on the other hand, will move you toward self-liberation, even if it disrupts your comfort or exposes your insecurity.

When you learn from life, you deepen your investment in the **Essential You**. You provide the commitment to learning. The **Essential You** provides understanding, insight, talents, strengths, and guidance. Sometimes it offers life-altering realizations and moments of enlightenment. It's your job to then anchor what you gained by turning it into action and practice. Remember: without these anchors, the forceful nature of the **Limited You** can easily re-assert its control.

LEARN FROM MISTAKES & PAIN

Mistakes are perfect opportunities for learning. But you can't learn if you're consumed with unproductive self-criticism or shame (or embarrassment, humiliation, or disgust). The **Limited You** is a reluctant learner. It will often fixate on a mistake and use it to berate you, or pretend you didn't really make a mistake. The **Limited You** is quite capable of using denial or blaming to mask your part in a mistake and bypass learning.

The **Essential You** will make a choice to learn and will rein in the tendency to deny your part in the problem, or blame someone else. It won't take you off the hook, but it will be patient and kind with what you discover. The **Essential You** won't save you from painful realizations, but it will help soothe the pain and find ways to manage it.

Painful, overwhelming, or frustrating experiences are windows into potential learning. Life often provides valuable feedback through these experiences, as if to say "something isn't working." If you can accept the pain as a teacher rather than pushing it away, you'll be in a better position to learn. Through an active learning process, you may find more creative or productive ways to approach a painful situation and even discover how to minimize pain in the future.

We should learn from the mistakes of others. We don't have time to make them all ourselves.

Attributed to GROUCHO MARX, comedian

If you make a commitment to extract a level of learning that is equivalent to any pain or suffering you have endured, you'll become a great learner. This attitude helps to ease bitterness and can make you receptive to more learning. The goal of all this learning is to reduce chronic, debilitating suffering by accepting moments of necessary pain.

The **Limited You** is embedded in chronic pain that it inflicts on itself over and over again. The **Essential You** will find the path out of that unproductive cycle by choosing to accept the acute pain that comes from learning and observe what is really going on around you and within you. As a leader, you need this abil-

By accepting and working with acute pain, you can find freedom from much chronic pain.

ity to see people and circumstances clearly, so your vision is grounded and you can realistically assess what is needed.

BE GRACIOUS ABOUT NOT KNOWING

Grounded vision often means accepting that there are foggy patches where you simply can't see or don't understand what is going on. There are times and circumstances when vision is limited. Just admitting that you don't know can be helpful. Of course, how you communicate

How do I work? I grope.

ALBERT EINSTEIN,
physicist and
Nobel Prize winner

your *not knowing* to others, especially when they are relying on you, is a sensitive matter and you would be wise to proceed cautiously. But you can be thoroughly honest with yourself about what you know and don't know.

Sometimes, when you feel as if you're walking in a fog, you need to move forward even though you can't see clearly. When visibility is limited, it's usually best to take just one step at a time and reassess as you go. As the fog clears, you can once again pick up the pace.

When your vision is obscured, your footing isn't secure, or you simply don't know what is going on, the **Limited You** can be triggered. These are times when you can choose to respond from the **Essential You**. For example, you might feel demanding, critical, and angry about being in the fog (the **Limited You**), but you might also question some of your operating assumptions and consider alternatives (the **Essential You**). When you discover that you're working from a flawed operating assumption, the fog often clears and you gain clarity.

> ◆ *Think of the last time you were in a situation in which you didn't understand what was going on or what was expected of you.*
> ◆ *Did you engage in any defensive strategies?*
> ◆ *Did you use any integrative anchors?*

Some questions don't have an immediate or certain answer; you need to live with them until the answers are revealed. Try this out by asking an important question that needs a solution or requires deeper understanding. Then keep asking the question and stay open to answers as you go.[3] This challenges the tendency to try to make answers appear on your time line—which isn't always possible. It will also help you stay open to what you still don't know.

The ability to investigate and ask mean-ingful questions rather than operate with uninvestigated assumptions will help you consistently engage with yourself and oth-ers in a productive way.

> *Ongoing inquiry supports learning, even when there is no immediate or certain answer.*

GET A REALITY CHECK

You can get a reality check anytime you test your assumptions about what is going on around you. For example, a business may need infor-mation about what its customers really want. At work, you may need feedback from people who can support or inhibit your success. At home, you may need to know how the people you are close to feel about you.

♦ *What are two or three situations in which you could benefit from a reality check?*

♦ *Is anything stopping you from getting the needed information? Are these valid reasons?*

A reality check is like going to the doctor for a checkup. It's uncom-fortable being probed. Waiting for test results is anxiety-provoking, but at least you'll know what you're dealing with. Even if the news is bad, you are generally better off finding out about a potential prob-lem before it worsens.

Regular reality checks will help you cut through limiting illusions and equip you to deal with what is really going on. You'll find out if you're doing anything that could leave you vulnerable to unnecessary damage. Feedback is the only way you can see a blind spot that could undermine your success.

Everyone has blind spots, where they can't see themselves or their impact. Blind spots, by definition, operate outside your awareness or field of vision. They are fertile ground for the **Limited You**. But when you bring a blind spot into awareness, your enlightened edge expands. Consider asking for feedback anytime you realize you need missing information that may be critical to your success in a significant area of your life or work.

Even though a reality check may be initially uncomfortable, the process gets easier with time. When you become used to dealing with what is really going on around you (rather than your untested assumptions), your relationship with reality gets friendlier. This puts you in a great position to learn.

Other people see you in a variety of ways, and they rarely see you the way you see yourself. Feedback is often full of surprises. Most people who go through the process of acquiring direct feedback from others get insight into some of their defensive strategies, but are often most surprised by how positive and encouraging the feedback is.

> *To believe is very dull. To doubt is intensely engrossing.*
>
> OSCAR WILDE, writer and poet

If you stay open and curious, learning can be fascinating. This assumes that you've sufficiently calmed down the defensiveness of the **Limited You**. Offering reassurance to yourself that it's safe to receive feedback, makes it much easier to take in what others have to say.

The **Limited You** may not focus on the positive feedback and may instead fixate on the possibility that a blind spot may be exposed. It will typically feel anxious about the possibility, but will do nothing about it. The **Limited You** could also confidently career into a potential disaster, in complete ignorance. On the other hand, the **Essential You** will get the information it needs, even if it's uncomfortable.

In the following example, Sandy sought feedback in a situation that was difficult to read. It helped her put her anxiety to rest and adjust more easily to a new role.

Sandy

Sandy was the leader of the American sales division of a large company that sold health care products. She was in her early forties and was used to having her bonus linked with her sales numbers. After a big organizational shake-up, she was moved out of sales and into a role that supported sales and marketing. The new position was a lateral move, with less immediate reward but higher potential for advancement.

She was ambivalent about the new role because it required many new skills and the rewards were not well defined or directly within her control. Sandy also wasn't sure if her manager intended the move as a promotion or as a demotion; she didn't know if he put her in the new position because he respected her potential or because he was in some way dissatisfied. She was chewing on this for weeks when it became clear that she needed a reality check.

Sandy had a candid conversation with her manager. She asked for clarification of his reasoning regarding the new position, and he did so happily. It was very reassuring to hear that he was highly invested in her leadership potential and that he saw this new position as providing the necessary challenges for her development.

Her manager also pointed out a gap in her ability to collaborate. He hoped the new role would help her to strengthen her collaborative skill set. Sandy's response to the conversation was initially mixed, but she quickly assimilated the information. The reality check helped her settle into the new role and to take on the challenges wholeheartedly.

If, like Sandy, you're proactive and get a reality check when you need to, you'll be able to catch any troublesome blind spots. The new information can help you test your assumptions, expectations, and concerns. This ensures that you're really on track with your best efforts.

Sometimes you get a reality check from life without asking. This could be in the form of structured events, like a performance appraisal, year-end revenue figures, or a quarterly team review. It could also come in the form of feedback from others in casual conversation, through a structured feedback session, or in an assessment. It could also come completely uninvited in the form of a crisis.

Learn From Crisis

When a crisis comes crashing in, it is saying in no uncertain terms: "Attention! You have to deal with reality, whether you're prepared to or not!" Life teaches through reality and sometimes through crisis.

If a crisis does occur, there is always the opportunity to learn from it. When you learn from what a crisis can teach, you'll be more likely to survive, recover, and even thrive.

> Most people live…in a very restricted circle of their potential being. They make use of a very small portion of their possible consciousness… Great emergencies and crises show us how much greater our vital resources are than we had supposed.
>
> WILLIAM JAMES, psychologist and philosopher

As a leader, others count on you for guidance, especially during a crisis. Your willingness to learn from what is going on will be like a beacon for others to do the same. But don't wait for a crisis to demonstrate your receptivity to new information and learning.

The **Limited You** may be comfortable pretending that everything is okay even if a potential crisis is brewing. This very popular defensive strategy adds to the likelihood that the situation will actually culminate in a crisis.

Some crises cannot be averted, but many can be prevented. If you take the initiative and get a reality check from time to time, the information you gain can show you where you need to focus to help avert a potential crisis.*

The following two-part exercise will give you a chance to identify where you may need a reality check.

Exercise: Need a Reality Check?

PART 1: Blind Spot?

Answer the following questions to identify where you may have a blind spot or could benefit from a reality check.

Yes ☐ No ☐ Am I fulfilling my potential as a leader?

Yes ☐ No ☐ Are my direct reports (subordinates) fulfilling their potential?

Yes ☐ No ☐ Are my informal partners (customers, vendors, peers, business groups) developing their potential?

---

* For information on how to deal with and avert a crisis: *12 Tips for Leading Through Crisis: Seize the Opportunity to Create a Better Future.* Available for free at **http://Contact PointAssoc.com/tools_leaderdev.html.**

If you answered Yes to all of the above, it appears that you and your organization are thriving. But before assuming that all is well, consider the questions in Part 2.

If you answered No to any of the above, you know something isn't quite right. Asking the questions in Part 2 will provide some clues about where the power leak or blockage is occurring.

If you're not sure how to answer some of the questions in Part 1, you are lacking vital information. The questions in Part 2 will provide some insight.

PART 2: Where Are You Losing Power?

In my current role, am I often:

Yes ☐ No ☐   Angry, irritated, or annoyed

Yes ☐ No ☐   Depleted, discouraged, or disappointed

Yes ☐ No ☐   Confused, fearful, or anxious

Are my direct reports often:

Yes ☐ No ☐   Angry, irritated, or annoyed

Yes ☐ No ☐   Depleted, discouraged, or disappointed

Yes ☐ No ☐   Confused, fearful, or anxious

Are my informal partners often:

Yes ☐ No ☐   Angry, irritated, or annoyed with my organization or me

Yes ☐ No ☐   Depleted, discouraged, or disappointed with my organization or me

Yes ☐ No ☐   Confused, fearful, or anxious about my organization or me

If you answered Yes to any of the above, deeper investigation is warranted.

If you don't know how to answer the above questions, further investigation is even more important because there is a serious information gap that could leave you needlessly vulnerable.

If you answered No to all of the above questions, you may indeed be walking on water, or you may be fooling yourself. If you feel quite certain that all is well, seek an objective opinion from someone who has nothing to lose by being honest.

After doing this exercise, you may have some ideas on where you need to make adjustments or get feedback. This is all fuel for your enlightened edge; be sure to use the new awareness or information constructively to strengthen the **Essential You**.

Now we'll look at some of the ways to get an honest, useful reality check from other people.

How to Get Feedback

There are many ways to get feedback. The simplest way is by sincerely asking for it. But you have to really be sincere in your request; others will sense if you truly want them to be honest. It's up to you to make it easy, comfortable, and safe for others to give you feedback. If you don't do this, you can be pretty sure you're not getting the full story on how others see you.

Even if you do your part, others might not be completely honest. It isn't easy for another person to give challenging feedback *even if* you've asked for it. Maybe the other person doesn't want to hurt your feelings or make you uncomfortable. The other person may also avoid the discomfort of delivering unpleasant news.

Perhaps the other person doesn't feel safe. This is completely understandable in anyone you have direct power over. Feedback from someone you have authority over often isn't possible, unless it is provided in a highly safe, confidential manner. This is where assistance from others in getting feedback can help.

One way to get feedback is through a multi-rater assessment, often referred to as a "360," which gathers information from a wide variety of sources in order to provide perspective from many angles. Sources of feedback can include those who report to you, your peers, your supervisor, and the board of directors, as well as your customers and vendors. A multi-rater instrument may already be available through your company. There are also many online resources, which are familiar to most consultants and executive coaches.

One of the best ways to get highly relevant feedback is by hiring a skilled coach or consultant to interview the people who are most strategic to you, to your success, and to your development. After the interviewing is completed, the coach consolidates and delivers the information to you. When feedback is acquired and delivered in this way, it is usually very well received.

When others are interviewed regarding a leader, it sends a positive signal; that the leader is invested in his or her growth and cares about the opinion of the person being interviewed. Often the leader earns respect and is even admired for being so courageous.

As you build a solid basis for trust with your coach, he or she will also be able to help you identify where to focus the interview questions. While conducting the interviews, your coach should be able to identify relationship, organizational, and political dynamics that might otherwise remain hidden.

This information can be brought back to you in a way that allows you to understand what is going on. It also becomes the basis for an action plan to address needed changes.

If you have a coach and are comfortable being observed "in action," this can be another fruitful way to get feedback. Receiving feedback following observation is sometimes referred to as shadow coaching.

Workshops and training, when carefully chosen, may also offer feedback in specific areas.

PROCESS FEEDBACK

You'll need to sort through the information people give you. Will it be the **Limited You** or the **Essential You** that processes this information? The **Limited You** will look for information that either reinforces your core insecurity or helps you defend against it. The **Essential You** will look for information that clarifies or helps you understand what is really going on. It will be more concerned with what's true than what you may feel comfortable with.

> People say I don't take criticism very well, but I say, what the hell do they know?
>
> Attributed to
> GROUCHO MARX,
> comedian

Look for patterns and pay special attention to themes. Don't fixate on the one or two bits of information that idealize or demonize you, but don't ignore them either. They mean *something*.

Taking feedback in or shrugging it off can be limiting if you haven't first clearly assessed the information. You'll need to evaluate the information before you can apply it effectively. If your tendency is to push away feedback, then take a few minutes longer to consider that the person who gave the feedback is indeed talking about you. Don't dismiss or ignore it. Don't minimize it because of the limitations of the person giving it. Take it in and try it out as information about you.

> *Clearly evaluate feedback from others before you dismiss it or apply it to yourself.*

Alternatively, if you tend to pull in and internalize the opinions and feedback of others without thoughtful evaluation, you can be thrown off balance and lose personal power. If you have this tendency, carefully assess whether the feedback can be best understood as information about you or as information about the other person. This distinction will support you in not taking things so personally. Without this evaluation process, you could be easy prey for manipulation by others who may or may not have your best interests at heart.

♦ *When you get feedback from another person how do you respond to it?*
♦ *Do you tend to take it in or shrug it off?*

Whenever you get feedback, look for the kernel of truth. Search out the opportunity to resolve issues that have been exposed. Put aside your defensiveness or anger and listen to what is being said. Be willing to deal with the discomfort and tension so you can learn something new. If this feels too challenging, work with a coach who can help you. This will build the **Essential You** and raise the ceiling on your leadership potential.

♦ *If you have some new but uncomfortable awareness about yourself, can you bring an attitude of warm acceptance to yourself?*
♦ *Can you now add some kind, generous curiosity to the mix?*

We've looked at how important it is to expand self-awareness, to learn from many sources, to get a reality check, and to process feedback in order to strengthen the **Essential You**. A spirit of curiosity and adventure is especially helpful as you continue to gain self-awareness through feedback from others. If you bring warmth and kindness to what you discover, your journey will be much more enjoyable. This warm curiosity also makes it easier to link *thinking and feeling* in order to stay involved in constructive learning.

The next chapter will build on your commitment to ongoing learning, as we turn our attention to acceptance. We will focus especially on accepting reality. This includes distinguishing the reality of *what is* from ideas about how reality *should be,* and working with the tension between these two perspectives.

8

ACCEPT WHAT IS

Face reality as it is, not as it was or as you wish it to be.
JACK WELCH, former CEO, General Electric

AS a leader, your capacity to learn from, accept, and creatively respond to reality will have a profound effect on any group or organization you participate in. When you accept reality, you can see your options, resources, and choices more clearly. Acceptance builds upon the ability to expand awareness and learn. It creates a non-violent relationship with reality and with other people. The **Essential You** puts down the weapons of denial, distortion, and blame, and stops fighting with reality. It observes and accepts the reality of *what is* and sets aside the impulse to argue, fight, attack, or defend. Accepting reality can bring immense relief and peace.

Acceptance is a core quality of the **Essential You**, but the **Limited You** struggles with acceptance. The nature of change, the difficult aspects of reality, and the tension between *what could be* versus *what is* are challenging for the **Limited You**. This chapter will focus on these themes and clarify the role of acceptance as we establish another cornerstone in the shift from the **Limited You** to the **Essential You**.

DYNAMIC ACCEPTANCE

When you are fundamentally willing to accept *what is*, you're in a better position to assess the situation clearly and take appropriate responsibility. The challenge you face is accepting reality as it is, with all its changeability and possibility. When reality isn't distorted, masked, or avoided, creative opportunities are more visible. You can then act on these openings to help shape reality into something more positive.

> *Acceptance is not passive. It requires active involvement with the reality of WHAT IS.*

Acceptance is not passive. It's dynamic, because there may indeed be action to take, but the action is based on acceptance of *what is*, rather than a cherished illusion harbored by the **Limited You**.

The nature of reality has been explored, argued over, and written about for thousands of years, but this isn't the place to discuss philosophy. We'll keep it simple here. We will refer to reality as *what is going on* in the here and now. *What is going on* is the result of everything that has occurred prior to right now.

> ◆ *Think about how many things had to occur in order for you to be where you are, reading this sentence.*
> ◆ *You had to be born, the alphabet and printing had to be created, you had to be educated to read, this book had to be written, and the book had to find its way to you.*
> ◆ *Consider the innumerable people, the hours of effort, and the confluence of forces that preceded the existence of this one event.*

Prevailing conditions are what you must deal with in the present because of everything that preceded this moment. It's impossible to fully comprehend the vastness of prevailing conditions. It *is* possible to respect those conditions and collective forces and to recognize that at this moment you are subject to constraints that are profoundly complex, and for the most part, beyond your direct control. As such, it's best to accept and deal with them whether you like it or not.

Imagine for a moment that you are part of a small group that has worked together for many months. One person in this group appears to influence outcomes in ways that lack integrity. His or her interests are served in ways that often are not in your best interest and that work against the greater good of the group. The reality of the situation is one you may not like, but it does exist. It is rooted in many complex dynamics that have their own momentum. There is no way to make the situation not *what it is*. This is the time to accept the circumstance *as it is*, so you can find a constructive way to work with it.

Reality has never stopped being what it is because someone didn't like it. Acceptance of reality, prevailing conditions, and *what is going on* is the basis for a well-adjusted leader who is rooted in reality.

Accountability, Not Approval

Acceptance doesn't mean you necessarily approve of what is going on around you. It really has nothing to do with approval. Acceptance simply acknowledges *what is*, independent of judgment about whether you approve or agree.

Acceptance doesn't mean failing to hold others (or yourself) accountable, either. In fact, accountability is based on acceptance of *what is*. First, you accept *what is*, and then you establish accountability. You do so by creating standards, communicating expectations, getting agreements, and following up in a consistent and clear way with feedback.

After you establish accountability, you may need to accept that others aren't taking responsibility for their commitments and aren't following through. This points to the need to accept something else: that other people will still do what they do for reasons you have virtually no control over. But whether others do their part or not, you can accept and monitor what is going on, and hold yourself and others accountable.

The Dalai Lama is an example of a leader who embodies the dynamic nature of acceptance. He has accepted the presence of the Chinese in Tibet as a fact, but this in no way means he has sanctioned their political presence or activity. He has spent a lifetime trying to establish accountability in a specifically non-violent way.

CHANGE IS INEVITABLE

Some change occurs no matter what you or anyone else does. For example, the seasons come and go, bringing change. We are born and die and ride the wave of many events that profoundly alter our lives. Change is inevitable. The **Limited You** can argue endlessly about control and change. But the **Essential You** simply accepts the impermanent nature of existence.[1] It also accepts what it can't control, and it chooses carefully how to participate with change.

> If we can recognize that change and uncertainty are basic principles, we can greet the future and the transformation we are undergoing with the understanding that we do not know enough to be pessimistic.
>
> HAZEL HENDERSON, futurist, author[2]

The **Essential You** brings purpose, clarity, kindness, and joy to the change process. The **Limited You**, on the other hand, fears change and loss. It will cling even to what is painful in order to avoid change. The **Limited You** is like a hand holding a cactus. It doesn't know when to let go. It can't accept *what is*.

The warm acceptance of the **Essential You** can often help the **Limited You** release its grip and accept non-negotiable losses. Even when you can't choose your losses, you can always choose your attitude and responses to change. This much *is* in your control.

♦ *Have you ever resisted change that you had no control over or that was forced upon you?*

♦ *Did you learn anything through this about how to accept change more graciously?*

♦ *Is there anything you learned about accepting change that you could instill in those you lead?*

Leadership requires patience with change, with yourself, with others, and with complex organizational systems. Carving a new path is often rough and awkward. The new way often won't feel as familiar or comfortable as an old, well-worn path. How you, as a leader, facilitate and guide change will have a big impact on those who are affected by that change.

Invest enough time and resources in yourself to ensure that continued growth can take place. If you have power through your position or role, be sure to give enough time and resources to other people and to new projects to ensure that they can grow successfully.

You'll have more control and impact in some situations than others. By accepting *what is*, letting go when necessary, and investing wisely in what is possible, you'll minimize ill-considered lines of action that could be harmful, wasteful, or regrettable.

TENSION WITH REALITY

To accept reality is quite a radical undertaking. It requires not only a deep acceptance of *what is*, but also the ability to temporarily suspend what you think *should be*.

*What **is** going on* is usually very different from *what you think **should be** going on*. The conflict between these two positions creates considerable tension in dealing with reality. For the most part, *what is going on* is not exactly the way we want it to be. In fact, in many cases, *what is going on* doesn't even come close to the way we think it *should be*.

> Adaptive work consists of the learning required to...diminish the gap between the values people stand for and the reality they face.
>
> RONALD HEIFETZ, faculty, John F. Kennedy School of Government, Harvard University[3]

Imagine for a moment that you manage a team that did not meet its year-end goals. Even though you believe the goals should have been achieved, the team fell short. Here, you have reality coming up against an idea:

*REALITY refers to what **is** going on.*
(The team didn't meet its goals.)

*IDEA refers to what **should be** going on.*
(The team should meet its goals.)

How do you deal with the tension between these two points of view? One way is to get angry, blast the team with what it should have done, and threaten them using the *dominate-punish* pattern. Or activate the *rescue-control* pattern by blurring and distorting the goals so it looks as if the group may have achieved them. Or find a way to not focus on the results. It's also possible to feel defeated and lose faith in what the team is capable of. There are endless ways to bypass acceptance of what happened.

The following diagram illustrates the tension that is generated when reality converges with ideas about reality.

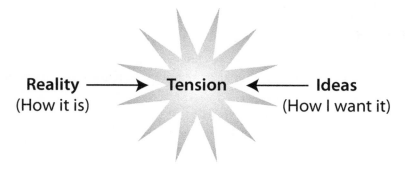

Reality ——▶ **Tension** ◀—— **Ideas**
(How it is)   (How I want it)

The tension between the reality of *how it is* and your ideas *about how you want things to be* or *think they should be* is here to stay. It's there in any important relationship or in any goal you really care about. There is no negotiating it. The question is *how* you deal with it.

> ◆ *Think of the last time you felt tense in a meeting. Do you recall if there was a conflict between what was going on and what you wanted to happen?*
> ◆ *Can you identify two or three areas of your life where there is tension between reality and how you want reality to be? For example:*
>   Reality: Not getting enough exercise
>   What I Want: To be fit and at ideal weight

The **Essential You** will accept reality unconditionally. It will also relinquish the tendency to distort reality in order to make it more palatable. It will then *work with* reality to create desired outcomes.

The **Limited You**, on the other hand, will distort or obliterate reality, using any number of defensive strategies to force or manipulate reality into compliance with its ideas about what it thinks should be happening. It uses its ideas as weapons against reality.

IDEA VS. REALITY

The word *idea* is being used here in a very general way to include any kind of thought, concept, opinion, conviction, ideal, principle, belief, or notion. It also includes vision, fantasy, and the vast contents of the imagination.

Ideas can be imaginative, creative, and powerful. They can be used destructively or to great benefit. Ideas are always dancing around reality, which *just is*. Ideas can be fanciful or purposeful, as with strategic visioning. But ideas aren't the same as reality.

Ideas can include what you think should be, must be, or might be going on, what could have happened, might be going on, or could happen in the future. Reality is more straightforward. It is simply what is going on now.

The following table summarizes the distinctions between ideas and reality:

IDEA		REALITY
What should be going on	vs.	What is going on
How I want it	vs.	How it is
Past or future focused	vs.	Here and now
Concepts and principles	vs.	What is
Beliefs and ideals	vs.	What is
Vision and goals	vs.	What is
Fantasy and stories	vs.	What is

Ideas are not the problem; you can use them to build defensive strategies or to construct integrative anchors. Ideals, fantasies, and visions can either contribute to a problem or to a solution.

Reality isn't the problem either. It is often very annoying, unpalatable, and sometimes truly horrible. But it can also be stunningly beautiful and awe inspiring.

To reiterate, the problem isn't ideas or reality. Both can generate difficulty; both can be a gift. The problem—and the challenge—

for the **Essential You** is *how* to bring yourself and your ideas into relationship with reality.

IDEALS: INSPIRING OR TOXIC?

Far away in the sunshine are my highest aspirations.
I may not reach them, but I can look up and see their beauty, believe in them, and try to follow where they lead.

LOUISA MAY ALCOTT,
author

Ideals are highly charged ideas that can help to frame a vision for the future. Used in a wholly constructive way, ideals can inspire and offer guidance for what is positive and possible. The **Essential Self** utilizes them to light a path and lift spirits toward something greater. When used relationally with a healthy respect for differences, reality, and truth, ideals act as beacons of inspiration pointing the way to what is better.

But when used reactively or antagonistically, ideals are volatile and can incite violence. When an idea or ideal is used to annihilate reality rather than to *relate to* reality, the situation becomes toxic. Used in the service of the **Limited Self**, toxic ideals have been used as fuel for terrible atrocities throughout the history of the world. Consider the Crusades, the racial idealism of Hitler, McCarthy's anti-communist reign of fear, Mao Tse-Tung's cultural revolution, or the "virtuous" suicide bomber, to name just a few examples.

Ideals can be used to inspire and uplift or to annihilate.

Toxic ideals often reinforce a feeling of righteousness. The pairing of righteousness with a toxic ideal is an especially powerful catalyst for violence or aggression. You'll know that an ideal is being used in a toxic way when it:

♦ Is used to justify aggression or harm to others (or to self)
♦ Refuses to accept and relate to reality as it is
♦ Is linked with hatred, fear, or disgust for life, self, or others
♦ Sanctions the righteous elimination of disagreement or differences
♦ Is paired with perfectionism or an attempt to control what cannot be controlled

The alternative, used by the **Essential You**, is to accept reality as it is and then engage ideas about reality in a mindful and heartful way. This also includes a decision to refrain from using force to get what is wanted. The **Essential You** is reluctant to use force and will not impose personal will if it's likely to do harm.

TENSION IS NECESSARY

While the tension between *what is* and *what could be* can be difficult to manage, it is also a source of energy that can be used creatively. Constructive work is fueled by the tension between reality and what we want reality to be. In Chapter 10, we will discuss in depth how to work creatively with this tension. The goal for now is to accept the tension as a necessary part of change and leadership.

It can be a challenge to accept reality and honor your ideals at the same time. Reality and what you see as a possibility can be *so* different. But the ability to hold these two elements together is a crucial feature of the enlightened edge.

Recall from Chapter 4 that two of the defining characteristics of a core truth are:

- ◆ Acceptance of reality as it is
- ◆ Honoring the potential in yourself and others

If you are to act from your core truth and strengthen the **Essential You**, you'll need to work with the tension between reality and potential. If you can learn to tolerate the tension between your ideals and the reality of how things are here and now, you will be much more effective in actually shaping the future you desire.

Toxic Discharge

When the tension between what you think *should be* versus *what is* gets too intense, the **Limited Self** may find the situation intolerable, and it will seek a release. It may then use an ideal in a toxic fashion to provide relief from the tension.

Imagine a group meeting that has a high potential for conflict, such as a tight deadline and a leader who has low tolerance for disagreement. The **Limited Self** of the leader draws on a toxic ideal, such as "we all must think exactly the same." He or she insists on the importance of consensus, demands conformity by punishing those who disagree, and effectively wipes out any differences in opinion. Voila! The tension is dissipated. The leader then doesn't have to deal with the reality of divergent points of view. This minimizes superficial conflict, but the differences continue to operate in ways that aren't visible. There is no exchange of constructive ideas, and the leader can feel gratified by having ideas that remain unchallenged.

Discharging tension in this way is toxic because it uses force to impose idea over reality. Any attempt to obliterate reality is fundamentally aggressive.

Toxic discharge is a primitive way for people to relieve themselves of the sometimes intense frustration and tension that is inherent in reality; it often leads to subtle and occasionally overt violence. This violence is usually expressed emotionally, but under some circumstances it can become physical.

> When it rains,
> I let it.
>
> 113-YEAR-OLD MAN,
> in response to a
> question about the
> secret of his longevity

Instead of discharging tension reactively, the **Essential You** holds the tension between an idea and the reality so that both reality and the idea can continue to exist and shape each other in a creative fashion. This is the essence of creative activity. We'll return to further discussion of holding tension in Chapter 10.

To summarize, the goal is to accept reality before trying to change it. Adjust to the facts. Get to know *what is*. Stay in a steady, thoughtful, non-reactive, and non-violent relationship with *what is*, and *then* go about shaping it. This will help you generate more sophisticated ideas and will support a better execution of those ideas.

DEFY OR ADJUST TO REALITY

Working constructively and creatively with reality rests heavily on the ability to accept it. This is often much more difficult than coming up with ideas on how to change reality. Both are necessary, but the heavy lifting is often acceptance of what feels impossible to accept.

Everyone resists reality to some extent. Most of us even have times when we hate reality. This is a natural defense against what may be unpleasant or unbearable. There are times when creating a buffer against reality is necessary and useful. For instance, when someone has gone through a trauma, it's important to pull away from its harshness in order to regroup. The problem arises when a person takes a position against reality and stays stuck there.

Even though reality is non-negotiable, it is human nature to try to bargain, and if bargaining doesn't work, we sometimes dig in and take a position of defiance.

> *The certain test of sanity is if you accept life whole, as it is.*
>
> LAO-TZU, Chinese philosopher

Reality is here to stay and will have its way whether you accept it or not. It operates completely independently of your wishes, hopes, and dreams. The choice you have is to accept reality and work creatively with it or not. This is an especially important choice for leaders.

A leader with a hostile relationship to reality may still be very charismatic and powerful, but his or her leadership presence and impact will be negative in the long run.

A leader with a weak connection to reality may simply avoid unpleasant aspects of reality. He or she often ignores facts, data, and feedback. Lack of attention to the facts then leads to poor decision making, poor execution, and impaired systems. The leader could prevent many of these problems just by paying closer attention to facts and reality.

> *When fantasies and reactions override acceptance of reality, a reality adjustment is needed.*

When *how things are supposed to be* collides with *how they are*, it's easy to discharge the tension in a toxic way and go into a reactive pattern. Reactivity is an indication that you are in defiance of reality and that you are in need of a reality adjustment.

Jamal's experience illustrates the collision between reality and the fantasy of how things should be. It also shows how creating a false story about someone can make dealing with an unpalatable reality temporarily easier, but it won't help a person learn and readjust to the reality at hand.

Jamal

Jamal had been working in the quality control department of a large company for four years. He had been designated a "high potential" and was on the fast track for promotion. Opportunities for moving upward weren't abundant in the quality control arena, but he was hopeful.

When Jamal was passed over for a promotion and watched his friend and colleague receive it instead, he felt surprised, disappointed, and envious. Jamal believed he should have received the promotion. The reality of what happened was completely unacceptable to Jamal. He felt himself turn against his friend, even while they shook hands and smiled.

He found himself making up a story about his friend that was very distorted. In his imagination, Jamal saw his friend plotting against him and laughing triumphantly at his expense. He wondered if he was being paranoid, but the fantasy persisted. It served a purpose. The fantasy protected him from the tension of trying to accept the unacceptable: that he was not the one chosen.

Being passed over for the promotion triggered Jamal's basic insecurity in a big way. By turning against his friend with an emotionally charged, negative story, he made use of a defensive strategy that masked his core insecurity.

He also felt some Shadow Gratification™ at being "wronged" by his friend, and this made it even more difficult to accept reality. In the end, he clung to the idea that he was the one who was "supposed to win," and his friend became the enemy. His friendship couldn't hold up against his unresolved bitterness.

Jamal's plight illustrates how reality often doesn't make sense or seem right. It doesn't fit with how we see things. Reality can be very difficult to accept and adjust to. Jamal told himself a story about his friend trying to sabotage him. Believing this story was easier than accepting and learning about why he was passed over for the promotion. The latter would have been threatening to his **Limited Self** and how he saw himself.

Fantasies that are held in defiance of reality are very important defensive strategies for the **Limited You**. It's not easy to give them up, since they were designed to mask painful, frustrating or frightening aspects of reality. These fantasies or stories create an illusory veil over reality, but reality is still there; it hasn't changed. The problems with reality are still waiting to be addressed.

For example, imagine that you have a business partner and close friend whom you want to believe has integrity. Despite your beliefs about your partner, there are some strong indications that he is systematically manipulating the accounting and financial reports in his favor. If you need to preserve your fantasy about your friend and his trustworthiness, you might not follow up. Further investigation would not be an option. If you are reluctant to challenge a fantasy about yourself as a trusting friend, you might say nothing and do everything you can to ignore the suspicious indicators.

In the above example, the fantasies about trust are held in defiance of reality. When fantasies aren't challenged with a healthy reality check, integrity and accountability are sacrificed. For example, dreaming of winning the lottery can be an enjoyable fantasy, but buying lottery tickets to deal with financial challenges is an unrealistic strategy that can contribute to loss of financial accountability and integrity.

> ◆ Is there some area of your life where you are holding a fantasy that defies reality?
> ◆ What do you stand to gain or lose by letting go of the fantasy and working with the reality?

There is an alternative. The **Essential You** can step in and create a reality adjustment by getting some facts. Even though the reality may be difficult to face, you'll be able to distinguish what is true and real from what is false and illusory, and restore integrity. This provides a better foundation for moving forward.

LIMITING STORIES

Some stories and fantasies are pleasant, creative, and inspiring. Some are depressing, destructive, and disabling. Limiting stories are ones that reinforce your core insecurities and help to justify your most reliable defensive strategies. They are designed to serve the **Limited You**.

Limiting stories don't tell the whole truth, even though they usually carry a grain of truth.[4] They defy some important aspect of reality rather than accepting and adjusting to it. They also make simplistic assumptions about *what is going on*, rather than accepting and working with the complex richness of *what is*.

Your most familiar limiting stories usually weave core insecurities and defensive strategies into a compelling fantasy about who you are and who other people are. Most people aren't aware that they are telling themselves well-worn stories. They usually don't even think of their stories as such, or examine their automatic assumptions, interpretations, and judgments about what is going on. This is how illusion works!

> **Fantasies are life-supporting when they support integrative anchors.**
>
> **Fantasies are aggressive and harmful when they support defensive strategies.**

When you use stories and fantasies to help you to deal with reality more effectively and to create integrative anchors, they are great.

When fantasies operate in defiance of reality, they can be severely limiting to you and the people around you.

Fantasies and stories are not the problem; they can be creative expressions of imagination. However, imagination is best channeled constructively. Don't let your imagination carry you into stories that don't serve the best in you. Do use your imagination to work constructively with reality.

In order to expand your leadership potential, you will probably need to relinquish certain fantasies and stories—not all fantasies, just reality-defying ones that you cling to when the facts and reality say otherwise, or that feed the **Limited You**.

Your own limiting stories may be based largely on what you inherited from your family of origin, as they were for Lynette, whom you first met in Chapter 5. As you continue to read about Lynette, notice how well her limiting story serves her defensive strategies and ultimately her **Limited Self**.

Lynette, continued from page 83

Recall that Lynette, the VP of human resources, had a new director, Dan, who was inundated with information about Lynette from other people in the department. They complained about how she micromanaged, offered unwanted advice, and intruded in ways that were offensive. Dan was looking for a way to give Lynette feedback about her impact but hadn't found an opening.

Since Lynette was a VP, she clearly had authority that made it difficult for her subordinates to speak up and offer feedback. Considerable tension was developing between her and Dan. As the tension became more intense, Lynette tried to address it by being overly helpful. This was a manifestation of her heavy reliance on the *rescue-control* pattern and the tendency to respond to most tension by trying to fix something.

At one point, in a moment of micromanaging helpfulness, Lynette actually reached over and picked up a piece of paper that Dan had been making notes on.

Dan finally spoke up. He asked her, "Do you even know what you just did? How disrespectful that is?" She looked stunned. She then began to explain in a defensive fashion that she was just trying to help. Dan stated that it wasn't helpful, and furthermore, that it was insulting to him, just as it was for others in the group when she barged in with unwelcome help.

Lynette was very surprised to hear this because she saw herself as kind, supportive, and respectful. She became angry at the accusation. At this point, she didn't ask Dan for more feedback but instead retreated. She went into a sulk with her familiar story for a few days. She felt hurt and angry. The story she told herself was:

> *"No matter how hard I try, no one really appreciates me or my efforts. But I have to keep trying."*

This was her core insecurity, her main defense, and her most familiar story.

Interestingly, her mother had the same story. Her mom was married to an alcoholic who didn't live up to his family responsibilities. She tried too hard with her husband and was not successful in getting him to take responsibility for his addiction. Without realizing it, Lynette had emulated her mother. When she realized this, she could see the seductive falseness running through the story.

Lynette finally decided to open up to *what was really going on*. She came out of her angry withdrawal and asked Dan for some real feedback. It became clear to her that by persistently trying too hard to help, she was alienating others. She began to see where her efforts were welcome and appreciated, and where they weren't. This became the basis for her core truth.

Once you see that a limiting story is not the carrier of truth, it often loses its grip. The trick is to bring the story into focus so you're fully conscious of it. You then have greater freedom; you can choose to align with reality and a more complete truth rather than being stuck within the constraints of the story. Through this process, you may even discover a core truth or an integrative anchor.

The following exercise will give you a chance to bring your own limiting story into focus. You'll revisit the **Limited You** and identify some of the elements of fantasy that hold it in place. If your core insecurity isn't clear yet, this exercise may help you to bring it into focus. Some people find this exercise difficult, but almost everyone who completes it finds it worthwhile and often revealing. Many people have fun with it too.

Exercise: Your Limiting Story

PART 1: Elements of Your Story

Refer to Chapter 5 and your sketch of the *Limited You*. Review your core insecurity and defensive strategies.

Think of a time in the recent past when something happened that you didn't like, that threatened you, or that triggered your core insecurity—such as losing an account, getting bad news, having a hostile encounter with a co-worker, or not getting enough work done.

Focus on just one event. Reflect on how much you didn't like what happened and how you reacted to it.

Go to the place inside that has a hard time accepting what happened.

Now write down five things you told yourself regarding the event. For example: "That person is just stupid." "I should have tried harder." "That's what I get for trusting someone like that." "He is just covering his butt." "I didn't want to go there anyway."

1. _____
2. _____
3. _____
4. _____
5. _____

PART 2: Write Your Story

Get a fresh sheet of paper to write on. Look at the five things and write one or two paragraphs telling a mini-story or parable, using all of the key phrases you just jotted down.

Here is an example of a mini-story, written very quickly, using the phrases from the example above:

"Once there was a young man who always knew he should try harder to get ahead in life. But he was ambivalent about his own success and what he wanted for his future. When he stumbled or failed at something new, he said, 'I didn't want that anyway.' As he got older, he blamed others, thought of them as stupid, and in this way covered his butt so well that he forgot all about what he really wanted. Along the way he stopped trusting others, but what really happened was he stopped trusting himself."

Now set your timer for five minutes and try to write your story in that period of time. If necessary, set your timer for five more minutes, but don't take longer than ten minutes.

Make it simple. Don't overthink. Be creative and expansive. Enjoy being a storyteller. Trust what comes up. Start your timer.

PART 3: Review

Now look at what you've written and see if it applies to you in any way. Does any of it help support your defensive strategies or your core insecurity? If so, look for the parts of the story that aren't true.

The main thing here is to distinguish story from reality and to remember that the **Limited You** is invested in protecting itself, not in discovering the truth. Use any new information from the story you just wrote to modify the sketch of the **Limited You** that you started in Chapter 5.

Once you see a limiting story as just a story, you have a new perspective and vantage point for assessing how true it is. Look for ways the story distorts the truth. If the story is very negative, pay special attention to how it makes your situation worse than it really is.

Take a look at the story and see if it intensifies any negative emotions such as fear, anxiety, desire for revenge, anger, or resentment. If the story creates added fear, check to see if your imagination is running loose. An active, unguided imagination can make up scary stories and imagine awful possibilities that serve no productive purpose.

GET FRIENDLY WITH REALITY

The following ten points summarize many of the ways you can create a friendly relationship with reality. Use them as guidelines and reminders as you challenge your core insecurity and build integrative anchors.

1. Repeatedly choose to be aware of and accept *what is*.
2. Deal solidly with *what is going on,* rather than *what you think should be going on.*
3. Address the facts as they are rather than what you imagine them to be or wish them to be.
4. Suspend reactions (witness, observe) until you have a complete picture.
5. Assess and investigate what is going on here and now before you take action.
6. Create accountability for aspects of reality you want to see changed.
7. Use ideals and fantasies to assist and uplift rather than to defy or destroy reality.
8. Make reality adjustments as needed.
9. Recognize that things are as bad as they are, but not worse than they are.
10. Don't make up scary stories or imagine horrible possibilities that serve no productive purpose.

♦ *How you would feel if you could do all of the above in a masterful way?*

♦ *What kind of impact would this have on your leadership?*

Imagine how solid and confident you would be if you knew you were seeing and responding to issues clearly rather than being bound by destructive fantasies, limiting stories, and illusions. Think about how much others would respect and appreciate your clarity and the benefits you could provide to them.

The impact on your leadership would be immense. Think of the mistakes you could prevent, the opportunities you could take advantage of, the people you could rely on as allies, and the confidence you would have moving forward. These are just a few of the reasons to continue the vital work of dealing with reality, managing the **Limited You**, and working with your enlightened edge.

Reality isn't an easy subject, and no one knows this better than the **Limited You**. The next chapter will focus on what you can do to make life better for this part of you. Remember, the **Limited You** isn't your enemy; it is yours to rein in and hold, to care for, and to take responsibility for.

9

TAKE CARE & TAKE CHARGE

Firmness of heart is needed for achievement…
RUMI, poet

I T'S probably becoming increasingly clear that the enlightened edge for leaders is deeply rooted in internal leadership. This ability to guide yourself toward a vision, even when multiple obstacles are in your path, qualifies you to lead others through similar territory. When you ask others to do what you have already demonstrated to yourself, your authenticity as a leader is secure.

Guiding yourself through the obstacles posed by the **Limited You** requires skill, firmness, and a generous attitude. By turning the warm light of acceptance and compassion directly on the **Limited You**, you create a cozy, safe place inside. This makes it much easier for the **Limited You** to align with the **Essential You**.

When you can soothe your core insecurity, you'll find it easier to contain, manage, and lead yourself. In fact, if you don't know how to soothe the anxiety that plagues the **Limited You**, its insecurity will invariably provoke a cascade of emotions and predictable reactive behaviors that will make it almost impossible to stay in productive contact with other people. This in turn can seriously affect your credibility as a leader.

The **Limited You** has a whole array of limiting stories, fantasies, and defensive strategies that keep it trapped in a fight with reality. By taking the **Limited You** firmly and securely in hand, you make it easier to accept reality and to relinquish many of your defensive strategies.

The fear and aggression that fuel the **Limited You** don't dissipate easily. If you ignore, punish, or deny these emotions, they continue to operate subversively and without the benefit of your guidance. You need to meet the compelling emotional states that drive reactivity, with the power of the **Essential You**. This chapter will show you how to contain and soothe the **Limited You** by approaching it with a combination of kindness and firmness. These skills will help you ignite your power and equip you for enlightened internal leadership.

KIND & FIRM

Anticipate that some situations will trigger your reactive tendencies. The **Limited You** will become activated, especially in challenging circumstances. This is inevitable and is not a sign of failure. It is a sign that you're alive and have some work to do. Your goal is to manage and contain the reactions and impulses so they don't take over.

Kindness and firmness work together when you're in a relational state. When you're reactive, one of these qualities drops away. The *dominate-punish* and *defy-subvert* patterns are not kind. The *rescue-control* and *comply-complain* patterns are not firm.

Enlightened leadership is kind and firm.

Linking kindness and firmness will optimize your ability to lead yourself. This kind-firm combination is necessary for any type of effective management.

Remember that the **Limited You** really does have a limited perspective, limited options, and limited personal power. It needs your benevolence and strength. The more effectively you manage it, the more it will trust you.

As you shift to the **Essential You** and become a reliable source of guidance and support, the **Limited You** is soothed and can settle down. You earn its trust. It becomes willing to follow you because you are acting as a wise, benevolent leader. You are then freer to respond to what is going on around you in more capable and constructive ways.

Soothe

If the **Limited You** is very agitated or anxious, you'll need to find a way to calm it down before taking further action. Greater calm will create the space and perspective to see more clearly what the **Limited You** may need, as well as how to care for and manage it.

For example, the **Limited You** may generate a feeling of urgency about something that isn't really urgent. This anxious pressure could alert you to the fact that something has triggered the **Limited You**. With that information, you could remind yourself to calm down, and think through and assess the urgency to see if it's misplaced.

> ◆ *Think of a time when something seemed very urgent at the moment, but later on the urgency seemed misplaced.*
> ◆ *What do you think was behind the sense of urgency?*
> ◆ *Can you imagine how the situation would have played out if you had soothed yourself and thought things through with a clearer, calmer mind?*

Many of the practices discussed in this chapter will show you how to calm, soothe, and support your self. They will also show you how to provide kind-firm self-care while taking appropriate responsibility.

Contain

Soothing and containing belong together, just as kindness and firmness do. Containment is a process of holding yourself in check—especially when limiting stories and reactive patterns go into play. By containing your reactions, you minimize harm to yourself and others.

Containment starts with pausing: stopping long enough to get some perspective and interrupt the momentum of the reaction. Then, with reflection, you may be able to identify any associated pleasure (Shadow Gratification™) and relinquish it. This will eliminate a lot of unnecessary damage and help to neutralize reactivity.

PAUSE–OBSERVE–REFLECT

It goes against the nature of the **Limited You** to pause, observe, or reflect. The **Limited You** is concerned with survival and thinks it already knows the best way to go forward. Yet pausing, observing, and reflecting is exactly what will help you best manage its fears and insecurities.

The **Limited You** may resist or even object to the *pause-observe-reflect* process. Through its defensive strategies, it does everything in its power to keep real change at bay and remain closed to anything new. It may find the process boring, unimportant, or a poor use of time, or it may say you'll never be any good at it, so why bother. This is normal. However, you *can* lead yourself and manage the **Limited You,** so that it doesn't mismanage you.

When you *pause*, you disrupt reactions and create the space to link with your essence, which is the source of power for the **Essential You.** It's then easier to remember your core truth.

When you *observe*, you allow new awareness and information that could potentially challenge your operating assumptions. This could also give you a stronger connection with reality.

When you *reflect*, you open yourself up to new possibilities and perspectives, which can be creative, brilliant, and meaningful. But they can disrupt what is familiar. No wonder the **Limited You** objects!

It's your job to lead the **Limited You** by taking its hand and showing it another way. This is the basic act of internal leadership. Try it now, by asking the **Limited You** to join you as you continue to read. Practice being kind and firm with it as you go.

> *This benefit of seeing... can come only if you pause a while, extricate yourself from the maddening mob of quick impressions ceaselessly battering our lives, and look thoughtfully at a quiet image... the viewer must be willing to pause, to look again, to meditate.*
>
> DOROTHEA LANGE, documentary photographer

Pause

The first step in gaining access to the enormous power of your essence is simply to pause. This is so obvious, yet can be so elusive. That's where you step off the hurtling train of reactivity (such as anger, irritability, fear, insecurities, and jealousy), take a deep breath, and regain perspective. When you come back to what needs attention, you'll see it with fresh eyes.

When you are in a reactive state, you are not only in it, but you are also defined by it, and that always limits your awareness of possible choices. Pausing and stepping back are usually the last things on your mind when you're caught up in a reactive pattern. The reactivity usually blinds you to the option of pausing to interrupt what is in motion.

Pause and step back from a task, activity, or reaction long enough to get perspective on what is going on and what you are doing. Often you will see some kind of pattern. With this awareness, you have a wider range of options, choices, and freedom.

Observe

After you pause, settle yourself down, and get some objectivity, you'll be able to observe more clearly. Then you can remember and focus on what's really important and what you're trying to achieve overall.

> ♦ *Take just thirty seconds right now to simply look around you and notice what you see as a neutral observer.*
> ♦ *Suspend judgment and commentary.*
> ♦ *What do you observe?*

Absolute objectivity isn't possible, but you can cultivate an attitude of neutrality about what you see. When your observations are unbiased and non-judgmental, your perspective will have much greater range.

Even if you see something you don't like, stay as neutral and as kind as possible. This attitude is sometimes called the "fair witness" or the "kind observer." If you slip into a judging or angry position against yourself or someone else, simply note that you aren't observing from a clear, neutral position yet. If you are harsh, scared, or angry, it means you are still in the **Limited You**.

The process is one of continuing to step back until you can see clearly what is going on. The goal is to observe through the kind, warm, curious acceptance of the **Essential You**. You may need to step back repeatedly. Keep at it until you can find a neutral point of observation. Practicing neutral observation will not only give you valuable data and allow you to see recurring themes, but it will also bring a sense of calmness and equanimity.

*If something emotional happens, it's very useful to try to observe your emotions...you try to see how much you can see. What do you **really** feel like, instead of what would you like to feel like, or what you ought to feel like.*

CHARLES TART,
psychologist

Reflect

After pausing and finding a neutral point of observation, you can start to reflect on what you see. The **Limited You** may rush in again with critical or distracting commentary. If it does so, you'll need to step back to a neutral place once more. Creating regular time to think, ponder, and reflect without interruption makes it easier to focus.

> Perspective is worth 80 IQ points.
>
> ALAN KAY,
> computer scientist
> and visionary

Once you stabilize your ability to observe, you can consider the implications of what you see. Reflection allows you the space to wonder, inquire, explore, and let possibilities roll around in your mind. Reflection also supports the ability to recognize meaningful patterns. Often insights and realizations occur spontaneously. Guidance, intuition, and vision are likelier during a period of productive reflection as well.

The following example shows how stepping back to pause, observe, and reflect can lead to powerful realizations and the ability to solve long-term problems.

Timothy

Timothy was an ordained minister and the director of strategic planning for a private Christian university. He had been working for two years with the instructors, deans, and senior leaders to move toward a consensus regarding educational direction for the university.

Timothy struggled for months to pull together the conflicting priorities within the university system and discover what tied the diverse views together. He had been addressing and documenting each specific concern as it came up. He hadn't stepped back to evaluate the larger system and get a broader perspective, even though he knew doing so would have value. He was lost in a thicket of detail and approaching a crisis as the deadline for the strategic plan loomed.

One weekend, he took time away from his sixty-hour-a-week schedule to drive to an important family gathering. During the solitary three-hour drive, he turned the music off and just drove, leaving his mind free to roam.

At the end of that time, he was in awe of how much he could then see and understand. He saw the vital thread that ran through each concern, identified the glitch in mutual understanding, and developed the seed of what would be an inspiring vision for the university.

Timothy was a little embarrassed at having given himself so little reflection time over the previous few years, especially when he knew how important it was for him spiritually. He realized he needed to pull away like that on a regular basis, even in the face of a deadline crisis. It was incredibly centering and the most productive time he had spent in three months. And it had taken only three hours!

Because some reactions will be triggered at the slightest provocation, you need to practice the *pause-observe-reflect* process. You can do so in a spontaneous, unstructured way, as Timothy did in the example above, or you can work with the process in a much more structured manner.

Using the *pause-observe-reflect* process with your reactive patterns can be very liberating. Try the following exercise for at least a week. Continue for longer if it is productive.

Exercise: Monitor Reactive Patterns

Start by identifying and jotting down three reactive patterns or problematic behaviors that you want to monitor. Refer to Chapter 5 for ideas.

1. _____

2. _____

3. _____

At the end of each day, *pause* for just a few minutes. Look back over the day *(observe)* and search for any of these patterns or behaviors.

Finally, *reflect* on:
  ▸ What triggered the patterns
  ▸ What the *Limited You* said about the incident

Conclude by:
  ▸ Challenging anything the *Limited You* said that wasn't entirely true
  ▸ Affirming what is more true

If remembering what happened during the day is too hard, keep a small notebook with you throughout the day and make a note each time you slip into a particular pattern. Then reflect on those slips for a few minutes at the end of the day using the process above.

Do you see how the *pause-observe-reflect* process can be a way to demonstrate kindness and firmness? Reflection, especially, provides an opening for you to guide your limiting tendencies in a way that builds internal trust.

Reactive patterns won't shift by themselves and will require vigilance on your part. Steady, regular use of the above exercise will help you guide your self as your reactive patterns shift to relational ones.

GUIDE YOUR FEAR

As you challenge your reactive patterns and defensive strategies, the fear that drives the **Limited You** may come to the surface in uncomfortable ways. You'll find your enlightened edge as you face and manage this fear. If you ignore it or deny it altogether, you may be missing some important information. If you collapse into it, you could find yourself scrambling to survive. If you stand up and fight with fear, the fighting might go on a long time and be exhausting. There is a better way.

Assume that fear might have a message for you. It can be the signal that says danger is present. Beyond that, it isn't a wise or reliable guide for taking action. If you let it control you, you lose. If you try to control it, you can't win.

Guiding fear is very different from controlling it. When guiding fear, you create safety for yourself. It's like being in a relationship with a scared kid. The child may be freaking out, with no ability to think clearly or create long-term solutions. It's *your* job as the adult to keep a clear head, and assess the situation while you soothe and contain the child's fears.

Acknowledge the fear. Respect it. Don't let it overtake you. Hold your center. Become courageous in the face of fear and take the kind of action you can be proud of. Lyle is an inspiring example of someone who did just that.

Lyle

Lyle was scheduled to speak at a strategic global corporate conference. He was terrified of speaking—not just scared, but drop-dead terrified. He was in a leadership position that required him to make effective presentations and he had to face this challenge or face serious career limitations.

He had a crucial meeting with himself and decided that no matter how much he sweated, how nauseated he felt, or how panicked he got, he would prepare and deliver. He prepared his talk for weeks, video recording himself at home and practicing for hours at a time.

Lyle talked to himself before and after each session, calming his fear and reaffirming his decision to stay with his plan. The practice sessions gradually got easier. The evening before the presentation, though, was hell. He practiced for six hours in front of a mirror until he was exhausted, but the next day, he was ready.

He delivered his speech with skill and power. Lyle was a corporate rock star for the day. His peers congratulated him, asking enviously how he could present so clearly, easily, and powerfully. In his private, politically astute way, he just smiled and thanked them.

Lyle's fear was very specific. Many fears are complex and multi-layered. Either way, the process of guiding your fear is the same. Stay in relationship with it. Soothe it as much as possible. Keep your head and heart together so you can make decisions and take action that will support you for the long term.

SELF-CARE

Self-care is another expression of kindness and firmness. It comes about when you couple compassion toward your self with personal responsibility for your well-being. If you offer compassion to others but not to yourself, or if you focus too much on responsibility for others, you'll probably neglect self-care.

Remember Shirley from Chapters 2 and 4? She illustrated how it's sometimes easier to take care of others than to take care of yourself. Lack of self-care hampers your effectiveness as a leader by making you vulnerable to reactivity. It undermines confidence and resilience and often broadcasts an image of low self-esteem to others.

You are as valuable as anyone else and are just as worthy of care. You are worth investing in, despite what the **Limited You** may say. When the **Essential You** establishes clear self-care practices, the world gets better for the **Limited You**. It won't have as much fuel for its stories of victimization and may object, as it does with many things, but it will also be soothed and reassured.

Self-care includes a wide range of behaviors that support who you are physically, emotionally, mentally, and spiritually. The *pause-observe-reflect* process, as well as the expansive practices and uplifting attitudes that we will discuss later in this chapter, play a part in self-care. If you'd like to assess your current level of self-care, you can download a free copy of the Self-Care Inventory.*

Almost everyone practices self-care to some extent already. But by taking yourself in hand and practicing a higher level of self-care, you'll enhance your resilience and balance, especially under conditions of stress. This is another aspect of internal leadership that will expand your enlightened edge.

> *Self-care stabilizes the ESSENTIAL YOU and prevents much needless pain.*

In the absence of self-care, there is always some kind of needless suffering. You suffer because you neglect important needs. Others suffer because you have much less to offer when you aren't whole and at your best. You can't give what you don't have. Leaders who neglect their self-care also become poor role models for others.

The **Limited You** is most often rooted in poor self-care, resulting in a loss of self-esteem, well-being, and personal integrity. In fact, poor self-care exacerbates all of the reactive patterns. Alternatively, excellent self-care promises to build your self-esteem and strengthen the

---

* The Self-Care Inventory is a simple test to help you assess your level of self-care and identify which behaviors to strengthen. Each of the forty behaviors listed in the inventory can be an effective integrative anchor. You can download a copy for free at **http://Contact PointAssoc.com/assess_selfcare.html**.

integrity of the **Essential You**. It leads to increased energy and a heightened sense of well-being. Because it corrects many imbalances at multiple levels, it also soothes anxiety and offsets depression. You build reserves through self-care. This makes you naturally more resilient and able to withstand even aggravating circumstances with greater equanimity.

> ◆ *Think of the last time you were really tired and how much harder it was to stay centered.*
> ◆ *Now think about the last time you had a great night of sleep and how much easier it was to function the next day.*

Self-care is so beneficial at so many levels and yet so often neglected. When you don't practice self-care, something is out of balance.

Disciplined Self-Care

Self-care takes both firmness and kindness. It requires taking responsibility for you. Only one person has been assigned that job—you.

As with any group of integrative anchors, good self-care requires discipline. You'll find that you need to practice certain behaviors over and over again. You can think of discipline as doing what is in your best interest, even when it doesn't feel easy or comfortable to do so.

Discipline is doing what you know is good for you, even when you don't feel like doing it.

Disciplined self-care is a choice, and like all choices it means giving up some things to get other things that are more important. Creating priorities, which is part of working with reality, always means making some trade-offs. The **Essential You** accepts this responsibility. It focuses on clear priorities and what is to be gained through smart self-care choices.

Disciplined self-care requires working in an ongoing way with many complex priorities and constraints. For example, you can't change the number of hours in the day, but you can change how you prioritize your time. You also can't change other people, but you can renegotiate their expectations of you.

The practice of taking care of yourself may go against other established patterns in your life. Some of your current habits may be quite comfortable; for example, you might draw considerable Shadow Gratification™ from being virtuous and self-sacrificing when in the *rescue-control* and *comply-complain* patterns. Taking care of yourself would mean giving up the gratification and learning to graciously say no when necessary.

When you practice self-care, you often need to work with others to reset the expectations they have of you. This is especially important in relationships that thrive at your expense. It can be a daunting task to initiate and sustain a change in a relationship that is built on a new premise. The other person's habits and your own can often collude to ensure that your self-care *isn't* a priority. However, if you are clear on what you need, you can negotiate new expectations and agreements.

RESPONSIBILITY

Taking responsibility for your self extends beyond self-care and into the world of relationships with others. Taking appropriate responsibility is perhaps one of the most important ways to take charge of your life overall. It is the firm counterpart to kindness. Although usually not fun, it is very powerful.

> Taking personal responsibility increases personal power.

If you take responsibility for your own limits, choices, and what you have the power to change, you'll be in a better position to learn and creatively adapt, especially if things don't go as planned. Equally important is standing behind your choices and accepting the consequences of those choices.

Your responsibility extends to your participation in events and relationships you are part of. This includes holding others accountable for their part in what is going on. When you do this in a way that is kind and firm rather than blaming, you demonstrate personal responsibility.

Blame

Blaming circumvents careful examination of personal responsibility and strips you of personal power. It is a very popular defensive strategy that accomplishes a great deal for the **Limited You**. Blame makes another person the target of responsibility and guilt.

It oversimplifies the issues, eliminates learning, and bypasses deeper understanding of a complex reality. Blaming is a strong tendency, especially with the *dominate-punish* and *defy-subvert* patterns.

Alternatively, taking responsibility for your choices, behaviors, and decisions will increase your personal power and make life easier in the long run. Discontinuing blame is an important corrective measure that can contain damage done by the **Limited You**, but it requires you to take responsibility.

In the following example, Carl illustrates how not taking responsibility for creating appropriate limits can lead to resentment and eventually to blaming someone else.

Carl

Carl's best work buddy and cubicle neighbor was Bret. Though moody and often angry, Bret had a quirky, irreverent sense of humor that Carl found entertaining. This made it easier to put up with Bret's dark moods.

One major point of friction was Bret's cigarette habit. When Bret went too long without a cigarette break, Carl knew it. His swearing and general negativity were audible. Smoking on the premises was forbidden, so Bret had to leave the office to smoke.

Before going out for a smoke, Bret left brief instructions for Carl on how to deal with people who were looking for him. Carl was interrupted more often at these times, but he was okay with it—for a while.

As Bret's cigarette breaks got more frequent and his own workload increased, Carl became more annoyed. Annoyance grew into deep-seated resentment. Carl said nothing. He remained silent and compliant, not wanting to bear the brunt of another one of Bret's angry moods. He failed to take responsibility for simply creating a limit.

When Carl had the opportunity to evaluate Bret in a confidential peer evaluation, he was highly critical of many things he had avoided speaking about to Bret. Carl said nothing that was technically untrue, but his comments were negatively colored by resentment and his own unexpressed annoyance. Carl took a cheap shot at Bret this way, getting back at him passively and invisibly. And he struck out at a time Bret could least afford it.

Carl was relieved at unloading some of his frustration, but he didn't grow in the process. Had he taken responsibility for his own limits, with Bret's cigarette breaks and other points of contention, he could have increased his personal power and prevented needless damage to Bret.

In the above example, Carl was in effect blaming Bret not only for the smoke breaks, but also for his own passive choice to not speak to Bret directly. He avoided taking responsibility for himself and bypassed the discomfort of making an assertive request. Instead, he delivered a righteous blow out of nowhere.

Taking Too Much Responsibility

Taking too much responsibility will feed the **Limited You** just as surely as blaming does, and you need to manage this issue with just as much care.

As a general rule, you aren't responsible for things that you have no power to affect. You're not responsible for the decisions and agreements other people make, nor are you responsible for their level of integrity, self-care, or self-awareness. Their behavior, intentions, and commitments are also not your responsibility.

You aren't responsible for the reactions of others, even if those reactions are linked with something you have done. You can't control how someone reacts to what you say or do; that person may hold you responsible in a misplaced way. Taking responsibility that isn't yours contributes to wasted energy and loss of personal power.

Taking inappropriate responsibility drains personal power.

The tendency to take inappropriate responsibility is especially common when the *rescue-control* or *comply-complain* pattern is operating. Joel is an example of someone who took on too much responsibility through his *rescue-control* pattern. As he worked with this tendency, he discovered some surprising things about personal power.

Joel

Joel was VP of operations for a mid-size electronics company. He had already discovered that he had a powerful *rescue-control* tendency, limiting his ability to manage others and bring out the best in them. He was struggling in the middle of complex responsibilities and was frequently triggered into a compelling emotional need to overprotect others.

Joel knew that his drive to fix what wasn't his responsibility was offensive to others. As he worked with becoming more aware of his *rescue-control* pattern, he saw that there was one employee in particular, Franka, who especially triggered his "need to fix."

Franka was a director in charge of procurement and a single mother. She was very competent but often had a sad, harried look on her face and a general mood of exhaustion. Joel felt empathy for Franka and jumped in to be helpful. He tried to take responsibility for something he didn't own (Franka's job) and for something he had no power to control (Franka's mood) and ended up micromanaging.

As Joel tackled his *rescue-control* tendency and pulled back on the needless control he was exercising with Franka, he began to see her in a different light. She seemed even more capable and a lot perkier as she took on new challenges. He was surprised that she seemed so different. He also found it worrisome that in some small way he missed the old Franka.

A few months into the new changes, Franka came to work late, a bit disheveled, and very tired after a long night with a sick kid. The old Franka was back. And he was shocked to see how much she reminded him of his own mother, who was also a single mom. The exhausted look was so familiar, and he felt the long-standing impulse to be helpful.

He stopped himself in the middle of his *rescue-control* reflex as he hovered anxiously. He stood back, took a deep breath, and then chose instead to give Franka some very thoughtful feedback on a project that was slightly off target. She received it well.

As he started to understand the connection between his *rescue-control* pattern and his early conditioning, he found it easier to see when he was going into the pattern and to shake it off.

He also took in the data about how well Franka was handling his hands-off approach and used this information to underscore with himself what his responsibility was and wasn't.

As Joel discovered, when you stop taking responsibility for what isn't yours, your personal power grows and so do the people around you. Even deep-seated patterns have a chance to shift when you base your actions on self-awareness and knowledge of appropriate responsibility.

Who Is Responsible for What

When you know who is responsible for what, it's easier to take appropriate responsibility and let go of responsibility that is inappropriate. Assessment of responsibility can be fairly straightforward with observable tasks, but is much murkier when it comes to internal and emotional states.

There is no way to draw the perfect line that defines exactly how much responsibility you have for your effect on others. What you *can* do is take responsibility for your own reactions and minimize harm. You'll be more able to do this if you stay open to learning about yourself and the other person.

The following guidelines will help you sort out your part in an emotionally charged exchange in which the other person may be upset, angry, or blaming:

1. You are responsible for containing your reactions and limiting any damage to the other person. This means refraining from delivering a counterattack like blaming.

2. You're responsible for limiting potential damage done to you. It means creating an adequate filter for any blame or attack coming from the other person so you don't "take it personally" in an unfiltered way. This may require keeping a safe distance.

3. You're responsible for learning about what is emotionally important to you and how others affect you.

4. You are responsible for learning about the other person. This includes listening to the person's complaints or issues and

viewing his or her emotional reactions as information about what is important to that person.

5.   You are responsible for learning about how you affect other people and how you may trigger their reactions. This is not the same as taking responsibility for their reactions or their emotions.

Going through the above guidelines won't ensure resolution, but it will ensure you're doing your part to make satisfying resolution possible. As you work with this list, pay attention to the way kindness and firmness with yourself and with the other person can help to calm the reactions and support you in finding relational ground.

> ◆   *Can you recall a recent incident at work or at home in which you had a reactive exchange with someone who was important to you?*
>
> ◆   *If it was resolved, did you touch on each item in the above list along the way?*
>
> ◆   *If it wasn't resolved, was one or more of the items in the above list missing?*

Reactions As Information

When reactions start to fly, blaming and responsibility often get tangled. If you keep a clear boundary regarding responsibility for reactive emotional states, you'll find it easier to stay centered.

The person who goes into a reactive state is the one responsible for it. If you are reacting, the reaction is yours and you are responsible for it. If the other person is reacting, he or she is the one responsible for the emotional or reactive state.

A reactive state *always* provides information about the person who is reacting. Sometimes the person reacting has valuable information for the person he or she is upset with, but not always.

Each person owns and is responsible for his or her reactions.

If someone is upset with you, that person is *primarily* giving you information about who he or she is and how you affected him or her. First, you need to assimilate the information about the other person.

Then, depending on who the other person is and what that person said, you can assess how the information applies to you, and take action or not. Remembering this sequence will help keep the boundaries between you and others much clearer.

The integrity of the **Essential You** will grow stronger as you take responsibility for only that which is yours. To do this requires kindness-firmness with yourself and others and soothing-containing the **Limited You**.

It's much easier to take responsibility for the **Limited You** when you can step out of reactivity and gain perspective on what is going on. The guidelines for what you are responsible for, along with the *pause-observe-reflect* process, can help you do this. We'll turn now to a wide range of practices that have the power to gently disrupt reactivity and help you to center yourself.

EXPANSIVE PRACTICES

A variety of techniques can help you to shift out of fear and reactivity, and into a more expanded mindset. The following techniques will supplement the *pause-observe-reflect* process, especially the ability to pause and observe. Many of these techniques are meditative in nature and are designed to bring about clear awareness, perspective, and objectivity, which will support greater personal presence.

These practices will soften the **Limited You**, help loosen rigid patterns, and make life easier overall. They enhance the **Essential You** by reinforcing and enlivening this aspect of who you are.

These expansive activities can offset *normal craziness* and reactivity. However the **Limited You** is not overly fond of stepping back from what it is attached to. It may resist. You may find that as you approach and work with these practices, patterns of reactivity, negativity, or resistance pop up, often unexpectedly. The **Limited You** may also say "I can easily do that," but then not take time to engage in the necessary practice.

This is the time to practice kindness and firmness. Put your arm around the **Limited You** and ask it to sit down. Reassure it that you really do have its best interests at heart and that this practice will help it feel better, even if it doesn't agree with you.

Breathe

Slow down and pay attention to your breathing. Take slow, deep, full breaths and relax as you exhale.

Move

Move intentionally and mindfully. For example, try meditative walking, yoga, or a martial art.

Create

Express yourself in some creative way. Consider expressive writing, painting, cooking, singing, dancing, or other creative pursuits.

Aliveness

Notice the life force in your body. Take some moments to feel this energy radiating from every part of you.

Here & Now

Keep your energy in the present. Your point of power is right now, not before, not later. [1] Stay rooted in what is going on right now, even when you are planning for the future.

Nothing Else

Try doing just one thing at a time for a period. For instance, peel and eat an orange. Do nothing else and focus only on what is in front of you.

Stillness

Look for and listen to stillness. The stillness may come from a quiet environment, but you can also find it inside, when your mind is temporarily quiet.

No Agenda

Sit and look out a window, without any agenda, for a few minutes.

Watch Thoughts

Sit for a few minutes each day and watch your thoughts arise. Briefly acknowledge any reactive patterns that come up.

These practices are useful when something triggers a reaction in you, or you're facing fear. When you're calm enough, the *pause-observe-reflect* process is your best ally in increasing your overall awareness. This process is most useful when done in a mindful and heartful way. It utilizes your ability to think and feel at the same time.

UPLIFTING ATTITUDES

When you are in transition from the **Limited You** to the **Essential You**, your attitudes will have a pervasive effect. Uplifting attitudes are deceptively simple yet powerful, just as the previously mentioned meditative practices are. The following attitudes also utilize the *pause-observe-reflect* process with a special emphasis on reflection. They often have an indirect way of connecting you with the **Essential You** and bringing perspective.

Gratitude

Gratitude unlocks the fullness of life. It turns what we have into enough, and more. It turns denial into acceptance, chaos to order, confusion to clarity. It can turn a meal into a feast, a house into a home, a stranger into a friend. Gratitude makes sense of our past, brings peace for today, and creates a vision for tomorrow.

MELODY BEATTIE, author

Appreciate and be grateful for who you are, what you have, and the people in your life. Feel gratitude for things that may be normal for you and that you take for granted, such as abundant food, shelter from the cold, the ability to move without pain, and the ability to see.

Beauty

Look for beauty around you. Bring beautiful or pleasing sights, sounds, smells, and tastes into your life. Then pause to abundantly appreciate the beauty and let it nurture you.

Nature

Look to nature for guidance. It offers abundant examples of how to live creatively with tension. For example, you can take creative inspiration from the seasons, the rhythm of light and dark within a day, and the cycle of seed-plant-flower-seed.

Balance

Don't take on more than you can handle or create an overwhelming situation. Stay steady and self-respecting with the challenges you agree to. Balance is elusive and never stays in place for very long; it requires active, consistent cultivation.

Play

Playfulness is the lighthearted pathway to renewal. A playful attitude brings fun and joy to life. When you seek ways to be less serious and to find amusement in everyday activity, even a dark mood can become lighter.

Humor

Look for humor, even in the direst of situations. Humor offers both perspective and stress relief. It's also good for healing.

Optimism

Develop an optimistic, life-affirming attitude toward what is going on in your life. This is also known as thinking positively.

Compassion

Compassion is often paired with an attitude of loving-kindness. It is a warm softening in your heart when you witness suffering (in yourself or others) and a wish for the suffering to be relieved. This is especially important when adversity strikes. Compassion eases the pain and keeps the door open to further learning. Practicing compassion will greatly increase your sensitivity to others and expand your emotional intelligence. It is part of the foundation for self-care.

♦ *Review the previous list of expansive practices and uplifting attitudes. Do one or two of them seem particularly powerful for you?*

♦ *If so, refer to the sketch of the **Essential You** on page 118 and record it as an integrative anchor.*

♦ *Keep the sketch of the **Essential You** close by so you can remember your integrative anchors when you need them.*

HOLD YOUR VALUE

The **Limited You** will almost always neglect some aspect of your self-care. The **Limited You's** core insecurity will also hamper your ability to hold your value. Without a solid grasp of your value, you can easily inflate, deflate, or skew your significance and contributions. You may become overconfident or underconfident. Both of these distortions in self-perception can lead to ungrounded and unwise actions.

Holding your value in a clear and unbiased way is a very powerful expression of taking care of yourself and taking charge of who you are in the world. It depends on your ability to recognize and validate both your intrinsic value *and* your relative value.

Your *intrinsic* value is your birthright as a human being. You take up space and resources on this earth and have as much right to be here as anyone else. You have essential value that is no more and no less than anyone else's. When you validate this for yourself, the result is intrinsically balancing and stabilizing.

Holding your *relative* value is a little different. You are valuable to some people for some things. However, to other people you may have no value at all. Under certain conditions, even your greatest strengths will have no value. It's a mistake to think you can be valuable to everyone under all conditions.

Holding your relative value means standing behind your strengths and acknowledging what you bring to the table. As a leader, it's very important that you do this for yourself and not rely too much on the validation of others.

Too much reliance on others erodes your personal power. While it's important to know how others value you, it's also up to you to hold that value and not let it drain away when external reinforcement wears thin.

Holding your value gets dicey when your usual ways of feeling validated and rewarded are challenged. For example, changing jobs can disrupt familiar rewards such as money, status, and positive feedback from others.

A new level of leadership asks you to re-establish your value in a new context and often with different rewards. In a very real way, you need to prove yourself under new circumstances. Holding your value is essential in these situations. In the following example, Shelly faced this challenge during a job transition and, as a result, established a much deeper level of self-care.

Shelly

When it came to a job change, Shelly was feeling very shaky about her value. For the first time in her ten-year career in the computer software industry, she was taking a sales position. She would be paid a base salary plus commission on both sales amount and volume. The commission offered the potential to be highly successful and make big bucks. She was both excited and a little horrified at the possibilities.

She prepared herself by meditating on her unconditional, intrinsic value. She spent five to ten minutes quietly breathing and reminding herself of her place in the world. When she felt calm and centered, she turned her attention to her relative value. She wrote down her strengths and the personal value she brought to her potential customers. She also clarified the value of the product she was selling.

Then she and her coach worked out three ways to anchor her value in the upcoming weeks and months:

1. Learn and respond to what the customer valued in her
2. Validate and stand behind what she valued in herself
3. Stay connected with her intrinsic value

She made a commitment to these steps. They acted as integrative anchors for her **Essential Self**, strengthened her integrity, and kept her up to date on the relative value of what she was offering. As a result, she was able to stand behind her value to the client and hold her value for herself.

Shelley developed high trust, high profile, and high profit relationships with her clients. It was an extremely rewarding transition for her, not just because of the outward success, but also because of the deep, internal confidence that she felt.

Identifying both your intrinsic value and your relative value is very helpful when you need to establish an unshakable feeling of confidence. Holding your value becomes second nature when you acknowledge your worth internally and also express it outwardly in your life.

> ◆ *Think of the last time you felt a loss of confidence.*
> ◆ *Did you experience doubt about your value?*
> ◆ *If so, was it your relative value or your intrinsic value that you questioned?*
> ◆ *Do you need to stand behind or affirm your value in some way?*

It's up to you to care for and contain the **Limited You** so it doesn't do damage. By taking care of the **Limited You** with kindness, and taking charge of it with firmness, you build internal trust and confidence. You reach for its hand and guide it.

> ◆ *Are you developing some compassion for the **Limited You** at this point?*
> ◆ *Are your feelings toward the **Limited You** too harsh? If so, try more kindness.*
> ◆ *Are you too accommodating or slack with yourself? If so, get a little tougher and establish greater accountability.*

The *pause-observe-reflect* process creates the space to sort out and stop automatic reactions. This stabilizes the **Essential You** so it can take wise action. Occasionally pausing to reflect on you and your life is necessary if you are to gain enough perspective to bring about change. Meditative practices and uplifting attitudes reinforce the *pause-observe-reflect* process and can be powerfully centering and calming.

As you work with your defensive strategies, they come into focus and need to be managed. Refraining from blame and taking clear responsibility encourages learning and helps to contain negative consequences. This helps to minimize harm and provide real relief from inappropriate expectations.

Self-care soothes the **Limited You** in profound and inexplicable ways, releasing tremendous energy that the **Essential You** can use. Self-care, holding your value, guiding your fear, reflection, and renewal go hand-in-hand to reinforce each other and support the emergence of a more vital, alive, inspired you.

In the next chapter, we will look at how to deepen your center of balance and strength by working with the tension between the **Limited You** and the **Essential You**. Your leadership potential can ignite as you work creatively with tension at multiple levels.

10

CREATIVE TENSION & IGNITION

To fly we have to have resistance.

MAYA LIN, architect and sculptor

YOU'VE probably been told to release tension, not hold it. That's true when you're holding *excess* tension in your body. On the other hand, if you don't hold *enough* tension in your body, you won't be able to move or function, nor will you be able to creatively think or work. Tension is a necessary part of life.

Tension creates the heat and passion that drives creativity. It can ignite your personal power, but needs to be managed. You can manage it best when you're significantly centered and grounded in the **Essential You.**

Holding creative tension is an active, reflective, internal state that encourages greater awareness. The *pause-observe-reflect* process supports this by giving you the internal space to become more aware of what is going on within you and around you. It also allows you to reflect and sort out your thoughts and feelings in a meaningful way. With a greater capacity to hold tension, you'll minimize anxiety and reactivity.

The ability to hold the tension that goes with new and sometimes disruptive information will help you work constructively with your enlightened edge. For a leader or high performer, holding tension can mean being able to acknowledge, understand, and address:

◆ Both sides of an issue
◆ Differing sets of needs
◆ Competing systems
◆ Opposing viewpoints
◆ Differing business agendas

Have you ever noticed that if you take sides on an issue, you can no longer pay attention to the totality of the issue? It is only from the larger vantage point that you can see the whole situation; you lose perspective when you align with just one side.

When you hold the tension between two sides of an issue, you acknowledge the merit of and show due respect to both sides. When you don't do this, you're more likely to identify with your preferred side and react against the other side. Your goal here is to suspend your reactions, hold the tension a little longer, and participate in leading others to a beneficial, constructive solution.

When you take sides, you may release tension but bypass creativity. If you can temporarily resist the impulse to take sides or prematurely rush to closure on an issue, you'll find it easier to see clearly and understand what is going on. With some objectivity, you can bring a more complete perspective to what you see, rather than being caught in the reactivity of one position.

For example, let's say you have a manager who is insecure and controlling and really does *not* want to hear challenging feedback. But you have some bad news on a high-profile project that is clearly off track with both time and budget. To give him the bad news will require working with considerable tension. You will have to consider both:

◆ His vested interests and your own
◆ His emotional reactions and your own
◆ His view of the project as well as your new information

Imagine that you are holding one end of a rope and the manager is holding the other end. Your goal is to keep enough tension on the rope so it's firm, not slack or too tight.

Keeping adequate tension on the rope means standing solid in yourself as you address the interpersonal dynamics and the business issues. It means forging ahead with the conversation even though your manager may react in unpredictable ways. You must also manage your own reactive judgments and do your part to generate a constructive discussion about solutions.

> ♦ *Can you think of a situation in which you pulled too hard on "the rope"? What was the result?*
> ♦ *What about a time when you let "the rope" go wobbly? What happened?*
> ♦ *Try working with the rope metaphor for a few days. For most people, it can act as a simple but powerful integrative anchor.*

APPROACH THE CREATIVE TENSION

In order to hold tension constructively, it's best to start by simply accepting the current conditions in your life and work.

The line of least resistance often is to withdraw from tension. But in order to successfully hold tension, you need to approach it in a friendly way rather than retreat from it. A little tension may be uncomfortable initially, but as you get used to the sensation, it becomes more comfortable and can even be exciting. It's like saying, "I'm going to play with this and see what happens."

For example, let's say you have an unpleasant task ahead of you, such as filing papers or making a difficult phone call. To get the job done, you must meet the tension associated with the task in some way. The more friendly and playful you are with the task, the more likely that it may be fun, creative, or at least less painful.

> ♦ *What would it be like if you didn't deny, bypass, or try to vanquish any aspect of yourself or your life?*
> ♦ *What if you accepted it all?*
> ♦ *Would friendly acceptance make it easier for you to hold the tension and work with it?*

Leadership requires you to approach tension in significant ways and at important times. When you approach creative tension in a friendly way, hold it, and work with it, the energy will ignite your personal power and presence as a leader.

UNDER PRESSURE

Being an effective leader is a lot like being a pressure cooker. It's your job to hold and regulate the tension that builds up in your "cooker." As the heat in the pressure cooker increases, it cooks the contents quickly and releases the pressure safely.

> ♦ *Think about two or three main areas of responsibility you have as a leader, such as the revenue from your organization, your team's morale, and prioritizing commitments between work and home.*
>
> ♦ *Think of each of these areas of responsibility as food in your pressure cooker.*
>
> ♦ *Do some areas need more pressure? Less?*

Your goal is to regulate the tension or pressure so there is enough heat and energy to generate the strategies and results you want.

A diamond is a lump of coal that did well under extreme pressure.

UNKNOWN
SOURCE

When you regulate tension, people around you aren't as likely to fearfully and unproductively scurry around, be pushed beyond their limits, get burned out, or go into crisis due to too much tension. At the same time, you hold enough tension to challenge any slackness, create accountability, and drive high performance.

RELEASE TENSION AT THE RIGHT TIME

You don't have to hold tension forever, that's not required, desirable, or even possible. There is an optimal time to release tension. Hold it just long enough to allow a creative solution or a new outcome to emerge. Then, when you do take decisive action, it doesn't have to be *against* anyone or anything. It can be *for* something you're trying to create. Holding tension for long enough, and releasing it when the time feels right, will increase your chances of success, especially when initiating changes.

Often a person releases tension too soon or holds it too long. Think of what happens to the rope or the pressure cooker when tension is released too soon. The rope goes slack, and pressure dissipates from the cooker before the food is done. When you yield prematurely, something inside collapses or caves in and you feel like you've compromised your integrity. This tendency to release tension too early is more likely when you're operating from the *rescue-control* or *comply-complain* pattern.

◆ Can you think of a time when you released tension too soon?
◆ What did you gain through this?
◆ Did you limit your potential in doing so?

Now think about what happens to the rope or the cooker when tension is *held too long*. Either the rope breaks or whatever is on the other side of the rope breaks down. The pressure from the cooker may erupt explosively, or stay contained but burn the food. When you hold on too long or push too hard for reasons that aren't productive, you're likely to harm someone or something, especially when you're operating from the *dominate-punish* or *defy-subvert* pattern.

◆ Can you think of a time when you held tension too long?
◆ Did you gain anything?
◆ What was the cost associated with the gain?

Regulating tension is an art requiring the full power and presence of the **Essential You**. In the following example, Patricia worked very intentionally with her tendency to avoid the tension between herself and her supervisor.

Patricia

Patricia was a hard-driving senior director of sales in a large retail clothing company. She motivated and drew out the best in her sales team. They felt thoroughly challenged and respected by her.

The situation was different with her peers, the other four directors in the sales department. Three of them resented her for appearing arrogant. They didn't speak to her about it, but they did make comments to their manager, the VP of sales.

During the last five minutes of her annual performance review with the VP, Patricia learned that her peers saw her as abrasive and professorial. That critique cost her one point in a five-point rating system.

Patricia was astonished. When she asked her VP for further clarification, he dismissed her. As usual, he needed to get to another meeting. She was upset about the feedback, and even more upset with how it was delivered, yet she didn't follow up with him. He had a long history of canceling meetings with her and generally avoiding one-on-one contact.

When Patricia was challenged by her coach to get further feedback, she was reluctant. She didn't want to speak with her fellow directors or the VP. Instead, she smoldered.

She did take the initial feedback to heart, though, and worked on correcting what was clearly a *dominate-punish* pattern with her peers. This was difficult because she was so angry with them, but she took responsibility for her behavior.

She also became aware of a *comply-complain* pattern with most authority figures, including her VP. Patricia came to see that with people who had more power, she avoided any appearance of non-compliance. However, with her peers, where power was more or less equal, she was very competitive.

Her safe haven was with her own sales group, where she was well respected, the lines of authority were clear, and she was in a solid position of power.

Her coach began to address her tendency to avoid conflict. Over the years, her tendency to pull away from personal conflict and slide into compliance hampered her ability to advance her career.

She and her coach discussed how odd it was that she could be so demanding and performance-oriented, yet she had this avoidance streak. It became clear that she could push hard and even deal with a high level of conflict when it wasn't personal, but when the conflict had anything to do with her personally, she retreated.

Patricia began to see how she avoided tension. She saw the way she was reluctant to hold the tension around her own need for clear feedback when it pushed against her VP's tendency to avoid one-on-one meetings.

She finally decided to address the situation, first by holding onto her need for further discussion, and then by insisting on a clarification meeting with her VP, who was slightly annoyed with the request. In that meeting, she had to deal with the tension in the room as she pressed for clarification on his original feedback about her peer relationships and what she could do to improve communication.

Finally, Patricia spoke to her peers, one at a time, using the same process with them. She accepted and came to terms with her own need for clear feedback first. Then she asked her peers for direct, honest feedback. They were uncomfortable and so was she, but everyone dealt with it.

In the process, she claimed significant personal power, gained deeper respect from her VP, and repaired some relationships with her peers that had been in sore need of attention. The work group as a whole was stronger and more productive as a result.

Patricia challenged her **Limited Self** and built one of the necessary features of her **Essential Self**: the ability to tolerate tension. She was gathering her power.

When you take similar action, such as making a necessary request, entering into a challenging conversation, or holding another person to an agreement that isn't being honored, you build personal power and leadership strength.

There is always some kind of tension in relationships, especially if the other person is angry, threatened, embarrassed, squirmy, or defensive. In Chapters 11 and 12, we'll look at what you can do to deal with both your own discomfort and the discomfort of others when tension mounts. You'll learn skills and techniques that will help a great deal in working constructively with the tension.

TENSION: THE LIMITED YOU & THE ESSENTIAL YOU

As you work with the **Limited You** and the **Essential You**, the tension between these very different aspects of who you are becomes increasingly apparent. Both are hard at work, trying to define you. They each have a different way of viewing not only who you are, but who others are, what the world is like and how it operates, and how you think all of it could or should be different.

> How you manage the tension between the LIMITED YOU and the ESSENTIAL YOU will affect everything you do and everyone you meet.

How you handle the tension between the **Limited You** and the **Essential You** will affect everything you do and everyone you come into contact with. It will determine how you respond to the needs of others, the decisions you make, the way you handle pressure, and your ability to influence others.

> Creative tension comes from seeing clearly where we want to be, our "vision," and telling the truth about where we are, our "current reality." The gap between the two generates a natural tension....Individuals, groups, and organizations who learn how to work with creative tension learn how to use the energy it generates to move reality more reliably toward their visions.
>
> PETER M. SENGE,[1] author and organizational consultant

Your enlightened edge expands as you work creatively with the tension between the **Limited You** and the **Essential You**. As a leader, you may need to hold tension, even when others cannot. This means holding differences long enough for a creative solution to emerge. Your goal as an enlightened leader is to accept and work with challenges in a firm, kind, and beneficial way.

The following diagram illustrates how the **Limited You** and the **Essential You**, with their supporting processes, come together to generate tension that you can use as fuel for creative activity.

Let's assume, for example, that you're up against a deadline. You know that you tend to get highly critical of others at these times. You also know that others don't respond well to this approach, and you'd like to find a way to meet the deadline without alienating others. There is an element of internal tension here that you can view as a creative challenge.

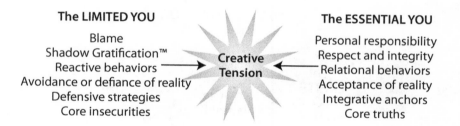

The LIMITED YOU

Blame
Shadow Gratification™
Reactive behaviors
Avoidance or defiance of reality
Defensive strategies
Core insecurities

Creative Tension

The ESSENTIAL YOU

Personal responsibility
Respect and integrity
Relational behaviors
Acceptance of reality
Integrative anchors
Core truths

In order to work creatively with the tension between the **Limited You** and the **Essential You**, you must accept both aspects as part of the picture. This is easier said than done, especially if you have a tendency to blame, shame, or make yourself wrong.

Do you ever find yourself making the **Limited You** the enemy? If so, you've probably found that it doesn't help matters. Taking an antagonistic position against another part of yourself is a tactic used by the **Limited You**, which often attacks itself. This tendency is often found in high-performing leaders and points to a need for greater self-acceptance or loving-kindness.

A more useful approach is to accept the fact that the **Limited You** is quite established and the **Essential You** probably still needs further development. Remember that the **Essential You** never attacks you. It will always work with you in a benevolent, constructive way.

Eventually, the **Essential You** will be powerful enough to thoroughly enfold the **Limited You**. Along the way, the **Limited You** will learn to trust in the love, power, and skill of the **Essential You**. It will choose to align itself with the **Essential You** and give up what doesn't work.

The following diagram illustrates the dual role of the **Essential You**. The smaller ellipse shows how the **Essential You** is part of the tension with the **Limited You**. The larger ellipse suggests that from a more expanded perspective, and with greater development, the **Essential You** can hold both the **Limited You** and the tension associated with it.

The dual role of the **Essential You** can appear paradoxical. It can be a source of tension for the **Limited You** because it challenges the controlled and controlling identity of the **Limited You**, but as we saw in Chapter 9, the **Essential You** also helps resolve tension for the **Limited You**.

The **Essential You** works with tension in a practical way when you are leading yourself or others. You need realistic ways to regulate pressure and find balance in an environment that is in a constant state of change. Fortunately, there's quite a bit you can do to stabilize your center of balance so you can better handle demanding leadership challenges.

DYNAMIC BALANCE FOR WORK & LIFE

> *The best and safest thing is to keep a balance in your life, acknowledge the great powers around us and in us. If you can do that, and live that way, you are really a wise man.*
>
> EURIPIDES, Greek playwright

One of the biggest challenges for high-performing leaders is managing the tension between the competing demands of work and personal life. Finding a respectable balance in your life will give you a steadier internal compass. Without this stabilizing balance, many other issues become more pronounced and difficult to manage.

Finding that balance is its own challenge. Work-life balance is loaded with tension. It's easier to manage the tension in this territory if you think in terms of *work-life integration* rather than dividing work and life into separate camps.

Often when people think of work-life balance, they assume that work and life are pitted against each other. The overly simple solution is to just work less. But this doesn't address the complex reality that work and life need to be integrated, not split apart.

Work and life are not two separate things, just as relationships and life aren't two distinct things. They are different aspects of one thing.

Work-life integration requires awareness and respect for the totality of your life. Your life includes everything you do; work is just one of many life activities. The goal of work-life integration is to juggle life activities so they can support both personal integrity and high performance. This will help you feel more alive and present both at work and at home.

Dynamic balance comes about when the **Essential You** takes charge of how you *prioritize* what is important to you and how you *choose to act* on those priorities on a daily basis. If you assume balance is dynamic, not static, you'll be better able to adjust quickly and in ways that serve your priorities.

If you'd like more information on your own work-life balance, you can take the *Work-Life Effectiveness Assessment.*[*] It includes four focus areas for work-life balance: self-care, managing your relationships, investing in your potential, and deepening your resilience.

The **Limited You** may have an agenda and priorities that work against balance. For example, it may try to sabotage self-care or prevent clarity in agreements. But as the **Essential You** takes charge, the **Limited You** may begin to trust the new changes and feel less anxious.

The ability to show up at your best is vital to high-impact leadership. By realistically managing your balance, you can rely on yourself to be present and effective when you need to be.[2]

The following six principles will help you to prioritize and make choices that support dynamic balance. They are rooted in realistic assumptions rather than unmanageable expectations. They will also help the **Essential You** carve out some new possibilities for choices that are more realistic. As a consequence, your efforts will be more successful.

---

* To take the *Work-Life Effectiveness Assessment*, go to **http://contactpointassoc.com/ assess_wl.html** for details. The website will also provide information on the *Performance & Balance Training* for groups. Look also for *Balancing on the Edge: Tools for Peak Performance in Work & Life*, a complete tool kit for work-life effectiveness for individuals.

Working Less Doesn't Ensure Balance

Balance does *not necessarily* mean working fewer hours. As previously mentioned, working less to find balance can be a simplistic approach to a more complex issue. Hard work is a necessary element of high performance. For many people, it is also an important way to find true contentment. Pushing yourself to meet a challenge or responding to a "calling" can be a very rewarding and creative part of living.

Working More Doesn't Ensure Success

You'll never get everything you want through work. Success at work is only one aspect of true success. Trying to get everything you need from work sets you up to be a workaholic, with work defining your life. When work rules you, you lose your ability to be realistic about what you can accomplish, so look at the price you pay by overworking and evaluate the rewards that work can actually provide.

> Take heed that when effort is too strenuous it leads to strain and when too slack, to laziness. So make a firm determination that you will adopt the middle way, not allowing yourself to struggle or to slacken....
>
> THE THERAGATHA,
> Buddhist scripture

Balance Exertion and Recovery

When training as an athlete, you build muscle and strength by exhausting your capacity. What do you do after an exhausting workout? You recover; if you don't, your chances of decreased performance or injury increase. The same is true with any kind of intensive effort at work. You build your work and professional muscles by working all the way to capacity.

Most leaders and high performers must be disciplined about their need for recovery after a period of heavy exertion.[3] They need to make adjustments when they're out of balance and create habits that support ongoing balance. In the following example, Jonas learned the hard way about overexertion and the need for recovery.

Jonas

In his late twenties, Jonas was the CEO of a high-tech start-up company that failed after three years of excruciating effort. He had pushed himself all the way to the ragged edge too many times, without sufficient recovery. After the collapse of his company, he dropped into an agitated depression that left him irritable, unable to sleep, and impossible to live with.

When his girlfriend moved out, he began to examine the many painful losses that were piling up around him. His health was threatened by high blood pressure. All of his relationships had incurred some damage, and he had lost his love of simply being alive.

After many weeks of honest self-reflection and a series of provocative conversations with friends and health care professionals, he started to recover. He remembered how much he loved rock climbing, snowboarding, and the excitement of waking up ready to attack a new day.

His sleep and health finally stabilized. He could think and feel clearly again. Jonas then made a promise to himself. He would never again let himself get so far out of balance that he compromised his life force. His personal litmus test was his ability to love and appreciate life. The application was simple: if he couldn't feel his love for life each day, he needed to make an adjustment.

With this new standard in place, he started his next business venture. He pushed himself hard as usual, but was disciplined about pulling back and recovering when he felt "compromised."

Jonas was surprised at one of the side effects of his new practice: better decision making. Brief recovery periods gave him the time and perspective he needed to make business decisions that were wiser and more strategic.

Balancing heavy exertion with recovery is part of self-care and requires discipline. By taking charge of your life in this way, you can establish both a sustainable pace and reliable pattern of elite performance.

You Can't Have It All—Establish Your Priorities

Accept that you can't have it all. Having it all is impossible, and trying to do the impossible can make you crazy. Inevitably, you'll drop some balls. For example, if you're sandwiched between young children and responsibility for aging parents, you'll feel the squeeze and will need to be very careful in assessing your priorities. This might mean not keeping up the house or yard as well as you'd like. Or maybe you'd cut back on socializing, or include family more in your social engagements.

You can't please everyone or keep everyone happy; it's not possible. The best you can hope for is to please some people and not others. So evaluate whom you can please, when, and for what purpose.

If you don't remember to care for yourself along the way, you will almost certainly fall out of balance. This is one ball that costs too much to drop. Self-care is vitally important, even if your culture or family doesn't support it. As we discussed in Chapter 9, self-care provides a foundation that helps you stay out of reactive patterns and helps strengthen the **Essential You** so you can make smart choices at home and at work.

Every decision will cost you something; it's just a matter of what that may be. Consciously facing this reality will make it easier for you to establish your priorities, make trade-offs, and accept the consequences. Accepting full responsibility for those choices will give you a greater sense of personal power—an essential ingredient for high performance and effective leadership.

There Is Always Inequity–Look For Balance Over Time

Accept that there will always be some inequity in the division between home and career. At times, you will have to put in long hours at work at the expense of domestic responsibilities, if you are to fulfill your potential. At other times, it will work in reverse: you may focus on home or your personal life at the expense of work in order to fulfill other areas of life. Your goal is to find a dynamic balance between work and life, not a mathematical split between the two.

Look for balance in the long run, over the course of your life. Different times in your life will require different choices, commitments, and periods of chosen "imbalance." For example, marriage, kids, aging parents, and demanding travel schedules will all demand a different type and length of investment from you.

You Can't Create Time–But Can Increase Energy

Time is limited, but energy can be greatly expanded through a variety of strategies. For example, energy is more abundant with basic self-care. Getting plenty of exercise, developing good eating and drinking habits, and getting enough quality sleep will all increase your energy.

You can then use greater energy to enhance both your performance and balance. When you apply the previous principles and develop your own priorities and habits for renewal, you can expect greater energy.

If you are strategic about your plan for renewal, implementing it will take less time and you'll enjoy the process more. You'll also find it easier to remember what is really important to you. In the following example, Marissa developed just such a plan.

Marissa

Marissa was a business manager in a busy legal firm, and also the mother of three-year-old twins. Her husband owned his own small business and was swamped with work.

The first phase of her plan for renewal in the middle of a very demanding lifestyle was to make some changes in her work schedule. Her new schedule called for her to work four days a week, ten hours a day, and take calls from work during specific times on the fifth day.

The second phase of her plan was to allocate time each day and each week to refill her reservoir. Each day when driving home from work, she turned off her cell phone, mentally put work aside, and started to focus on her family. Within a couple of miles of home, she pulled over to a quiet spot and parked for a while. She set her cell phone timer for fifteen minutes, put the seat back, closed her eyes, and rested. When she came in the house after a long day, she was ready for her kids and a full evening.

On her fifth, partial workday, she took an exercise class after dropping her kids off, had lunch with a friend afterward, came home to take her work calls, napped, and, after some errands, picked up her kids. She found that exercise, girl talk, and catching up on her sleep were vital for her well-being.

A year prior to these changes, Marissa never imagined she could make these changes and feel so good about herself, but she was open to an attitude adjustment. Once she made up her mind, she was disciplined in her action.

Marissa brought energy and attention to the goal of creating greater balance. As a consequence, she gained even more energy, but she had to work with many levels of tension in order to bring this about.

> ◆ *Can you recall a time when you invested time and energy in yourself?*
> ◆ *Did it help you become more productive?*
> ◆ *Did it help you manage tension more creatively?*

When the **Essential You** orchestrates adjustments and choices that bring you into balance, it's easier to work creatively with tension. This is an important safeguard against burnout and loss of power.

Establishing priorities and making wise choices is not an automatic process. It requires stepping back from the pressure of everyday activity and assessing what has integrity for you. The *pause-observe-reflect* process helps to create the space to find clarity, and you need to hold some tension as you consider what is most important.

Often the best course of action isn't obvious. This is especially so when you're actively changing and shifting out of old habits. Inspiration or guidance can help you find your way and chart a path.

GIVING & RECEIVING GUIDANCE

To be a trustworthy guide to others requires that you have access to some kind of guidance—direction or advice about a decision or course of action—for yourself, whether from an internal or external source. Enlightened leaders usually want to both receive and offer, the wisest counsel possible. When you see a path forward and can chart a course, you're able to offer guidance to others.

There are many situations in which you may provide guidance to others. For example, when you teach or offer advice, you act as a guide.

You probably offer guidance through your role as a parent, consultant, coach, manager, or group leader. But what is it that guides you?

The **Limited You** may dismiss this question, assuming that it already knows what to do and what is best, or it may feel unworthy of guidance and assume it has to flail in the dark. The **Limited You** often tries to bypass the creative tension between you and what may be wiser than you, by providing pat answers to questions that it hasn't investigated.

Being open to guidance presumes there is something wiser than you, and that by linking with this source, you can be assisted in some significant way. Guidance can come from external sources such as a mentor, coach, therapist, good friend, spiritual advisor, or family member whom you trust.

Internal sources of guidance can be just as varied and reach into territory that goes beyond the scope of this book. We'll keep it simple by focusing on a process for linking with *what is greater* rather than outlining potential sources of internal guidance.

♦ *Do you have a way to connect with internal guidance?*
♦ *If you don't believe you need guidance, can you imagine a situation in which you might need it?*
♦ *If you don't feel worthy of guidance, could this be a defensive strategy that limits your leadership?*

INTERNAL GUIDANCE

What is greater can be seen in a variety of ways. You could think of it as your soul or essence, as God or spirit, as natural grace, as wisdom, courage, inspiration, acceptance, love, purpose, or enlightened awareness. For this discussion, it doesn't matter what you call it. What does matter is that there is something in the universe you can trust that is greater than the **Limited You**.

When you align with your core truth, act on your integrative anchors, and open up to *what is greater*, you generate positive momentum. This momentum is like a "carrier wave" for the **Essential You**. You gain a sense of being carried along and supported in positive yet inexplicable ways. You may feel lighter and more positive, with a greater sense of well-being.

What is greater can show up in subtle or obvious ways. Here are a few examples of how people experience the benevolent presence of *what is greater*:

♦ Feeling encouraged, hopeful, or comforted after a period of difficulty

♦ Sensing a meaningful connection between inexplicable events

♦ Being supported or treated favorably, even when it doesn't seem as though you earned it

♦ Feeling awake, alive, perky, or bouncy

♦ Receiving support from surprising places

♦ Receiving wise nudges from the quiet, still voice inside

If you feel you don't have a relationship with *what is greater* or with a reliable source of guidance, you may find, as you continue to read, that you rely more on it than you thought. You may also discover that it operates in the background and just needs to come more into the foreground. As is true of any relationship, the more you nurture your connection with *what is greater*, the more it can grow and flourish.

When you have a relationship with *what is greater*, you can begin to rely on its guidance. This is indeed tricky territory and there is much to learn about discernment regarding any source of guidance. There are reliable techniques for doing just that, including staying grounded in the reality of *what is going on* as you proceed. The following five steps provide a reliable sequence for connecting with your own guidance and linking to *what is greater*.

1. Get Centered

Getting centered is the first step in receiving guidance. This is basically a process of settling down inside, minimizing external distractions, and helping to calm down the internal chatter. Any simple repetitive physical activity or action that requires intense focus can help. Many of the expansive practices mentioned in Chapter 9 will assist you in getting centered. For example, exercise, meditation, gardening, martial arts, yoga, and singing can all help to calm the mind.

Letting go of reactivity and Shadow Gratification™ is also important in shifting from the **Limited You** and establishing the centered **Essential You.**

2. Ask for Guidance

The next step is asking for guidance. There are many ways to ask. You can use internal imagery, sit in silence, listen to intuition, pray, or consult oracles. The act of asking sets the stage to receive what you ask for. After you ask, it's a matter of opening up to receiving it. Look and listen deeply. Pay attention to your intuition.[4] The point is to ask a meaningful question and then wait for the response.

> *I call intuition cosmic fishing. You feel the nibble, and then you have to hook the fish.*
>
> BUCKMINSTER FULLER, architect and innovator

3. Wait

Waiting can be the hardest part. Sitting in silence with no answer isn't comfortable for most people. However, the wisest guidance often comes from a quiet, subtle place inside that can easily be ignored or overridden by louder voices. Sometimes it takes longer to show up than you hoped. When you do receive guidance or have an insight or flash of realization, be sure to write it down. These moments are often elusive and hard to remember later on, if you don't anchor them.

♦ *Can you remember a time when you needed to make an important decision, weren't sure of the direction, and then the path suddenly became clear?*

♦ *Try to remember what you were thinking, feeling, or doing **just before** the sudden clarity. (Being relaxed or doing nothing of substance often precedes small moments of enlightenment.)*

4. Assess

Evaluate and test out the guidance you received. Sort, sift and filter it. This may mean talking it over with someone you trust or checking it against other things that you know in your heart are true. Make sure that you also check it against what you already have established as having a high degree of integrity. Reliable guidance should fit the criteria for a core truth or integrative anchor (accept reality, be truthful, honor potential, and be relational).

5. Take Action

Finally, take some kind of action, based on the guidance you received. Guidance that you act upon often serves well as an integrative anchor.

Guidance can often be quite soothing, but it can also be intensely challenging. You may have a tendency to resist or refuse guidance, even when you know it to be highly reliable. When this happens, view your resistance as an indication that the tension between the **Limited You** and the **Essential You** has become activated and needs to be managed.

You always have choices in how you respond to *what is greater* and to guidance. A sense of purpose can help guide these choices and keep them highly relevant.

PURPOSE

A guiding purpose can be balancing and centering, and it can help you make wise choices in the middle of considerable tension. When issues get muddled and murky, a clear purpose offers focus. A guiding purpose provides direction and inspiration when you have to make a tough decision or a judgment call.

> *What man actually needs is not a tensionless state but rather the striving and struggling for some goal worthy of him. What he needs is not the discharge of tension at any cost, but the call of a potential meaning waiting to be fulfilled by him.*
>
> VIKTOR FRANKL, psychiatrist and Holocaust survivor[5]

The **Essential You** grows stronger when your intention or central purpose comes into focus and provides a stabilizing reference point. Purpose acts as a powerful catalyst in bringing together your strengths and integrative anchors. This helps unify who you are and what you want to achieve, and moves you forward.[6]

When it's necessary to take a realistic risk in the face of potentially frightening consequences, purpose helps to activate courage and conviction. You can consider and measure risks in light of the guiding purpose. Purpose also makes it possible to live by those tough decisions, especially the ones that carry a heavier cost.

Just as receiving guidance enables you to offer guidance, it's more useful to have your own purpose clearly in mind in order to lead others purposefully. This is the reason for developing a *leadership purpose statement*. A summarized statement of your leadership purpose says, in your own terms, why you exist as a leader. Organizations often create a purpose or mission statement. It's just as important for you individually as a leader to do the same.

> *Clear purpose unifies your strengths and propels you forward.*

A well-crafted leadership purpose statement will always acknowledge and respect your potential. It will distill and pull together what you most deeply care about. It should inspire you, but not be so idealistic that it's unattainable.

The result is a laser-like focus that can cut through the confusion to what is true and clear. Your leadership purpose statement will help you:

- Amplify your core truth
- Act on integrative anchors
- Be inspired and energized
- Strengthen your integrity

Ideally, your individual leadership purpose and your organizational purpose will be aligned and without conflict; one should enhance the other. If there are conflicts between your individual and organizational purpose, they warrant a closer look, because power can leak away through the misalignment.

A leadership purpose statement doesn't arrive at your doorstep. You craft it, often with the assistance of a coach, a workshop, or a good book on the subject.[7]

The following exercise won't tackle the goal of creating a leadership purpose statement, but it will help you focus on the areas of tension that you need to manage, and it will provide some guidance. Set aside thirty to sixty minutes to do this exercise. Think of it as a self-managed mini-retreat that will provide deep perspective and contribute to your evolving leadership.

Exercise: Support & Guidance

Consider the pushes and pulls in your life and the tension you are trying to manage. List three different levels of tension that you are working with. For example:

- ► Want to play vs. too much work to do
- ► Feel confident vs. waves of self-doubt
- ► Feel like I'm letting others down vs. the need to limit commitments

1. _____ VS. _____

2. _____ VS. _____

3. _____ VS. _____

Decide which area of tension is the most important for you right now and highlight it. Focus on this for the rest of this exercise.

Find a quiet place and a comfortable position, either sitting or lying down. Take a few deep breaths. Reflect on what you trust that is greater than your everyday sense of self. For example, you may think of this as a wise inner guide, or as God, or as your intuition.

Formulate a question for your trusted source of guidance. Make sure it relates to the area of tension you are focusing on and write the question below. Take your time. There is no need to rush.

_____

_____

_____

Now close your eyes and feel or visualize your source of guidance. Ask the question written above. Wait. Pay attention. Listen. Feel. Intuit. Stay open to something other than a pre-formulated answer.

When you get an answer or inner response, you may feel a sense of relief, a release of some kind, or a wave of relaxation. The guidance should support your sense of well-being and feel "right."

Write the response below.

_____

_____

_____

Imagine you are trying out the above recommendation. Envision it in as much detail as possible. Does it help you deal with the tension area you are focusing on? Are you more balanced? More purposeful? More centered?

If the answers to the previous questions are generally positive and the guidance seems sound, then express gratitude to your source of guidance. This may be a simple "thank you" or more elaborate. It acknowledges that you have been assisted. Expressing gratitude for guidance will help keep your heart and mind open to further guidance.

Finally, commit to taking the necessary action.

Working at regular intervals with the process outlined in the previous exercise will support all of your other leadership goals in immeasurable ways. If you are in a period of transition or are working with a complex issue over a period of time, consider doing the exercise a couple of times a week. Frequent connection with your inner guidance will help build quick rapport so you can get guidance when you need it.

We've looked at tension from a number of perspectives: the **Limited You** and the **Essential You**, the pressures associated with leadership, the demands of work and life, and the process of linking with something greater. Throughout this discussion, we've emphasized holding tension so you can work with it creatively. By expanding this capability, you can minimize much of the reactivity, needless pain, and wasted effort generated by the **Limited You**.

- ◆ *Do you see how creative tension can ignite your leadership?*
- ◆ *Are there any areas of tension in your life that need special attention?*
- ◆ *Can you remember one or two times when you felt the presence of something greater than you?*

Another major area of creative tension is the Contact Zone™, that intense interactive field where people can have significant impact on each other. This will be the focus of the next two chapters, where you'll learn how to work constructively with the tension generated in the Contact Zone™ to create productive and nourishing contact. This happens when the **Essential You** manages your participation in the Contact Zone™.

11

ESTABLISH CONTACT READINESS

We are caught in an inescapable network of mutuality,
tied in a single garment of destiny. Whatever affects one
directly affects all indirectly.

MARTIN LUTHER KING JR., civil rights leader

A S a leader, you are frequently called on to deal with a high degree of internal and interpersonal tension. In this complex territory, emotional intelligence[1] and communication skills are more important than ever. Positioning yourself internally and interpersonally, prior to entering a highly charged situation, will support your ability to skillfully manage the many unknowns that can arise.

Tension intensifies when you enter the Contact Zone™, the space where people come into contact and can have significant impact on each other. You're in the Contact Zone™ when you are negotiating, having an intense conversation, trying to influence someone, closing a deal, giving difficult feedback, or really connecting with someone. In each of these examples, there is considerable potential for impact on both parties. The meeting space between people that we call the Contact Zone™ is illustrated in the following diagram.

When you relate to others, you contend not only with the internal tension between the **Limited You** and the **Essential You**, but the tension between you and those around you. While you may be able to hold and manage your own tension, you can't be sure exactly what will happen when another person enters the picture. His or her decisions and actions will affect you in ways that you can't possibly control. Fortunately, you can often anticipate certain possibilities and prepare yourself.

The Contact Zone™ is, by definition, an unsettling space. Because the stakes are high (materially or emotionally), you and the other person can potentially have a profound effect on each other. This can be energizing and exciting, but also uncomfortable. You know you're in the Contact Zone™ when:

- You feel some tension or intensity
- Equilibrium is at least mildly upset
- You and the other person can significantly affect each other
- There is something important at stake

Because of the potential for impact, there is often a higher level of perceived threat in the Contact Zone™. When a lot is at stake, the potential for reactivity is higher.

If even one person is highly reactive and *acts upon* that reaction, someone will get hurt. Maybe that person will hurt only him or herself. Maybe he or she will hurt the other person. Or maybe both people will be hurt. If both people act on their reactions, the potential for damage escalates. Relationships can be seriously damaged and often don't thrive or endure when reactivity is too high.

Activity in the Contact Zone™ can lead to either significant benefit or harm.

With a lot at stake, the potential for relational activity can be higher as well, but this is possible only if the **Essential You** is powerful enough to weather the storm of insecurity that the **Limited You** can generate.

When you contain and manage the reactivity of the **Limited You**, you can see, listen, feel, and think with greater range and nuance. This allows you to learn about the other person, make clear choices, and respond in ways that will optimize positive contact.

Relationships can be strengthened and charged with liveliness and purpose when relational activity is present. Significant connections can bloom, grow, and mature in the Contact Zone™.

The Contact Zone™ will test you. You'll find out how much resilience you have and how far you can be pushed before you fall into a reactive pattern. The Contact Zone™ can get very hot and isn't for the fainthearted; however, it will build your leadership capacity.

> *Ignite your power as a leader by becoming skillful in the Contact Zone™*

The intensity of the Contact Zone™ is more pronounced when there is a power difference between the people making contact. This difference in power heightens the potential for reactivity. Generally, more is at stake for the person with less power. That's why it's especially important for leaders who have formal authority or power through their position, to manage their own reactivity as well as they can and to be aware of the consequences of not doing so.

Preparing for contact in stressful or high-impact situations will help you navigate potential minefields with skill. For example, it's not always immediately obvious how to proceed when others are behaving badly. In certain situations, it's not always clear how to avoid your own reactive pattern. However with enough preparation, you'll have your wits when you need them and won't be pulled into mind-numbing or toxic reactivity.*

INTERNAL CONTACT READINESS

Before we focus on the interpersonal activities that can prepare you for the Contact Zone™, let's review what you can to do *internally* to prepare for the Contact Zone™. The following exercise takes many

---

* If you'd like regular reminders on how to thrive in the Contact Zone™, subscribe to the free *Expand Your Personal Power in the Contact Zone™* tips series. For more information, go to **http://contactpointassoc.com**.

of the themes already discussed and summarizes them as simple and complex skills that you can practice. They will assist you in moving from a reactive to a more centered position.

These skills and processes represent the internal work of preparing for high-impact and constructive contact. When you master them, your confidence and personal power as a leader will expand. You'll then be more prepared to work with the complex interpersonal and organizational dimensions of leadership.

Exercise: Assess Your Internal Contact Readiness

Review the following skills and processes and place a √ beside those skills and processes that need further development or that you need to pay special attention to.

☐ Observe when you are in a reactive state and how you feel in your body. Stop. Breathe. Consider the consequences of continued re-activity. Take time out to reflect and to "get your head straight."

☐ When a reaction is triggered, ask yourself "What happened?" Make note of the event that triggered your reaction. Focus on just the facts, without interpretation, until you can see the reactive patterns clearly.

☐ Notice any premature judgments, familiar stories, or litanies of complaint that are aggravating you. Challenge anything that isn't true and acknowledge what is true.

☐ Notice any tendency to generalize prematurely, leave out chunks of information, or distort information. Stay focused on specific, accurate, complete information that is aligned with reality.

☐ Notice any Shadow Gratification™ that could drive reactivity. Give it up, if possible. If you don't want to do so, consider the long-term cost.

☐ Stabilize and center yourself. Some possibilities are relaxation, deep breathing, exercise, creative self-expression (writing, painting, singing, dancing), meditation, yoga, and martial arts.

☐ Accept necessary losses and frustrations. This includes unmet needs, which can be physical, emotional, mental, or spiritual.

☐ Face your fears or insecurities and soothe any needless anxiety until you can think clearly again.

☐ Keep your energy in the present. Your point of power is right now; not before, not later. Stay rooted in what is going on right now, even when you are planning for the future.

☐ Notice when you are fixated on how things "should be" or on un-realistic control. Let go of what you can't control and come back to what you can realistically do to improve a situation.

☐ Learn from everything. Commit yourself to learning from whatever life throws at you. Mobilize this commitment especially when you make a mistake. This guarantees progress.

☐ Ask for guidance. Allow for benevolent support to be present in your life. This is a direct line to the **Essential You.**

☐ Develop compassion. This is the desire to relieve suffering. Direct it to both yourself and to others.

☐ Engage in those spiritual practices that nourish and make sense to you.

☐ Identify your guiding life purpose. It can bring you to your best on the worst of days.

Refer to this list especially when you feel seriously challenged or are struggling with a reactive pattern.

Internal preparation for contact is especially important when you feel aggravated, challenged, or off center. Use the above checklist often!

♦ *What are the two most important skills or processes from the checklist that would be most strategic to your success?*

♦ *Do you need to get any further information or support to gain strength in those areas?*

We'll now turn to contact readiness at interpersonal levels. This is warranted whenever you expect contact with others to be challenging, when you anticipate a high level of tension, or when the need for quick, creative solutions is high. In these situations, you can prepare by setting the tone and establishing a friendly attitude.

SET THE TONE

Part of managing yourself in the Contact Zone™ is holding onto your center and setting a positive emotional tone, even if those around you are pulling in a reactive, destructive, or negative direction.

Most people have no idea how much they affect others. Your behavior, attitudes, and emotional state all have impact. You already affect those around you in important ways, even if you aren't aware of how you do it or the effect you have.

You have impact that you may never fully realize.

Emotional communication is crucial in setting the tone for a relationship and often has greater impact than verbal communication. First impressions are an example of non-verbal assessment and communication that can have a lingering effect for many years.

♦ *Think back to the first meeting you had with one or two important co-workers and colleagues.*

♦ *You probably exchanged some very specific and tangible information. But do you remember a more subtle process operating?*

♦ *Do you recall "feeling out" the other person and assessing him or her at a gut level?*

♦ *Looking back, were your first impressions accurate?*

As a leader, even your seemingly insignificant behaviors can create a powerful ripple effect on others and on the emotional climate of your organization. You can safely assume that you are a huge contributor to the prevailing mood of your organization. This in turn affects morale and productivity.

The emotional mood of a group tends to be contagious, so what you affect directly can have an indirect effect somewhere else in the organization. Leaders are often surprised at how offhand comments they made created serious concern and disruption elsewhere in the organization.

The contagious aspect of moods is easier to see when it's between two people. To illustrate this, let's look at Scott and Ryan, who meet regularly as part of a leadership team.

Ryan & Scott

Ryan and Scott, both VPs, are part of a lively leadership team in a large high-tech company. Scott is VP of marketing, and Ryan is VP of research and development. They have worked together for four years, and have a history of exchanges that have been both hostile and friendly.

Ryan is moody, energetic, and emotionally transparent. Scott is inquisitive and engaging, but emotionally cloaked. When Scott is in a mischievous mood, he makes comments and assertions that are provocative and unproductive. He regularly "stirs the pot" for reasons that aren't clear. Often his taunts are directed at Ryan, who too often takes the bait. Ryan gets triggered and reacts angrily while Scott sits back with a satisfied smile.

Ryan has learned that he loses his center by getting overly upset. He loses credibility with other members of the leadership team as well. At these times, the emotional storm between Scott and Ryan takes over the room. As a result, the team loses focus. Side issues often take center stage and strategic thinking is derailed.

When Ryan is feeling especially clear, he can resist Scott's invitation to fight. He then acts as a stabilizing influence for the other team members, who find it easier to stay focused, even in the face of Scott's complex and persistent pattern of disruption.

As in Scott's case, the tone you set can be powerful. And like Ryan, you will probably vary in how well you hold onto your own emotional center when another person's mood is troublesome.

Your ability to hold onto yourself and set the tone you want is a measure of how well you manage yourself in the Contact Zone™. Difficult meetings at work can provide excellent feedback on how you manage both the interpersonal tension and the internal tension between the **Limited You** and the **Essential You**.

Just like moods, the attitude you have toward others will affect what happens in the Contact Zone™. Your attitudes are also somewhat infectious, and you communicate them in many obvious and also subtle ways.

> ◆ *Think about the last time you were in a highly charged*
>   *meeting with an agenda that was threatened.*
> ◆ *How well were you able to "hold onto yourself"?*
> ◆ *Were you able to remain powerful and positive enough to*
>   *continue to influence the outcome?*

FRIENDLY ATTITUDES

Contact always generates some kind of tension. You can use this tension creatively to affect others in positive ways or destructively, generating a negative impact. This is why it's so important to work with interpersonal tension in conscious, responsible ways, and to make use of friendly attitudes. We'll now look at some of the basic attitudes that support relational activity in the Contact Zone™.

Minimize Harm

Do as little harm as possible to others or yourself.

The commitment to minimize harm can act as a fundamental guide for all your interactions with others. This intention is at the heart of being a responsible, trustworthy leader.

Developing a practice of minimizing harm makes you someone to be trusted, someone who can be relied on for ongoing partnership. It is crucial to do as little harm as possible if you want a relationship to succeed in the long term.[2]

Keep your thoughts positive because they become your words. Keep your words positive because they become your behaviors. Keep your habits positive because they become your values. Keep your values positive because they become your destiny.

MOHANDAS GANDHI,
non-violent resistance leader

Minimizing harm doesn't mean you don't hold others accountable. It doesn't mean being a pushover either. It will always be important to hold firm with what you stand for and to create ongoing accountability with clear consequences. It is equally important to limit your use of force and let go of inappropriate control.

If you restrain the tendency to use force, you will probably become more resilient, which may feel a bit more flexible, but don't confuse lack of rigidity with lack of power. If you combine *minimizing harm* with *holding firm* when needed, you'll exercise a resilient, relational form of power that you can use quite productively.

Show Respect

Everyone wants and needs respect. Strong relationships are built when you demonstrate that you truly respect, value, or appreciate the other person. By bringing respect to another person, you open the door to greater understanding. The toxic alternative, often expressed through the *dominate-punish* pattern, is humiliation or ridicule.

> ◆   *Think about how important respect is to you personally.*
> ◆   *How did it feel in the past when you **didn't** have the respect of someone important to you?*
> ◆   *When you **did** have respect, how did that feel?*

Communicating your positive or negative regard for another person publicly is even more powerful. Public expression of respect through recognition or appreciation has added impact. And the toxic impact of humiliation, shame, or ridicule is also more intense.

When you show respect, even to your enemies, the playing field changes. Giving respect and expecting it in return demonstrate a willingness to play on a level field. As people feel respected and valued, reactivity often drops a notch or two. Everyone has some insecurity, and feeling valued is a powerful antidote to most insecurities.

The ideal attitude here is to hold both yourself and others as worthy of basic respect. If you can't maintain respect for either yourself or the other person, it indicates that you're moving off center into a reactive pattern.

Showing respect is a way to acknowledge the value of another person. It doesn't mean you respect everything that person stands for. It simply means you're showing basic respect to another human being who has human value, *even if* he or she does things you don't approve of. Sometimes simply respecting differences rather than condemning them is all that is needed. If you look carefully enough, you'll see that everyone deserves respect for something.

Expect Respect

Expecting to be respected establishes you as someone with a significant presence that will not be dismissed or taken for granted. This attitude is essential if you are to establish a leadership presence. In all of your important relationships, you should clearly communicate that you expect to be taken seriously. If you don't assume you are worthy of respect, you can become a target for those who might take advantage.

Remember that you are always to be included in the circle of who is valued. However, even if others don't validate your worth in ways that you want, you can still carry yourself with dignity and as deserving of respect.

> *People don't care how much you know—until they know how much you care.*
>
> JOHN C. MAXWELL, author

Understand & Empathize

When you indicate to another person that you sincerely want to understand what he or she is going through, you'll almost always get a favorable response. Most people don't like being put under a microscope and analyzed, but they do want to be deeply understood.

When you empathize with another's situation, or what that person is going through, he or she feels seen and understood in a positive way. Many people have a deep, unmet hunger for this kind of contact, and when it occurs, they feel powerfully connected to the person who "gets it."

Be Kind

True understanding and empathy aren't really possible unless an attitude of kindness is also present. Kindness is a heartfelt attitude of generous benevolence. When you look at others through a filter of kindness, you are better able to understand who they are and to connect better.

We often reserve kindness for people we like, but if you need to work with someone whom you don't like, it can be just as important. For example, if you report to someone you dislike or manage someone you don't enjoy, you'll still need to navigate the relationship as skillfully as possible. In difficult relationships, remember that kindness doesn't cancel out firmness; nor should firmness erase kindness.

Kindness is often sacrificed for truth and necessity. It doesn't have to be. You can deliver a message with kindness, even if it will be difficult for the other person to hear. For example, if you need to give difficult performance feedback, you can create a positive context for the feedback and say what needs to be said, but choose your words with care. You can do all of this in a warm, friendly way.

> *Something has happened*
> *To my understanding of existence*
> *That calls my heart to be filled with wonder And kindness.*
>
> HAFIZ, Sufi poet

Commit to Relational Solutions

Stay in a productive dialogue when you are feeling challenged. This requires mobilizing your determination to stay solidly centered in the **Essential You**. Often this includes listening to and considering diverse points of view. The effort needed can be taxing, but it keeps the doors open to exchanges that will give you vital information.

When you are very determined to hold the tension no matter what, you'll find internal resources you didn't know you had. When the heat is on, re-affirm your commitment to finding a way through the complexity—a way that works well enough for everyone involved.

Relational solutions don't mean everyone gets all they want; that's rarely possible. It does mean that the process is respectful, collaborative, and considers the bigger picture, including both you and others.

> ◆ *Which of the friendly attitudes just discussed is most important for you at this time?*
> ◆ *How would practicing it consistently affect your leadership?*

The rest of this chapter will build on these friendly attitudes and show you how to become more contact ready at political and strategic levels. For example, before an important meeting, a high-profile presentation, or a difficult conversation, you can prepare in specific ways. You can do the following work in preparation for many of the challenges you face in the Contact Zone™. Some of the suggestions will prepare you in a general way, and some will help you in specific situations.

IDENTIFY VITAL RELATIONSHIPS

Leadership, commerce, and business are all built on a complex network of relationships. Vital relationships are those that are strategic to your success. Because of this, they need special attention. When you assess these relationships, you expand your awareness of the intricate network of influences in your life and work, and you can pick out the ones most pivotal to what you are trying to achieve. As you manage and nurture the relationships that are most important, you can also gather support for your goals.

The relationship may be with someone you like or with someone you find distasteful. If it has the power to affect you in significant ways, even a relationship with an adversary could be vital.

Vital relationships need extra attention and care. This means staying connected, centered, and attentive. When you make contact, your goal is to do your part in making sure that the exchange is as productive and beneficial as possible. Giving regular attention to vital relationships will help you keep your finger on the pulse of what is going on around you. It will keep you in the loop politically and more able to spot opportunities as they arise.

One of the big benefits of identifying your vital relationships is being able to recognize your base of support: your fans. These are the people who like and respect you. They're often very loyal and will go out of their way to back you up. Be sure to acknowledge them. Don't take them for granted. They deserve to be treated with extra care.

The following exercise will give you a chance to identify your key relationships.

Exercise: Vital Relationships

Take a few minutes to think about those relationships that are vital to your success, personally and as a leader. First consider the following personal relationships and the ones that are vital for you.

- ► Spouse or lover
- ► Ex-spouse, especially if you are co-parenting
- ► Kids and stepkids
- ► Parents and in-laws
- ► Siblings, step, and half siblings
- ► Friends and neighbors
- ► Spiritual community

Write down the names of people who are especially strategic for you.

_____

_____

_____

_____

Now consider the following work relationships and the ones that are vital for your success.

- ► Senior management
- ► Direct manager and those you report to indirectly
- ► Direct reports and those you manage indirectly
- ► Support staff
- ► Peers, team members, and colleagues
- ► Clients and customers
- ► Competitors
- ► Professional organizations
- ► Media connections

Write down the names of people at work who are especially strategic to your success.

_____

_____

_____

_____

Review the names you have written and highlight or circle those that are the most important. Keep these people in mind as you read on. Remember that you need them.

Managing and caring for your vital relationships is a powerful strategy for expanding your political intelligence and influencing others. Make sure you connect from a position of integrity, and frequently update your awareness of who is vital.

- ◆ *Is there one person you identified from the above exercise whom you need to tend to right away?*
- ◆ *What might you gain (or not lose) by taking action?*

GATHER INFORMATION

When you are about to go into a high-intensity meeting with someone, gather your information first. Pull together what you've heard, seen, and learned about the person in the past. Connect this with the bits and pieces of information you have on hand from the Internet or from written materials. Be sure to include your intuitive sense about the person, any gut feelings, and any subtle patterns. Pay special attention to:

- ◆ The person's reactive patterns, typical responses under pressure, and hot buttons
- ◆ What is really important to the person, including what he or she is invested in personally and professionally

If you have a lot of information, summarize it in a few strategic bulleted points that can help you remember what is most important. Remember, you aren't connecting with just *anyone*; it's always *someone specific*. That someone has his or her own particular profile.

When you combine knowledge of your vital relationships with strategic information about those people, you have significant political intelligence available to you. How you use this intelligence will depend on whether you act more from the **Limited You** or the **Essential You**.

Going into important meetings prepared with background information will help you understand the other players better, guide you in how to show appropriate respect, enable you to influence more effectively, and help keep you out of trouble.

INFLUENCE BEHIND THE SCENES

Political intelligence can also be put to use *prior to* a meeting where an important decision will be made. By having informal conversations with the stakeholders or decision makers in advance of the final meeting, you can build your base of support before the formal decision is made.

A series of informal meetings will give you a way to discover the concerns, needs, and vested interests of the strategic players. They will also give you a chance to troubleshoot your ideas and come up with possible alternatives. At times, these informal consultations can lead to a new and even better direction.

If you've done your homework, what happens in the formal meeting often won't be a surprise, because you already know where people stand. This advance work also puts you in a more comfortable and powerful position in the formal meeting. It frees your attention to focus on what is currently occurring and how to influence the immediate outcome. The influencing process can continue seamlessly from before, to during, to after the meeting, especially when you've built the necessary relationships.

Antonio is an example of someone who worked actively to apply many of the skills previously discussed. He was successful in influencing outcomes and dealing with organizational politics and did it all with considerable integrity.

Antonio

Antonio was the director of marketing in an international telecommunications company. He was charming and attractive, with remarkable verbal acuity and wit. He used these assets in a natural way to influence others. His sharp but pleasing presence was instrumental in his rise to a director position; however, he hadn't tried his wings with political influence.

Antonio was assigned to a task force that would decide which parts of the company to phase out in the upcoming reorganization. The complicating factor was that his group was one of those being considered for the phaseout.

First, he needed to deal with the conflict of interest between his role as director of his own organization and his participation on the task force that would affect the future of his group. He agonized over this, but it became clear that including his group among those phased out would be best for the company as a whole. It was a painful decision, but one that had integrity for him.

Antonio then had to figure out how to help create a vital new role for his group. He knew his group was relying on him to go to bat for them. He didn't want to let them down. The need to influence effectively was paramount. He needed to learn quickly, and he did.

He met with other members of the team to brainstorm options for the groups and organizations that would be phased out. He asked smart questions and listened intently. As he did so, a potential new role for his group came into focus. He envisioned the creative opportunity and could also see the potential problems.

The vision became a clear set of objectives that would require considerable influence on his part to achieve. He thoroughly researched the issues relating to his objectives so he knew whom and what he was dealing with. He analyzed the data and its implications until he came up with an organizational solution that fit both his own objectives and those of the company. Antonio found the solution relatively easy because it drew on his natural analytical talents.

It was much harder to go about the next stage of actively influencing others in strategic ways. He ran into his insecurity—that he wasn't as worthy of respect as other people—but set up the strategic meetings anyway.

He had previously handled politically sensitive issues on the fly and with a fair amount of glibness. But he couldn't afford to be glib at this point. Being systematic about relational processes was new to him.

His coach suggested that Antonio make sure he knew he had the support he needed *before* the larger meeting that would decide the fate of his group. She also suggested that, in the best of all worlds, the decision makers would see his vision as a solution to *their* problems.

He went about planting the seeds of solution with the key stakeholders, weaving in his objectives along the way. By the time the decisive meeting occurred, his proposal was a fait accompli. All he had to do was formalize it. The decision makers were ready to see it as a solution to a problem they wouldn't have to struggle with.

In this example Antonio leveraged any number of skills. He also did some intensive work with his core insecurity and didn't let his

Limited Self get the upper hand. He actively worked with his **Essential Self** as he deepened his communication, relationship, and political skills. Throughout, he acted with integrity, which was one of his core values. As a result of these efforts, he had a positive and decisive impact. Antonio earned his success.

> ♦ *Do you have a current situation that could benefit from some "behind the scenes" influencing?*
> ♦ *Whom do you need to influence?*
> ♦ *Are there any ethical challenges in this situation that you need to consider?*
> ♦ *Do you have a plan for influencing that also establishes your integrity?*

We'll return now to a few more suggestions on how to prepare successfully for the heat of the Contact Zone™.

HAVE A PLAN

If you have an agenda in mind, be sure to put in place a plan or proposal that supports it. This is best done in advance of a meeting, when you have enough time to reflect and think clearly. If you need to discuss something that is emotionally loaded for you, this preparation is even more important. The reflection time will allow you to connect honestly with what you really feel and to sort out your reactions.

If you don't have a plan, you may be overly influenced by the well-formed agenda of someone who is more prepared. A plan can also help you stay clear when faced with the chaotic agenda of someone who is reactive; it will also keep you on track if you become distracted or tangential.

In your plan, be prepared to address the personal interests of the other person. If you know about his or her non-negotiables or specific needs, keep these in mind, so your plan is in line with the reality of who that person is.

IDENTIFY YOUR NEEDS & VESTED INTERESTS

When you are clear about your own personal needs, you put yourself in a better position to make balanced, wise choices that are in your best interest. Know what you really need and what is non-negotiable for you.

Non-negotiables are important, but they are also deal breakers, so assess them carefully; this will give you clear definition and boundaries. If you don't have firm enough boundaries, you will be vulnerable to manipulation by others and to your own reactions.

Your boundaries can act as integrative anchors. When your limits are firmly in place, you have greater freedom to negotiate. Firm boundaries will keep you clearer in the heat of an intense exchange and less vulnerable to the agenda of a highly persuasive person.

Go into conversations, meetings, and negotiations knowing what you want and need as well as what you don't want and don't need. This will help you define what you hope to accomplish overall as you guide the conversation and influence the outcome.

LEARN WHAT OTHERS ARE INVESTED IN

Find out what is important to other people. This is especially important with vital relationships that are strategic to your success. Everyone has their own vested interests at personal, social, organizational, and political levels. Behavior is usually organized around these vested interests.

Discover what drives, motivates, or feels rewarding to the people who are important to you. This information will help you predict how they will react and help you avoid walking on a land mine. It is essential for political intelligence[3] in the workplace.

CHOOSE THE LEVEL OF CONTACT

Be prepared to limit contact when necessary and not go into territory that is unwise for you. This may be as simple as limiting a meeting to an agreed-upon time, or as complex as skillfully bypassing an agenda that you know will be damaging. Be ready to say no to further contact, especially if your integrity or basic well-being is at stake.

On the other hand, it's important to stay in contact and take the heat at times, especially if you expect others to do the same. Recognize when too much heat is destructive for you. This distinction can be a fine line, but is part of both self-care and creating effective boundaries.

Don't take on more than you can handle, or it will most likely backfire and you'll find yourself in some kind of reactive pattern.

It's time to limit contact when you feel:

- Too anxious
- Too reactive
- Overstimulated
- Overtired

If you have a difficult time backing down from a challenge, remember that getting fried in the heat of the Contact Zone™ isn't your goal and won't help develop your leadership capacity. Your goal is to stretch yourself to meet challenges that are necessary and to build relational strength, and along the way, to make sure you do no needless harm to yourself or the other person.

CLARIFY THE CONTEXT

One way to keep your head above water when you are managing complex, multi-layered issues is to step back and clarify the context. Context is like the picture frame and matting around a painting. Leaders are the holders of context and vision. They frame the issues and in doing so create a way to view them.

Clarifying context comes about when you *pause-observe-reflect.* Then the context or pattern can pop into focus. If you aren't doing this as the leader, it's very possible no one is. When no one is providing context for an organization, there can be a contagious, unnerving feeling that no one is "minding the store."

You have probably seen how important context is if you've been in a strategy session that has gone either very well or very wrong.* An effective leader in a strategy session will help define and effectively communicate the larger context for what he or she is trying to achieve. Once the leader establishes context, it becomes much easier to create and generate buy-in for specific strategies.

Clarifying the context in relationships is equally important. Make it clear that the work you want to do with someone else is also respectful of his or her needs. For example, before a potentially challenging strategy discussion with a peer, you could greet the other person

---

* Vision, mission, and strategic planning sessions yield better results when you have a facilitator who can be neutral about the outcome. If you need a referral, go to **http://contactpointassoc.com/contact.html**.

warmly and inquire about his or her well-being. You could also affirm that you want a beneficial outcome for both of you.

Creating a business context that links your interests with the interests of your partners and co-workers is a very refined skill. It assumes you have done advance work to understand the other person's vested interests. It also requires you to think creatively about how that person's interests and yours can work well together.

A clear relational context and a comfortable emotional tone generate a harmonious resonance between you and others. When you contribute to making this happen, you amplify your ability to drive results in a relational way.

Developing skill in preparing for the Contact Zone™ is a demonstration of both internal and interpersonal leadership. Practicing these skills will help increase your emotional intelligence[4] and anchor the **Essential You**. Take a minute to do a quick review of the contact readiness checklist, the friendly attitudes, and the other main headings from this chapter.

> ◆   *What do you think are the tools most crucial for you in preparing to lead others?*
> ◆   *Do you see how these tools could help you move more swiftly from the* **Limited You** *to the* **Essential You**?

The skills that are most relevant for you can become integrative anchors that support more complex relational skills, such as collaborative problem solving and decision making.

The payoff for this preparedness will come when you demonstrate that you can effectively lead others through a challenging situation. How you function in the middle of the tension and heat of the Contact Zone™ will serve as both a test of your leadership and a catalyst for further development. The next chapter will show you how to deal more directly with others in order to strengthen the **Essential You** and your leadership in the Contact Zone™.

12

HANDLE THE HEAT IN THE CONTACT ZONE™

*The only way to make sense out of change is to plunge
into it, move with it, and join the dance.*

ALAN WATTS, contemporary philosopher and
interpreter of Eastern philosophy

YOUR impact is amplified when you're energized, ignited, and in contact. In the Contact Zone™, the energy of others is intensified as well. This is where you'll discover how you do under pressure. We all have some impact no matter what we do, but it is magnified in highly charged, complex situations that involve intensive contact. Some familiar examples of high-contact activity include:

- Giving or receiving a performance review
- Negotiating a contract or agreement
- Managing a serious misunderstanding
- Making a decision by consensus
- Restructuring an organization
- Launching a high-impact project

To safely manage yourself and your relationships in the Contact Zone™ requires some initial skill, but as you practice, you'll get stronger.

231

It's like learning a new sport, such as soccer. You need some information on how to play the game and a basic ability to run and kick in a coordinated fashion, but it's only by playing the game and focusing on certain skills that you'll become proficient.

The previous chapter showed you how to prepare yourself so you have enough initial strength, balance, and endurance to enter the Contact Zone™ relationally. This chapter will show you how to handle the heat that's generated so you don't get pulled into the reactivity of the **Limited You.**

With practice, and as the **Essential You** gets stronger, you'll be able to navigate and lead others through emotional, organizational, and political minefields. As you build the capacity and strength of the **Essential You**, your impact will be increasingly positive and powerful.

WORK WITH DIFFERENCES

So far, we have mostly focused on your challenges with the **Limited You** and the **Essential You**. But what about the **Limited Self** and the **Essential Self** of others?

You live in a world populated by people who have their own core insecurities and defensive strategies. They have an **Essential Self** that may be more or less developed. And they have a **Limited Self** that most likely is quite active and powerful.

Until now, we have focused more on you and less on others, because your greatest source of power is within you. You have virtually no control over others, but potentially vast control over yourself.

While human beings have a great deal in common, they are also very different, with unique conditioning and specific needs. These differences might be easier to accept if it weren't for the fact that we also want different, competing things at times. That's the rub. This competition for who gets what can lead to considerable ongoing tension in relationships. This tension in turn gives rise to many life-altering choices.

The following diagram illustrates how You and Other have choice in dealing with the **Limited Self** and the **Essential Self**. Each of you make choices that will determine to what extent you will engage in the Contact Zone™.

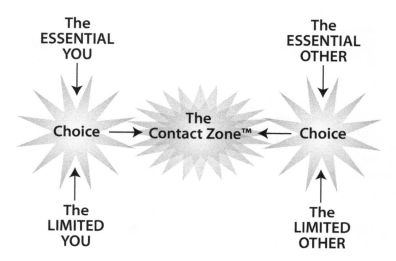

Both of you will also make internal choices that determine whether your impact on each other is more reactive and destructive or more relational and constructive. The important thing is that each person has internal choices. Your choices affect how you deal with other people. Their choices affect how they deal with you.

While you can't control the choices others make, you can certainly influence them. When you make clear, creative contact with other people, they will be more inclined to make choices that support your success.

LEADING THE LIMITED OTHER

Let's assume you are operating substantially from the **Essential You.** You've made some important shifts and have emerged as a more enlightened leader. You have more energy and choices available to you, but many people around you have not gone through a similar process. They are operating mainly from the core insecurities and defensive strategies of their **Limited Self.**

This is a typical situation for leaders and will test your leadership. As you meet with others in the Contact Zone™, the contrast between choices you make from the **Essential You** and the choices made by the **Limited Self** of other people will become even more apparent.

The **Limited Self** of another person could act as a roadblock to your ideas and goals. If you're locked into the **Limited You**, you won't be able to lead that person effectively. However, if you're rooted in the **Essential You**, your margin for influencing, guiding, and leading the other person can increase.

However, even when you try to make it safe enough for others to join you in creative, collaborative ways, they may be unable to do so. Such small things as simple friendliness or an authentic exchange may not be possible for them. When people are in too much reactivity, fear, or pain, they can become blinded to options. Remember, you can influence, but not control their choices.

This is especially difficult to accept when you are dependent upon the other person to promote you or represent your interests. In the following example, Allison illustrates how important and challenging it can be to represent your own interests when someone who should represent them fails to do so. She also demonstrates leadership from the **Essential Self**, while her manager is entrenched in his **Limited Self**. He doesn't shift beyond his **Limited Self**, but he can be influenced.

Allison

Allison was a director of finance in a large technical manufacturing company. She reported to Henric, the CFO. Henric in turn reported to the CEO.

The CEO was an intimidating figure who decided that a massive re-organization was needed to cut costs. This meant eliminating many positions across the company. Henric was to work with other members of the leadership team to come up with a plan.

When Allison and the other finance directors heard about this from reliable but unofficial sources, they felt threatened. One of the directors asked Henric in a staff meeting how the re-organization might affect the finance department. Henric's eyes darted and he looked away. As he changed the subject, the message was clear; he was very uncomfortable and didn't want to discuss it.

Matters were aggravated by Henric's highly compliant and overly accommodating way of dealing with authorities. He avoided conflict—especially with his peers and the CEO—at all cost. The result was that he didn't represent his directors or his department, and he didn't fight for their interests in the meetings with the leadership team.

All of the directors were frustrated, but Allison decided to do something about the situation. At the next one-to-one meeting with Henric, she pointed out how important it was to his success, as well as the success of the finance department, that they not lose key positions needlessly. He glared at her.

She took a deep breath and gently acknowledged that she understood what a difficult position he was in and how scrappy the CEO and other members of the leadership team could be. She went on to say that she wanted to work with him to make sure they would all be successful, but needed to know how to help. He continued to look very displeased with her but started to talk.

That discussion marked a small but significant change for Henric. He began to listen to his directors and discuss some of their suggestions about strategies for the re-organization. Allison's assertive but sensitive approach soothed him and helped to keep him from diving further into reactivity.

Henric still didn't negotiate effectively with the leadership team, but he implicitly encouraged his directors to informally influence the other members of the team. In this way, he allowed others to work around him rather than blocking their efforts.

Allison was about as effective as she could be, given the nature of the situation. She calmed her own fears well enough to deal with Henric in a non-reactive and supportive way. By indirectly asking him to take some responsibility, she raised the level of accountability, and in the face of ongoing frustration with his limitations, she supported the whole department with her positive leadership presence.

Even if you operate from the **Essential You**, the **Limited Self** of others may fail to appreciate you or could see you as threatening. If another person's envy gets activated, that person may become overtly or covertly aggressive, compete excessively, or undermine you in ways that are damaging or hurtful.

> ♦ *Has someone else's envy or hostility ever been hurtful or damaging to you?*
>
> ♦ *If so, did it trigger your core insecurity or activate the* **Limited You***?*

Hostility from others can trigger feelings of isolation and loss. If this happens, be sure to acknowledge the painful feelings and be especially kind with yourself. This will make it easier to stay connected to the **Essential You** and engaged with others. In these instances, your leadership and involvement are just as important as ever, even if they don't appear to be.

Sometimes others are stuck in their LIMITED SELF and there is very little you can do about it.

If you feel smug or superior when leading someone who appears more limited, you're no longer in the **Essential You**. The tip-off could be that you feel have nothing to learn, that you are above it all, or that you don't need to hold the tension anymore. It's always easier to discern someone else's pattern than it is your own, and it's more comfortable to see yourself as "fine" and the other person as the one with the problem. Usually, both of you are contributing to the problem in some way.

When leading others, you'll find that their **Limited Self** will show up in many ways. We'll now look at one of the more important ways this occurs, especially when you are in a position of power or are dealing with the tension of the Contact Zone™.

Projection

The assumptions you make about someone and those the other person makes about you can either collide or be confirmed in the Contact Zone™. The concept of projection[1] is useful in sorting out complex interpersonal situations that may otherwise make no sense. Knowledge about how projection operates will help you understand how others may respond to you, especially as you grow in your leadership.

Simply put, projection takes place when one person assigns qualities to another person that he or she is uncomfortable with, unaware of, and cannot accept as his or her own. Everyone does some projecting some of the time. You have your projections that you place on other people and they have ones they place on you.

We'll focus on the projections others place upon you as a leader. For example, someone you manage exaggerates your critical feedback and sees you as punishing when that's not the case. Or a team member assumes you disapprove of his or her work when you're actually neutral or slightly positive. Or you have an underfunctioning employee who sees you as responsible for solving his or her difficulties with work-life effectiveness, even though you don't have the power to do so. Or you have a peer who believes you are out to undermine and backstab him or her, when these aren't your intentions or behaviors.

Projections can be very volatile. They often get mixed up with feedback about you and your blind spots, but these are two different things. Projection is information about the other person and what that person can't see in him or herself. Feedback gives you information about you and may refer to blind spots that you can't see in yourself. Both things can be going on at once.

Let's assume, though, that you've worked with receiving feedback, as we discussed in Chapter 7, and have a reliable process for sorting it out. It will still be important to recognize projection when it occurs in others.

As you become more visible, you are like a screen for others to project their traits and motives onto. Because projection is almost always an unconscious process, addressing it head on usually isn't a successful approach.

- *Can you recall an incident when someone completely misread you and seemed to be reacting as though you were someone else?*
- *How did this feel?*
- *Did you understand what was happening?*
- *How did you respond?*

You can interrupt some projections by providing a reality check for the person who is projecting, but for the most part there is nothing you can do about it. Some people will need to see you the way *they need to see you*. Period. You can be aware of the projections of others and manage them, but you probably won't be able to stop them.

When others see you mainly through their projections rather than as you really are, you may feel lonely and isolated. They're too busy looking at you through their own idealizations and insecurities to consider how they are affecting you.

To keep this isolation to a minimum, it's helpful to maintain relationships in which you aren't idealized and you're free to be yourself. In these relationships, the other person won't be taking you more seriously than is warranted. Spouses and kids often play this role nicely!

A deeper understanding of projection gives some leaders pause; and it should, but it shouldn't stop you. It is just a reminder of how things work and underlines the need for clear communication, which will help you correct any mistaken operating assumptions.

INQUIRE–LISTEN–VERIFY

The most basic way to work with differences and to sort out projections is by communicating thoughtfully and respectfully,[2] using the following basic communication steps:

1. Inquire. Ask an exploratory question.
2. Listen to the answer. Pay attention at multiple levels.
3. Verify what you heard.

These skills are overlooked with astounding frequency. When you don't inquire or listen, the message you send to others is loud and clear: you don't care about what they have to say. Even if this is not the message you want to send, it's the one received. Others will tend to feel that their opinions don't matter to you, unless you ask a meaningful question and then listen to what they have to say.

Inquire-listen-verify. It sounds so simple, yet these are refined skills that often need further development. When you demonstrate these skills, especially under adverse conditions, you're displaying a high level of relational activity that will expand your enlightened edge as a leader.

Inquire

Inquiry is a way of exploring another person's position. Questions that can be answered with a simple yes or no usually don't leave much room for deeper investigation. They don't open the door to understanding what is really going on.

If you want the other person to join you in a real discussion rather than feel interrogated, then make sure your questions leave some room for more than a yes or no response. This is especially important when having a challenging conversation, because it helps minimize reactivity and keep possibilities open. Open-ended questions and a spacious discussion can make it easier to recognize options and discover pathways for resolving differences.

> *It is not the answer that enlightens, but the question.*
>
> EUGENE IONESCO, playwright

Listen

Ask a clearly constructed question and then listen intently. Everyone wants to be heard. This is at the heart of feeling connected and respected in relationships. Without it, there can be no new understanding.

> ◆ Do you want to be heard by people you lead? By your managers and peers? By your friends and family?
> ◆ Do you remember the last time someone listened to you at a deep level?
> ◆ How did you feel about that person afterward?

When feeling seen, heard, and understood by someone who is deeply attentive, people often respond with warm appreciation. Frequently this develops into generous loyalty and a forgiving attitude toward the listener. This is because authentic listening builds a friendly attitude of understanding and empathy.

Curiosity is your best ally when listening. Friendly or warm curiosity is even better. It invites the other person to open up and connect. It can also be an enjoyable state that supports learning and productive work of any kind.

> *Friendly, warm curiosity can be irresistible.*

In the following example, Suzanne tried listening with friendly curiosity in an emotionally charged situation.

Suzanne

Suzanne, a director of sales in a global software company, was used to thinking fast, making quick decisions, and acting on gut reactions. She had recently announced a minor change in the compensation package for her sales managers.

The following day, one of the sales managers, Jon, confronted her angrily. She was initially surprised at the intensity of his anger. Her energy mobilized to ward off the attack, and she quickly became dismissive of his concerns. As a result, she cut the conversation off, saying she didn't have time to talk. Jon left her office feeling resentful and offended.

Later on, Suzanne realized she didn't really understand what Jon was so angry about. She hadn't listened to his anger because of her own defensiveness. With a bit of coaching, she became curious about what was going on with him and why he was so angry.

When she approached Jon with sincere, friendly interest and mentioned the compensation package, his anger flared again. She listened this time and, after a few minutes, learned there had been a misunderstanding, which was easy enough to correct.

Suzanne was surprised that when she started listening in a friendly, attentive way, Jon's manner shifted dramatically. His anger melted away and he seemed more open. This happened even before she corrected the misunderstanding.

Even though Suzanne was surprised, the process was highly predictable. When people are listened to, they feel "heard" and valued. Most people really appreciate this. As a result, they will very often drop their guarded, angry position.

Listening can help you really understand something you simply didn't "get" before, but this requires you to pause, listen, and take in new data. Taking in new information may be challenging, but it's necessary if you are to stay in a creative working relationship with reality.

The communication skill that most leaders (and especially executives) need to develop is listening. When the other person speaks, it's time to listen and reflect. Give the speaker your singular focus.

When you ask a question, take the time to really listen to the response. This is very difficult to do if you are multi-tasking or busy constructing your own answer or rebuttal. You don't have to abandon your agenda; just set it aside long enough to take in what is going on with the other person.

> *Listening is a magnetic and strange thing, a creative force... When we listen to people there is an alternating current that recharges us so we never get tired of each other. We are constantly being re-created.*
>
> BRENDA UELAND,[3]
> author and journalist

You can develop listening skills at a number of levels. At the most superficial level, it just means zipping your mouth and not interrupting until the other person stops speaking. At a much deeper level, it means listening to emerging patterns, emotional needs, personal interests, political nuances, and even what *isn't* being said.

When it's your turn to listen, consider the following:

◆ Listen with respect, even if you don't respect the person's position.

◆ Listen to what the other person is actually saying, not your ideas about the person or what you expect to hear from him or her.

◆ Suspend your interpretations about what the person is saying or why he or she is saying it until you've really heard the person.

> *Courage is what it takes to stand up and speak. Courage is also what it takes to sit down and listen.*
>
> WINSTON CHURCHILL,
> British prime minister and wartime leader

◆ Suspend the tendency to agree or disagree. Your position may be important later on, but at the outset, it can impede clear listening.

◆ Feel what the other person is saying. Don't just think it.

◆ Resist the impulse to interrupt!

When the other person says something that triggers a reaction, keep listening, even if it's something you don't want to hear. This is especially important if it is a strategic relationship and you still need to know what is going on with this person.

Stay with reality, even if you don't like it. If you find your reactivity, agitation, anxiety, or anger escalating, find a way to calm yourself enough to keep a clear head.

As you listen, pay special attention to what the other person believes is true. This will show you what drives that person and what he or she is organized around. It doesn't matter whether you agree with the person at this point. What matters is that you recognize that he or she believes it and that you are demonstrating you understand this.

Verify

After you listen, be sure to verify what you heard. This accomplishes two things. First, it lets the other person know that not only were you listening, but that you heard the essence of what he or she was trying to say. Second, it allows you to sort out any possible misunderstandings before you go any further.

Verifying what you heard is one of the simplest ways to address communication difficulties. This fundamental step can prevent any number of communication exchanges from becoming impossibly entangled in misunderstanding.

When you tell another person what you heard, and do so in a way that is meaningful, that person will usually feel understood. Touchdown. You now have a potential ally. As we have discussed, feeling understood is a rare thing.

The following simple exercise will help you create a reminder you can use when practicing your communication skills.

Exercise: Reminder for Practice

Write the following words on a card that you can easily carry with you:

- ► Inquire
- ► Listen
- ► Verify

Now write down the three most important people to practice this with. Refer to your list of vital relationships (page 223) for ideas.

Beside each person's name, make a note of what you want to remember to ask about, understand further, or verify. Jot down your ideas below.

1. Name _____

_____

_____

2. Name _____

_____

_____

3. Name _____

_____

_____

Carry this card with you and use it as a reminder when practicing these skills. Notice how your relationships change.

Make notes on the card as you practice.

The *inquire-listen-verify* process lays the fundamental groundwork for building high-trust relationships. You develop further trust through exchanges that have a track record of integrity.

COME FORWARD WITH INTEGRITY

When you demonstrate your integrity in relationships that are already built on trust, your ability to influence others can be very high. This ability to influence with integrity is one of the pillars of enlightened leadership in the Contact Zone™.

Integrity is often used to mean honesty. While honesty helps to support integrity, the two aren't the same. Honesty refers to telling the truth and not being deceitful. Integrity indicates a state of completeness—of being whole and undivided. You gain integrity by being true to the essence of who you are and acting accordingly. You strengthen your integrity when you:

- ◆ Clarify what is really important to you
- ◆ Stand behind your cherished values, important needs, and self-respecting limits
- ◆ Act on your core truth, guiding purpose, and integrative anchors

Your integrity as a leader is visible when you communicate what you stand for in a way that is clear, responsible, considerate of others, and reality based. Communicating in this way shows others that you are thinking clearly, acting fairly, and in a lucid relationship with reality. This can be very reassuring! Leadership based on integrity often inspires others to trust and be open.

Integrity deepens and expands with the development of the ESSENTIAL YOU.

Integrity is a natural state for the **Essential You**, but for the **Limited You**, integrity is in a constant state of erosion. Its "truth sense" is flawed and can't distinguish illusion from truth. As a consequence, when it gets caught up in its pervasive, fearful fantasies and stories about your competence, value, or place in the world, your integrity erodes from the inside out.

You compromise your integrity whenever you operate from core insecurities, defensive strategies, Shadow Gratification™, or fantasies about how things should be rather than how things are.

When a leader lacks integrity, he or she often will disrespect other people and may even violate their rights. Such a leader may rely too much on domination and intimidation (*dominate-punish*), or invasive controlling (*rescue-control*). In a situation like that, you can expect others to react with passive compliance (*comply-complain*) or overt or covert aggression (*defy-subvert*). All of this will undermine the leader.

The **Limited You** can be too reliant on force or coercion. Alternatively, it may also shy away from influencing in order to avoid uncomfortable contact, difficult feelings, and unpleasant political dynamics. This kind of avoidance inhibits a leader's energy, presence, and power and doesn't do anything to strengthen integrity.

The following case study introduces you to Dianne, a reluctant leader who became highly influential while preserving her integrity and challenging her tendency to avoid conflict.

Dianne

Dianne was the talented senior director of research and development in a large pharmaceutical company. She was a positive, attractive woman in her early forties who met challenges with a smile and a consistent "can-do" attitude. The VP she reported to wanted to appoint her as his successor because she was so well regarded and competent. However, she lacked visibility across the larger organization and had a fairly low profile with the rest of the executive team. She wasn't concerned about this, but her VP was. He hired a coach to work with her.

Dianne was totally invested in her work, but she wasn't sure she wanted to be promoted. She also wasn't sure she wanted to "play politics" and had mixed feelings about the direction the company was going in. She carried a lot of ambivalence.

With deeper discussion, it became apparent that Dianne had a very high ethical standard that she was unwilling to sacrifice. As she realized she could call more attention to herself without compromising her integrity, she found ways to increase her visibility. She spoke up more with the executive team and participated in teams that would influence the direction of the company along lines she could stand behind.

The more challenging issue was her deep-seated tendency to pull back from conflict or disagreement. Her quick smile and affable manner were part of her gracious disposition, but they also covered a deeper pattern. When things got too heated, she pulled back, relaxed, and shifted into an easygoing posture.

Her laid-back attitude wasn't an act; that was the problem. When she was tempted to care "too much," she disconnected from her upset, angry, or agitated state. Rarely did anyone see the angry side of her. Rarely did she see this side of herself.

Her passion was under wraps. It was preventing her from finding out how powerful she could be if she let herself care fully. This would mean being upset more often and then figuring out how to manage her discomfort.

It wasn't easy, but Dianne used her positive attitude to take on the challenge. She learned how to "stay out there" during conflict, and to fight good and hard for what she believed in. She had considerable impact when she did this.

Her political capital increased accordingly. Within a year, her VP appointed her as his successor with the full support of the executive team and was enthusiastic about her potential as a CEO.

Dianne thoroughly resolved her reluctance to be a leader. Her maturity as a leader deepened as she discovered how to be visible and engage in ways that didn't undermine her integrity. She also developed skill in expressing and managing her passion. Her ability to influence was a natural extension of this.

Antonio from Chapter 11 is another example of someone who maintained a high level of integrity as he expanded his ability to influence and deal with a political landscape.

- *Do you have any reluctance about completely fulfilling your leadership capability?*
- *If so, is it tied up in any way with your feelings about integrity? Visibility? Workplace politics?*

As you can see, the decision to be more influential, and to do so with integrity, requires many other supporting skills, processes, and qualities. We'll now look at those skills that will further develop your enlightened edge in the Contact Zone™.

PRACTICES FOR SKILLFUL CONTACT

In the Contact Zone™, obstacles and challenges of all kinds can come into focus and demand attention. When working constructively in any high-impact situation, you often need to dig deep for skills and resources. By using obstacles as fuel for change, you'll draw on your strengths, expand your awareness, and master many skills.

The following practices, attitudes, and approaches will support your growth as a leader as you interact with others. They will help ignite and anchor the **Essential You** and assist you in finding a skillful path through the maze and haze of the Contact Zone™.

Use Authority Only As Needed

Set the stage for leading through influence rather than trying to force or control. Assume that your goal is to get another person or group to *choose* to join you. To do this, you'll need to rely less on your authority and more on your personal power. When people experience choice, they feel they're part of the process. They're then more ready, willing, and able to absorb the impact of changes that are put in motion. This bypasses the reactivity generated by misplaced use of force. The result is far less wasted energy and resources.

Give Up Being Right

Save the arguments about who is right and what exactly is true for very specific, necessary circumstances. It's quite often not necessary to establish who is right or what is true. More often, the argument about who is right is a defensive strategy that camouflages deeper insecurity. Relinquishing righteousness and the need to be right usually means also giving up the Shadow Gratification™, which so often goes with these defensive strategies.

Draw Out the Best

Look for the best in the other person, then keep reinforcing that. Acknowledge the other person's best qualities and encourage what you want to see more of. Show appreciation when a person is trying to deliver his or her best. Give praise generously when it is earned.

Make Requests

Ask for what you need in a timely, clear, and self-respecting way. Requesting is different than demanding. If the other person has a choice, it is a request. If the person doesn't have a choice, it's a demand or requirement.

A direct request can be positive and powerful. For instance, asking someone to do something that you both know will bring out the very best in that person can be beneficial. Asking the person to take responsibility for something that is in his or her arena of ownership can also be quite important.

Making direct requests can help you clarify where another person stands on an issue or in a relationship. Keep in mind that when you make a clear, direct request of someone, you put that person on the spot. He or she is obliged to say yes or no, or to negotiate. If the person is too uncomfortable or lacks negotiation skills, he or she may try to squirm away.

You can get valuable information about the person, based on how he or she deals with your request, but you may also trigger the other person's defensive strategies, so be mindful of this when making direct requests.

Create & Keep Clear Agreements

Clear agreements bind you with others and can act as glue to bring both of you back to a common commitment. Because agreements are binding, it's important that they be clear and respectful of you as well as the other person.

> The moment we cease to hold each other,
> the moment we break faith with one another,
> the sea engulfs and the light goes out.
>
> JAMES BALDWIN, writer and civil rights activist

When agreements, contracts, and promises are entered into with integrity, they serve as integrative anchors. For a contractual understanding to have integrity, it needs to be formed in good faith and without coercion. If you don't plan to keep a promise or aren't sure you can, then you haven't negotiated in good faith.

Agreements also need to be very clear if they are to serve their purpose. A murky agreement can be worse than none, since poorly formed commitments can lead not only to misunderstandings, but also to feelings of betrayal.

If a clear agreement was negotiated in good faith but isn't working, it may be because some basic aspect of your relationship has changed. It is usually better to redefine your purpose together and renegotiate your agreement than to have the agreement erode and lead to a loss of integrity.

Hold Accountable

When an agreement is in place, accountability is part of the deal. Sometimes it's necessary to ask others to take responsibility for what they have agreed to do. You can hold another person accountable by referring back to your mutual agreement and to his or her commitment to integrity. It's usually possible to do this graciously and with kindness.

When you hold someone accountable, don't judge his or her motives or intentions; that just gets in the way of clarifying what is going on. You can't possibly know what another person is dealing with internally. For example, taking responsibility may have very costly implications for that individual, or the person might have an intention and desire to take responsibility but not enough skill. Even though you don't know the full extent of what is going on (motives, circumstances, prevailing conditions) for another person, you *can* remind him or her of the agreement or commitment and find out what is getting in the way of fulfilling it.

Accept the Discomfort of Others

Sometimes the other person will be uncomfortable if you take action that has integrity. He or she may become visibly uneasy if you try to restore clarity to an agreement that has become blurry. This is especially so if you try to establish accountability with a person who doesn't want it. You can expect him or her to find your efforts disagreeable.

Sometimes people are distressed, upset, or even hostile for reasons that may or may not have anything to do with you, and there is very little you can do about it. After you've done your best with the friendly attitudes discussed in the previous chapter and made your best effort, it's time to stop trying to make the other person less upset.

At times you just have to accept another person's discomfort. If you go too far trying to make the other person comfortable, you can lose your ground and damage your effectiveness.

This ability to work in a kind but firm way with the discomfort of others is a necessary part of enlightened leadership. As you develop this ability, you'll be able to see the other person more clearly and with greater insight.

Have Strategic Conversations

Strategic conversations are ones that will further your own or your organization's success, impact, and agenda. These are conversations in which you can, for example:

◆ Find out what is important to the other person
◆ Get missing pieces of important information
◆ Build alliances
◆ Correct misunderstandings or repair a relationship that's been damaged
◆ Set the stage for a proposal or change initiative

Strategic conversations are often high impact and intense. Come to them at your best.

Deliver Value

You expect the best from others, and you need to deliver it as well. Make sure that what you offer—whether a product, service, presentation, proposal, or strategy—has real value to others. Don't assume that what you value is the same as what others value. Each individual you know has personal criteria for what he or she finds valuable.

Upon investigation, many people are surprised at how differently other people assign value. If you're not sure what has value, ask, listen, and verify that it has the degree of value you think it does. Then, if you can do it with integrity, deliver what the person wants, in the way he or she wants it, in order to provide maximum value.

Make Collaborative Efforts

A collaborative approach assumes interdependence and mutual respect among participants. It relies very heavily on trust, clear agreements, and resilience in dealing with challenges. This mind-set is very helpful for cross-group participation that bridges different functions of an organization.

In order for a collaboration to succeed, there may be times when you choose to relinquish some of your vested interests for the sake of the greater good, but pay close attention to your motives for doing so. Check to see if the *rescue-control* or *comply-complain* pattern is operating behind the scenes, or if you're getting any Shadow Gratification™. Sacrifices that don't have integrity can often harm the collaboration in insidious ways

The activity of the **Limited Self**—either your own or that of others—impairs collaboration. This can happen in any number of ways and when it does, trust is damaged or betrayed and clarity is clouded. At these times, you may need to draw on the **Essential You** to make a wise assessment. Then come up with a plan for repairing the damage or shifting the nature of the collaboration.

Despite the challenges of collaboration, there are many rewards. Some things can come about only through a collaborative effort, and there is a sweet joy that comes from working together with others for something greater.

The following exercise summarizes much of what you can do to move from the **Limited You** to the **Essential You** and optimize your leadership power in the Contact Zone™. It focuses on behaviors and skills that are interpersonal or that you can apply in the middle of an interaction with someone else. This checklist draws on many principles, processes, and skills that have been discussed. You'll find it beneficial to review this list on a regular basis.

Exercise: Assess Your Impact in the Contact Zone™

Review the following skills and processes and place a √ beside those skills and processes that need further development or that you need to pay special attention to.

☐ Correct any misunderstandings that have occurred. Often simple clarification is sufficient. Sometimes it's necessary to look at the bigger picture to understand what happened.

☐ Take responsibility for what is yours and give responsibility to others for what is theirs. When accepting or assigning responsibility, check to see if there is sufficient power to fulfill the responsibility.

☐ Acknowledge damage you have dealt. Repair it when possible. A sincere apology works wonders.

☐ Make it clear where you stand in a clear, non-combative, and non-defensive way. Directness, paired with kindness, is very effective.

☐ Create an environment of respect and understanding with others. Others will more easily trust you and be inclined to support your agenda.

☐ Say what needs to be said, even if it is uncomfortable. Say it especially when your integrity will be compromised if you don't say it.

☐ Ask clarifying, strategic questions. Find out who the other person is, what his or her vested interests are, and where he or she stands.

☐ Invite feedback in any area where you need a reality check. Use trusted sources.

☐ Listen deeply to the other person's response. Listen for patterns and undisclosed positions. Verify what you heard.

☐ Create clear agreements. Verify any agreements you think have been made. Base your future expectations on these agreements. Renegotiate them as needed.

☐ Pay attention to your intuitive feelings, gut sense, and hunches about the other person. These data points often provide insight you can't find any other way.

☐ Stay in a collaborative dialogue, even when feeling challenged, and especially with complex issues. Make sure the other person knows you are committed to a relational solution, even if it gets difficult.

☐ Articulate your vision for what is possible. Inspire others to activate their own potential by joining you.

☐ Hold the tension between you and others until something new happens. Don't yield to your insecurities, engage your defenses, or react to the other person's patterns. Stay with the exchange.

☐ Take in diverse points of view. Stay open to exchanges that will give you valuable, divergent information. Receive the information graciously, even if it isn't what you want to hear or disrupts your view of the world.

☐ Create a vital support system. Ask friends and family to support the changes you are making. Enlist the services of a counselor, coach, or consultant as needed.

Refer to this list especially when you feel challenged in a relationship. Review it from time to time to see if the areas that need focus have changed.

Your positive impact in the Contact Zone™ will be enormous if you practice the above skills. You don't have to wait for the other person to do his or her part. You can choose to act from your own center of integrity regardless of how the other person acts.

- *Do you see any similarities between the items you checked on the above list and the Contact Readiness list from Chapter 11?*
- *How would you feel as a leader if you could effectively address the gaps you've identified?*
- *What kind of a contribution could you make?*

When you're in the heat of the Contact Zone™ you have a greater opportunity to lead others and strengthen your relational skills. You have a variety of tools and skills to draw on at this point, including the *inquire-listen-verify* communication process and several practices for skillful contact.

The goal is to bring the **Essential You** forward and to contain the **Limited You**. Remember, the **Essential You** is a construction project. You are building a vehicle for enlightened leadership that will allow you to come forward with integrity and lead others, even when the situation is complicated by projections or entrenched limitations.

We'll turn now to our closing chapter and look specifically at your leadership presence and vision. The quality of your presence will, not surprisingly, be determined by how you work with the **Limited You** and the **Essential You**. A powerful, positive presence and an inspiring vision are natural results of working with your enlightened edge.

13

LEAD WITH PRESENCE & VISION

Thus, the task is not so much to see what no one has yet seen; but to think what nobody has yet thought, about that which everybody sees.

ARTHUR SCHOPENHAUER, philosopher

WHEN another person turns his or her full awareness toward you, it is unmistakable. It can feel wonderful, like a gift, or uncomfortable, bringing unwanted exposure. The positive or negative quality of that attention will depend on how well the person has developed his or her **Essential Self**.

When you are the one focusing attention on others, they will be in the spotlight of your awareness. If you're linked with the **Essential You**, most people will enjoy the positive attention.

You might be described as "present" when you are undistracted, here and now, fully attentive. Your full inner observer is usually attractive and respected by others and is associated with someone who is trustworthy.

If you use this mindful attentiveness to establish contact with another person in a positive way, you have a heightened capacity for impact on him or her. This makes you more able to influence others, build alliances, and achieve mutual goals.

Presence is attractive to others and inspires confidence.

255

Remaining attentive and non-reactive when others are off center tends to have a soothing effect on those around you. Your positive, centered leadership presence is even more important when a situation is disagreeable or upsetting. In these circumstances, you could be seen as a stable force, inspiring trust and confidence.

YOUR LEADERSHIP DNA

You transmit your leadership presence and impact through direct contact with others, and also in more subtle ways. As we discussed in Chapter 11, you contribute significantly to the emotional climate of your organization. Your leadership DNA[1] is like a signature that is replicated throughout your organization.

As you engage with others and create resonance,[2] you transmit your behaviors, attitudes, emotions, and overall presence like a wave that ripples outward, carrying your leadership DNA. Others beyond your immediate sphere of influence pass these qualities, traits, and bits of information on, sometimes farther than you thought possible, extending your leadership "brand."

Your leadership DNA is passed on to others like a wave, extending your sphere of influence.

An example of this occurs with successful service professionals who depend on referrals for most of their business. When they start to receive referrals from unknown sources or through connections they can't track, their DNA is getting around.

Another example is found with executives who are surprised that what they said in an off-hand way was transmitted like wildfire throughout the organization in ways they didn't anticipate. The organizational grapevine is a powerful transmitter of leadership DNA.

Your presence is already having an impact on others and radiating through the organizations and groups that you are a part of. The issue is how much and what kind of impact. What is the quality of your presence? What is it communicating to others?

We'll now take a look at your presence through a self-assessment. Remember, your level of presence isn't the same in all situations. It will probably be more powerful or more positive in one situation than another. For the following two-part exercise, just try to come up with averages. If you notice any huge variation as you consider the questions, simply make note of them.

Exercise: Your Presence

PART 1: How Powerful?

Rate yourself on the following scale by circling the number that applies to you.

Overall, how powerful is your presence as a leader?

1 = almost no presence
10 = extremely powerful presence

1 — 2 — 3 — 4 — 5 — 6 — 7 — 8 — 9 — 10

Imagine you are sharing this self-assessment with a group of people whom you respect. Write down three things that support the rating you gave yourself.

1. _____

2. _____

3. _____

PART 2: How Positive?

Rate yourself on the following scale by circling the number that applies to you.

Overall, how positive is your presence as a leader?

-5 = extremely negative
+5 = extremely positive

-5 — -4 — -3 — -2 — -1 — 0 — +1 — +2 — +3 — +4 — +5

Imagine you are sharing this self-assessment with a group of people whom you respect. Write down three things you would say to support the rating you gave yourself.

1. _____

2. _____

Check out your self-assessment by getting feedback. Consider actually asking two or three people who know you as a leader to assess your presence, using the above questions.

Is your presence as powerful or as positive as you'd like? If not, the solution is to develop the **Essential You** using the tools outlined in this book. Getting the personal, professional, and technical support you need to effectively apply these tools can make all the difference.

Your organization needs you,[3] fully ignited and acting from the **Essential You**. When your leadership presence is powerful and positive, it is reflected in the group you lead. As it reverberates through the group, it generates a positive resonance that can stimulate greater success for everyone.

IMPACT IN YOUR ORGANIZATION

You can also assess the quality of your leadership DNA and presence by looking at the climate of the organization you lead. When you keep your reactivity to a minimum and manage group reactivity, you'll probably see committed, motivated individuals and cohesive, collaborative teams. Energized, committed individuals and teams contribute to a culture of ongoing innovation and high performance.

> The mark of a successful organization isn't whether or not it has problems; it's whether it has the same problems it had last year.
>
> JOHN FOSTER DULLES,
> U.S. Secretary of State
> in the Eisenhower
> administration

If your organization is plagued with a lot of reactivity, productivity will no doubt suffer as well. If the climate is reactive but productivity is high, assess how sustainable this level of output is. Ongoing reactivity usually doesn't support high performance in the long run.

The following exercise asks you to take a look at the organization or group you are currently leading and to take its temperature. This will help you to see where more active leadership on your part may be needed. The patterns described refer to the collective activity in your organization and are a result of everyone's contribution. Part 1 looks at the reactive patterns, which are a result of **Limited Self** activity in the organization. Part 2 looks at relational patterns, which are a result of **Essential Self** activity in the organization.

Exercise: Assess Your Organization

PART 1: Reactive Patterns

If any of the reactive patterns listed below describe the group or organization you are currently leading, place a √ in the associated box.

☐ **Depressed, low-energy teams**

▸ Feelings of defeat and deflation (not voicing concerns, excessive sick leave, complaints to Human Resources)

▸ Diminished energy, hope, and confidence, (planning an exit strategy, avoiding contact, feeling overly sensitive)

☐ **Sabotage, anger, and violence (emotional or physical)**

▸ Anger or rage is unleashed (lawsuits, angry communication)

▸ Direct or symbolic acts of sabotage (turning customers against the company, cynical views about the company, stealing)

☐ **Obstruction to planning, work flow, and task completion**

▸ Ongoing, underlying, unresolved conflict and problems (frequent misunderstandings, miscommunication, unrealistic schedules and promises)

▸ Blockage that is often invisible (deadline slip, incomplete tasks, frequent delays, errors, redos, inability to collaborate)

☐ **Complacency based on reluctant compliance**

▸ Sustaining status quo with minimal growth (busy work, resistance to change, gossip)

▸ Lack of imagination, creativity, or initiative (unproductive meetings, tangential discussions)

If you checked any of the above boxes, congratulations on your willingness to take an honest look. The checked boxes indicate that there is work for you to do individually and with your group. Give some thought to how the reactive behaviors of the *Limited You* may be contributing to these outcomes.

PART 2: Relational Patterns

If any of the relational patterns listed below describe the group or organization you are currently leading, place a √ in the associated box.

☐ Individual and team commitment

- ► It's safe to be fully invested; group efforts are supported and respected; helpfulness, humor, enjoyment of others and of work
- ► Swifter recognition of real problems that need attention, heightened ability to address individual and team challenges

☐ Team cohesion

- ► Forces join to accomplish something greater, less time wasted with misunderstandings
- ► Energy flows with focus to the task at hand, improved capacity to effectively link human and technical functions

☐ Motivated employees

- ► Desire to contribute, providing and receiving useful feedback, desire and ability to work through conflicts and disagreements
- ► Higher performance when reward matches performance, greater efficiency, less rework

☐ Creativity and innovation

- ► Uniqueness and differences are accepted, creative risks can be taken
- ► Opportunities are recognized, assessed, and acted upon; creative strategies and alliances are forged; problems are solved synergistically

If you checked any of the above boxes, congratulations on your good work and good fortune. Give some thought to how to build on and anchor the strengths of your team as well as your own relational behaviors.

If you checked boxes in both Part 1 and Part 2, you're in good company. Commendable work is going on, but there is more to be done.

As you review your organization's patterns, keep in mind that relational patterns can offset reactive tendencies, just as they do with individuals. If your organization is like most, there is probably some work to be done. It's especially important to assess these patterns when you transition to leading a new organization, or are considering re-organizing a current group.

> ♦ *Were there any surprises in the previous exercise?*
> ♦ *How do you as a leader influence both the reactive and relational tendencies of your organization?*

The profile of an organization can be quite complex. Use this initial profile as a prompt to investigate further* if it seems warranted. With the right support and guidance, your organization *can* move from reactive to relational. For example, James, who was introduced in Chapter 1, had a significant effect on his organization when he shifted from a highly reactive to a more relational presence. Edward, whom you met in Chapter 5, illustrates in a similar way how a business can reflect both the dysfunctional and enlightened aspects of the leader.

VISIBILITY

With greater impact and presence comes greater visibility, which most leaders really want and too often really dread. It calls up one of the most basic desires (the need to be seen) and one of the most basic fears (the aversion to being seen and the impulse to hide).

> *Visibility can trigger your core insecurity but can also be exhilarating.*

Visibility can easily stimulate your core insecurity, which in turn can limit your confidence and presence, but visibility is non-negotiable for a leader. It goes with the territory. You need to be seen clearly, frequently, and in a good light. This is part of making contact and influencing others. It is part of the recipe for success as a leader.

Having the spotlight of other people's attention turned on you can be exhilarating. The opportunity to shine and be recognized is a potentially enjoyable, natural benefit of visible leadership. However, increasing your visibility is easier in some situations than others.

---

* The climate and dynamics of an organization are often assessed through a combination of interviews and surveys. They are most effective when targeted and tailored to the specific needs of your organization. Go to **http://contactpointassoc.com/contact.html** to discuss options or to get a referral.

It is usually much more difficult to be visible when you aren't sure how others will view or judge you. For example, if greater visibility on your part triggers a reaction in someone who has the authority to undermine your success, the situation can get dicey. At these times, any ambivalence or mixed feelings you have about visibility may surface.

The following example shows how Marion worked with her need to be seen and her fear of speaking in front of groups.

Marion

Marion was a product manager in a software company that had a highly competitive culture. She often needed to defend her ideas in small and mid-size groups that could be overtly hostile. Marion was very comfortable talking one-on-one, but speaking in front of a group terrified her. Her heart pounded and she feared being struck dumb (and looking dumb too) when she had to present in front of a group. The exposure, especially to criticism, was almost disabling.

It was so much easier for her to hide and avoid group situations in which she had to speak. But this defensive strategy was limiting her ability to influence others and to act visibly as an advocate for her very solid and creative ideas.

Marion knew she needed to learn how to articulate her ideas in front of a potentially antagonistic group. She found her courage, even though she felt inadequate, and took on the challenge of learning to speak in front of groups.

She used her analytical skills to break the challenge into manageable steps. She got the support she needed through Speaking Circles, Toastmasters, and coaching. These all helped her to move beyond her fears and defensive strategies so she could find and hold her own center, even when she felt threatened.

After several months, Marion found a new level of comfort and skill in mobilizing her brilliant ideas quickly. When she was put on the spot by aggressive questioning, she could respond in an orderly fashion. As a result, she gained greater respect and recognition. Her job became much more rewarding as well.

Marion's challenge in speaking up when feeling threatened is a common one. The movement toward greater visibility can easily trigger your core insecurity. In fact, any time you have greater visibility, you can expect the **Limited You** to become activated. That's the time to step in with your ability to lead yourself.

Being a Target

With high visibility, you can accomplish a great deal. When your presence becomes big enough and bright enough to catch the attention of those around you, many things can happen. Visibility brings energy and attention, which can be very positive. It can assist you in being successful, but it can also trigger negative responses from others and make you a target for their negativity.

Even if your presence is positive, it can activate the insecurities of others. With visibility, you may come under closer scrutiny. Others might emphasize or fixate on your mistakes. You might exaggerate your own mistakes as well. No wonder it's sometimes easier to stay undercover!

Greater visibility will make you a bigger target for either positive or negative responses. There are many ways this can show up. For example:

- Those who haven't found their own personal power may admire and try to emulate you, OR become envious and try to take you down.
- Your peers may become more respectful and want to join you, OR become more competitive and aggressive.
- Your manager may become more appreciative and help to promote you, OR become more demanding and undermine your success.
- People below you in the organization may see you as a more powerful authority figure and turn to you as a symbol of hope and inspiration, OR see you as someone to distrust and undermine.

Thankfully, not all of the above scenarios will play out, but you may have to face some of them. Greater visibility activates not only your own internal insecurities, but also the truly complex psycho-socio-political dynamics of those around you. You need to manage it all. This is why making effective contact is so important.

The more powerful and visible you become, the more others will project their hopes, fears, and angels and demons onto you. As a leader, you must be prepared for this. If you aren't prepared, you'll too easily misread a person or situation and then collide with reality in a way you simply can't afford.

Leadership can be a compelling and rewarding path, despite the challenges of visibility and being a target for the projections of others. This is especially so if you feel "called" or inspired to fulfill a vision of some kind.

COMMUNICATE YOUR VISION

> Good business leaders create a vision, articulate the vision, passionately own the vision, and relentlessly drive it to completion.
>
> JACK WELCH, former CEO, General Electric

We now turn to the final area of focus, your vision as a leader. Your success as a leader depends on the quality of your vision and your ability to communicate it effectively.[4] An inspired vision has the potential to mobilize the diverse talents and strengths of many individuals and bring them to a shared point of focus.

Your leadership vision paints a picture of what is possible and inspires the viewer to move toward that possibility. It outlines a realistic path toward an inspiring future.

> ♦ Imagine that it's three years from now and you're celebrating the completion of goals that took many years of effort. You feel satisfied and happy.
> ♦ What was accomplished?
> ♦ Who would you thank? What would you thank them for?
> ♦ What were the critical factors that supported this success?
> ♦ Consider using these points of reflection to develop a vision for the next three years.

When you communicate your vision, others learn about who you are, what you care about, and what you are committed to. When you deliver your vision precisely and purposefully, you also show others where you stand on issues that are relevant to them.

A clear vision defines who you are and also helps to neutralize the projections of others. In the presence of information about who you are as a leader, some projections will simply fall away. A powerful vision communicated with high visibility has tremendous potential to influence others.

> *A clear vision shows others what you really care about and what is possible for them.*

The act of communicating your vision will no doubt reassure some people, but will challenge others. It will create some ripples and probably some creative tension as well. How you communicate your position or vision needs care, so that you can use the resulting tension constructively. Before you verbalize your vision or position, ask yourself:

- ◆ Is it inspiring?
- ◆ Is it truthful?
- ◆ Is it relevant and necessary?

Inspiring

As a leader, you need to win hearts and minds. An inspired vision is something others can feel. People will more happily and easily join you if they are inspired. An uninspired group is very slow to move and respond.

> *If others can't feel you, they won't want to follow you.*

When others see and feel what you are passionate about, then your vision rings true and can be uplifting. Let them see who you are, not just hear your words. Sometimes this means sharing a specific experience or story that establishes your humanness in a significant way. Sometimes it means touching the hearts of your listeners. It always means connecting with something important to them.

- ◆ *If you don't have an inspired vision, what do you need to do to develop one?*
- ◆ *If you have a long-standing vision, is it still inspiring to you? Does it need to be refreshed?*

Truthful

If your vision is truthful, you should be able to personally commit to it without reservation. A truthful vision will also be one that is viable and achievable. Goals that can't be achieved are not fully honest, they are frustrating. Frustration limits the mobilization of resources and ongoing support.

You should also be able to speak to the potential challenges that the vision entails, so you don't mislead others. This doesn't always mean full disclosure of details. It does mean carefully assessing the needs of your audience, along with the impact of specific information.

If your vision poses some controversy, be sure to consider the outcome of speaking up or not speaking up. Think about what the cost may be to both you and others. Weighing this cost is part of developing greater integrity rooted in wisdom.

Relevant & Necessary

For your vision to be relevant, it needs to outline some kind of desirable change or transformation. A relevant vision will provide a creative solution to a pressing problem on the part of those you are leading. If it's linked with some other constructive change that is already in motion, that's even better.

You know your vision is relevant if other people become highly invested in it. When your individual vision becomes part of an organizational vision, its relevance is owned by more people, making it potentially much more powerful.

CONSOLIDATE YOUR FOUNDATION

When you ignite the power of the **Essential You**, you expand your sphere of influence in the world. With vision, visibility, and presence, you can mobilize and lead others toward a future they want and will participate in creating.

The final exercise will assist you in consolidating your foundation of power. It summarizes central themes to return to, helps you establish your most important leadership goal, and anchors your next steps in achieving that goal. Because this exercise distills what you've learned about yourself so far, it warrants at least thirty minutes of undistracted time. The time spent will be worth your investment.

Exercise: Your Foundation of Power

Quickly review the following and look for anything important you want to remember or that will help consolidate your leadership power:

- ▶ Scan the headings of what you've read so far
- ▶ Look at anything you underlined or made note of
- ▶ Review the exercises you completed and any important realizations
- ▶ Pay special attention to the Personal Leadership Goal you identified in Chapter 1 and the integrative anchors you identified in Chapter 4

Use the space below to make note of seven things that are strategic for you in solidifying or developing your presence, power, and impact as a leader.

1. _____
2. _____
3. _____
4. _____
5. _____
6. _____
7. _____

Of the above items, circle or highlight the three most important ones. Put a big star beside the one thing that would have the most profound effect on your leadership presence, power, and impact.

Now rewrite the starred item as a goal.

_____

_____

_____

Take another look at you core insecurity and defensive strategies, and write down three things that could get in the way of achieving the above goal.

1. _____
2. _____
3. _____

Take another look at your core truth and your integrative anchors, and write down three things that you could do to support yourself in achieving the above goal.

1. _____

2. _____

3. _____

What will it cost you in terms of business results and the success of your organization if you don't achieve the above goal?

_____

_____

What do you stand to gain by achieving the above goal?

_____

_____

Finally, identify three external sources of support that could help you achieve your goal.

1. _____

2. _____

3. _____

Take action, and make sure you have some means of creating accountability for yourself. You could enlist one of your external sources of support to help hold you accountable.

This last exercise pulled together some key information that will help you to act from the **Essential You** as you move forward. Consider repeating it again in six to twelve months, or whenever you're ready to create a new goal. Consistent, disciplined application of the tools and skills for managing the **Limited You** will ensure that you continue to stretch yourself and work with your enlightened edge. I wish you good fortune and abundant support with this important effort.

14

THE ENLIGHTENED EDGE OF LEADERSHIP

THIS book began with a challenge: that you become a more powerful, positive force in the world by working with your enlightened edge. Now that you have greater awareness of the **Limited You** and the **Essential You**, it is probably clearer than ever that the ability to lead yourself is at the heart of effective leadership. In fact, without internal leadership, your ability to lead others is seriously hampered.

The **Limited You**, with its reactive patterns, needs to be managed so it doesn't amplify the reactivity of others. Even though the **Limited You** may operate with good intentions, the outcome of its actions are often polarizing and damaging. The **Essential You**, with its centered nature, draws on relational patterns that can neutralize reactivity and contribute to collaborative, creative, and constructive outcomes.

Making the shift from the **Limited You** to the **Essential You** requires a deep and persistent effort. That change doesn't happen overnight, nor does it have precise, linear steps. But there are reliable, necessary processes you can rely upon to facilitate the transition.

By learning to accept who you really are, who others are, the effect you have on each other, and the reality of *what is going on,* you can steadily strengthen deeper levels of integrity.

Integrity, one of the core qualities of the **Essential You**, is anchored through disciplined self-care and appropriate responsibility. When you take responsibility for your actions, cultivate a lifestyle of balance, and bring loving kindness to yourself, the **Limited You** settles down and comes into greater alignment with the **Essential You**.

You can apply a similar process when leading others. If you expect others to take responsibility for their actions and respond with kindness and firmness as you establish accountability, those individuals will naturally respect you and have more reason to align with you as a leader.

Leadership, by definition, is a role that requires the ability to work creatively with tension. The tension between *what is* and *what could be* can be hard to tolerate for very long. However, when this tension is held long enough, the outcome can be elegant, brilliant, inspired, and sustainable. The *pause-observe-reflect* process, expansive practices, and uplifting attitudes will all help to build this capacity. And the efforts you make to stretch yourself will pay off.

The test of your ability to hold tension is never more obvious than when you're in a relationship with another person or group in the dynamic, volatile Contact Zone™. When your internal leadership is in place, you're not swept up in reactivity. Instead, you can focus your attention on the skills needed to navigate the ever-present relational and political minefields that are a non-negotiable part of leading others.

Practicing the skills and processes in the contact readiness checklist, using the *inquire-listen-verify* communication process, and cultivating friendly attitudes will support your centered personal power. This will put you in a position to be respected, listened to, and trusted.

An expanded, enlightened leadership presence is something you earn by anchoring the **Essential You**. With the integrity and energy of the **Essential You** backing you up, you can go forward with visibility, vision, and impact. Then you are in a much better position to leverage organizational tools and systems and to draw on the specific qualities and talents necessary for leadership in a specific situation.

MY VISION

Some lingering questions remain: What is this enlightened presence for? Who is it for? Do you serve something greater than yourself?

These are big questions for the end of a book. They deserve ongoing reflection and discussion. I hope that as you consider them, you'll link with your inner guidance and find your own private answers. Perhaps this will lead to a clearer, more inspired purpose.

My own purpose has called me to write this book and to articulate a foundation for leadership that I hope can transform your life and, through you, the lives of those you touch. My deepest wish is that through your leadership, you can express and bring into reality something luminous and expansive. Whether you focus on your team, company, clients, family, or country, you *can* make a difference in the world you live in.

You live at a unique time in history, with a unique purpose that can only you can fulfill. As a mobilized, enlightened leader, you have a role to play in your personal life and our collective life. The world needs you to develop your talents and strengths, use all your capacities to the fullest, contain and manage your self-limiting tendencies, and come forward with your full presence.

By joining others in the Contact Zone™, you'll be able to offer and receive support. With others, and with the necessary tools and resources, you can solve pressing problems and create wise solutions that have longevity.

I imagine clusters of creative, powerful, joyful alliances that could uplift life on a global scale. Together, we could reduce needless suffering, ensure that each person is treated with kindness and respect, provide tools for creating balance and wellness, commit resources for ongoing learning, and help to create a working environment that utilizes the gifts of each individual. We could do our part in creating the conditions for each person to be happy, peaceful, and free.

We have the choice to consciously participate in the evolution of humanity. Through our collective efforts, we can nudge reality, shape the world, and discover over and over again the creative, enlightened edge of leadership.

NOTES

CHAPTER 1

1. For more information on the role of meditation in developing mindfulness: Thich Nhat Hanh, *The Miracle of Mindfulness: A Manual on Meditation* (Boston: Beacon Press, 1975).

2. Source of quote: Chagdud Tulku Rinpoche, *Change of Heart* (Junction City, CA: Padma Publishing, 2003).

3. *Acting as though* was first introduced to me thorough the study of psychosynthesis. Roberto Assagioli, *Psychosynthesis: A Collection of Basic Writings* (New York: Penguin, 1993) and Roberto Assagioli, *The Act of Will* (Baltimore: Penguin, 1974).

4. Another resource for linking personal and professional growth: Stephen R. Covey, *The 7 Habits of Highly Effective People* (New York: Free Press, Simon and Schuster, 2004).

5. For an excellent discussion of authority and its basis in social trust: Ronald A. Heifetz, *Leadership Without Easy Answers* (Cambridge, MA: Belnap Press, 1994).

CHAPTER 2

1. The Hoffman Quadrinity Process works with negative behaviors, moods, and attitudes that are rooted in childhood. The goal of the work is to re-align and integrate intellect, emotions, body, and spirit.

CHAPTER 4

1. Source of quote: Eugen Herrigal, *Zen in the Art of Archery* (New York: Pantheon Books, Random House, 1953, 1981)

2. Black-white, primitive thinking are described in more detail: Mark Sichel and Alicia L. Cervini, "Black & White Thinking," http://www.psybersquare.com/me/me_back_white.html.

CHAPTER 5

1. To understand how brain and biochemistry are altered during times of stress: Bruce McEwen and Elizabeth Norton Lasley, *The End of Stress As We Know It* (New York: Dana Press, 2004).
2. This quote was taken from employee interviews: Kathleen D. Ryan and Daniel K. Oestreich, *Driving Fear Out of the Workplace,* 2nd ed. (San Francisco: Jossey-Bass, 1998).
3. Ibid.
4. Ibid.

CHAPTER 7

1. A well-established process for linking thought with feeling: Eugene T. Gendlin, *Focusing* (New York: Bantam Books, 1981).
2. Learn from life even in the most challenging of circumstances: Pema Chodron, *When Things Fall Apart: Heart Advice for Difficult Times* (Boston: Shambhala, 2000).
3. How to develop skill in the art of inquiry: Diana Whitney and Amanda Trosten-Bloom, *The Power of Appreciative Inquiry* (San Francisco: Berrett-Koehler Publishers, 2003).

CHAPTER 8

1. The impermanent nature of existence, a basic premise of Buddhism, is considered through interviews with 120 people and is accompanied by a DVD: David Hodge and Hi-Jin Kang, *Impermanence: Embracing Change* (Ithaca, NY: Snow Lion, 2009).
2. Hazel's new book: Hazel Henderson, *Ethical Markets: Growing the Green Economy,* (White River Junction, VT: Chelsea Green, 2007).
3. A discussion of leadership and the role of adaptive work: Ronald A. Heifetz, *Leadership Without Easy Answers* (Cambridge, MA: Belnap Press, 1994); also Ronald A. Heifetz, "The Work of Leadership," *Harvard Business Review on Leadership* (Boston: Harvard Business School Press, 1998).
4. Byron Katie has developed a simple inquiry process called "The Work" that assists people in disentangling themselves from limiting stories and identifying what is more true. Her website: http://www.thework.com/thework.asp.

CHAPTER 9

1. For instruction on how to be present in the here and now: Eckhart Tolle, *The Power of Now: A Guide to Spiritual Enlightenment* (Novato, CA: New World Library, 1999).

CHAPTER 10

1. Source of quote: Peter M. Senge, "The Leader's New Work: Building Learning Organizations," *MIT Sloan Management Review* (Reprint 3211, Fall 1990).
2. An article that challenges some of the myths regarding work-life balance and offers some smart alternatives: Keith H. Hammonds, "Balance is Bunk!" *Fast Company* (Issue 87, October 2004).
3. Excellent article discussing the need to recover energy after expending it: Jim Loehr and Tony Schwartz, "The Making of a Corporate Athlete," *Harvard Business Review* (Reprint R0101H, January 2001).
4. A classic text and perspective on developing intuition: Frances Vaughan, *Awakening Intuition* (New York: Doubleday, 1979).
5. Source of quote: Viktor Frankl, *Man's Search for Meaning* (Los Angeles: Washington Square Press, 1984).
6. For tools on how to establish a personal vision and purpose that is aligned with career: Richard J. Leider, *Life Skills: Taking Charge of Your Personal and Professional Growth* (San Diego: Pfeiffer & Company, 1994).
7. For a distinctly Christian focus in developing a mission statement: Laurie Beth Jones, *The Path: Creating Your Mission Statement for Work and for Life* (New York: Hyperion, 1996).

CHAPTER 11

1. Examination of four cornerstones of emotional intelligence for leaders: Robert K. Cooper, *Executive E.Q.: Emotional Intelligence in Leadership and Organizations* (New York: Perigree, Putnam, 1997).
2. A communication process for long-term relationships that is organized around non-violence: Marshall B. A. Rosenberg, *Nonviolent Communication: A Language of Life* (Encinitas, CA: Puddle Dancer Press, 2003).

3. Offers more empowered alternatives to traditional political strategies: Peter Block, *The Empowered Manager: Positive Political Skills at Work* (San Francisco: Jossey-Bass, 1991).
4. The importance of personal and social competence in an emotionally intelligent organization: Daniel Goleman, *Working with Emotional Intelligence* (New York: Bantam, 1998).

CHAPTER 12

1. Projection was viewed as a defense mechanism by Sigmund Freud as early as 1911. It is a widely accepted concept in the field of psychology.
2. Thoughtful, respectful communication utilizes a complex set of skills discussed in this anthology of fifty-one scholarly and popular readings: John Stewart, *Bridges Not Walls: A Book About Interpersonal Communication*, 10th ed. (New York: McGraw-Hill Humanities, 2008).
3. Excerpt from "Tell Me More," an essay by Brenda Ueland, reprinted by permission of the publisher from *Strength to Your Sword Arm: Selected Writings* (Duluth, MN: Holy Cow! Press, 1992). Copyright© by the estate of Brenda Ueland.

CHAPTER 13

1. Leadership practices for shaping an organization's DNA: Judith E. Glasser, *The DNA of Leadership: Leverage Your Instincts to: Communicate-Differentiate-Innovate* (La Crosse, WI: Platinum Press, 2007).
2. Resonance and leadership: Daniel Goleman, Richard Boyatzis, and Annie McKee, *Primal Leadership: Realizing the Power of Emotional Intelligence* (Boston: Harvard Business School Press, 2002).
3. The significance of leading an organization: John P. Kotter, "What Leaders Really Do," *Harvard Business Review on Leadership* (Boston: Harvard Business School Press, 1998).
4. How to mobilize others through the power of narrative and storytelling: Stephen Denning, *The Secret Language of Leadership* (San Francisco: Jossey-Bass, 2007).

INDEX

U

uplifting attitudes, 180–181

V

verify. *See* inquire-listen-verify
visibility, 261–263
    being a target, 263–264
vision
    leadership vision, 264–266
    perspective, 19–20
    reflection, 166

W

work-life effectiveness and integration, 196–202
    exertion and recovery, 198–199
    Work-Life Effectiveness Assessment, 197

ABOUT THE AUTHOR

Barbara Bouchet, MEd, President of Contact Point Associates LLC, brings over 25 years of experience in leadership coaching, systems change, relationship management, counseling, and adult education to her work with leaders and organizations.

Barbara draws on her rich experience and training as a coach, counselor, mediator, group facilitator, and trainer in her work with individuals and groups. She has worked successfully with leaders of small businesses and large corporations including Philips Healthcare, Amazon, Microsoft, and Costco.

Barbara is a Board Certified Coach and a licensed counselor, with degrees in Psychology, Sociology, and Educational Psychology. She has supervised and trained hundreds of professionals both privately and through university graduate programs.

Barbara is abundantly creative and committed to linking what is deep and wise with what is practical. She is the author of *The Contact Zone™: Power & Influence* board game and training workshop, *Balancing on the Edge: Tools for Peak Performance in Work & Life* toolkit, *Work-Life Effectiveness* assessment for individuals, *Performance & Balance* training for organizations, and *Clear Communication: How to Prevent Miscommunication* training program.

Barbara lives in Seattle with her husband, where they enjoy their kids, grandkids, and the natural beauty of the Pacific Northwest.

CONTACT POINT ASSOCIATES RESOURCES

The following resources will help support your shift to greater balance and personal power. They can assist you in shining your brightest as the leader of your life and being an inspiring example to others.

CONTACT: Phone: 206-361-4730
Email: BB@contactpointassoc.com

NEWSLETTER: The Enlightened Edge™

When you sign up for the *Enlightened Edge™* newsletter, you'll receive a free article with powerful action steps in each issue. You'll also get free access to the:

- *Self-care Assessment*
- *More True You Worksheet*
- *Tips for Expanding Your Personal Power in the Contact Zone™*

Go to **http://contactpointassoc.com** to sign up.

ASSESSMENT: Work-Life Effectiveness

Rate yourself according to 40 behaviors in order to:

- Find out how well you manage the competing demands of your work and personal life.
- Develop more ways to expand and anchor your real value.
- Discover what limits your personal power and what you can do about it.

The assessment includes your scores, a brief interpretation, and a copy of the *Work-life Effectiveness Tips* digital booklet. Go to **http://contactpointassoc.com/assess_wl.html** to take this assessment.

TIPS: Work-Life Effectiveness

For powerful tools to manage your work-life balance, take a look at the *Work-Life Effectiveness Tips* booklet. It contains 95 life-restoring tips. They're organized into the following areas: Self-Care, Managing Relationships, Investing in Your Potential, Deepening Resilience. Go to **http://contactpointassoc.com/tips_wl.html** to order and download your copy of this booklet.

TIPS: Expand Your Personal Power

This booklet provides 114 tips to become more powerful, balanced, and connected. These tools will help you increase your emotional intelligence, influence others, and work effectively with challenging relationships. Go to **http://contactpointassoc.com/tips_pp.html** to order and download your copy of this booklet.

TOOLKIT: Balancing on the Edge: *Tools for Peak Performance in Work & Life*

This toolkit will help you move through a stressful, busy, demanding life without becoming irritable, depressed, or exhausted. A more balanced, joyful and powerful life is possible for you. It is a life where you can handle frustrations without losing your center; where you can enjoy other people and your work, even when work is demanding; where you can be in charge of who you are and stop trying to control things you can't control; and where you find the renewal you need, when you need it so you can return to your activities refreshed. Go to **http://contactpointassoc.com/toolkit_wl.html** for more information.

COACHING

You can either call Barbara to schedule a free 30-minute coaching session or go to **http://contactpointassoc.com** and book a session through her online scheduler. Whether your focus is work-life effectiveness, career or professional transition, or becoming a better leader, you can take advantage of this free consultation to help you define your next steps and create the best life possible for yourself as well as those you care about and serve.

PROGRAMS AND TRAINING

The Enlightened Edge™ Program

These free teleseminars, live events, and coaching calls will bring the material from *The Enlightened Edge for Leaders: Ignite the Power of You* to life. They will help you focus more intensively on your own transformation. Whether you are an executive, a manager, a professional, an informal leader, a community leader, or simply a leader of your own life, these workshops and coaching opportunities will accelerate your expansion into the potential that is waiting for you. Go to **http://contactpointassoc.com/train_ee_seminars.html** for more information.

The Contact Zone™ Board Game

This interactive game provides intensive skill-based feedback for leaders and teams. Participants have a chance to quickly apply and demonstrate new learning as they try out new skills. It provides a safe, structured, and fun way to develop powerful relational skills. Go to **http://contactpointassoc.com/boardgame.html** for more information.

The Contact Zone™: *Power and Influence Training*

This training shows participants how to influence others by relying less on position power and more on personal power. They develop greater relational intelligence and a more versatile leadership style by working with limiting reactive patterns and corresponding relational antidotes. *The Contact Zone™ Board Game* is a central feature of this training. The training also helps build teams and provides tools for more effective communication. Go to **http://contactpointassoc.com/train_czpowerinfl.html** for more information.

Performance & Balance: *Dynamic Tools for Work & Life*

Sustainable, elite performance depends on more than hard work or busyness. If your organization needs to increase employee effectiveness, create better team morale, or retain talent, the *Performance & Balance Training* provides a solution. A healthier, happier, and more engaged employee has better focus, makes fewer mistakes, and has a consistently higher level of performance. This workshop provides the tools needed to create ongoing balance, satisfaction, and productivity. Go to **http://contactpointassoc.com/train_wl.html** for more information.

The Clear Communication Program: *How to Prevent Miscommunication*

When people are communicating clearly, concisely, and respectfully, work gets done! Too often, however, work and relationships are seriously hampered by miscommunication. This leads to unnecessary rework, conflicts, lost opportunities, and needless drain of resources that can have a profound effect on the bottom line. This can change. With the necessary skills in place, you and your organization can thrive. Effective communication can be learned though coaching, by taking the *Relational Communication Skills Survey*, and through training.

The Relational Communication Skills Survey

If miscommunication is a problem for you or your organization, this survey assesses the cause and points to the solution. It assesses 33 communication competencies and 160 behaviors that are the underpinnings of the competencies. It can be used as a self-assessment or as a 360 assessment. When an entire team is assessed, the sources of miscommunication can be identified and the behaviors to focus on are very clear. Go to **http://contactpointassoc.com/assess_comm_survey.html** for more information.

Say It: *Find The Words for Difficult Conversations*

Difficult conversations are necessary but often avoided. This half-day workshop asks each participant to focus on one difficult conversation that they currently face. They are given guidelines for how to say what needs to be said, practice saying it, and then receive feedback. Go to **http://contactpointassoc.com/train_com_miscom.html** for more information.

Precision Communication: *Building a High Performance Communication Culture*

This workshop helps prevent fragmented, ambiguous, or contradictory communication. It provides the skills necessary to be clear and to identify where the short-circuit has taken place, and to repair it. This is especially important in cross-functional teams, across sites, and when communicating with a different culture. Go to **http://contactpointassoc.com/train_com_miscom.html** for more information.

BOOK ORDER INFORMATION

To purchase additional copies of this book:

1. Visit **http://ContactPointAssoc.com** and use your credit card to order through the secure shopping cart, OR
2. Use the following order form. Fill it out and fax or mail it.
   Fax: 206-801-7220
   Mail: Contact Point Associates LLC
         10740 Meridian Ave N, Suite 203, Seattle WA 98133
   Phone: 206-361-4730 for special handling or quantity orders

ORDER FORM

ITEM	COST EACH	QTY	TOTAL
The Enlightened Edge for Leaders Autographed copy	$18.95		

SALES TAX (Washington residents only, add 9.5%)	
SUB TOTAL	
SHIPPING & HANDLING: $5.00 for the first book, plus $1 for each additional book, shipped US Media Mail.	
TOTAL AMOUNT	

❐ A check or money order for the total amount is included.
Please allow 5 to 10 days from receipt of your order for delivery.

SHIPPING & BILLING INFORMATION

Name _____

Company _____ Title _____

Address _____

City, State, Zip _____

Phone _____ Email _____